Size of China Compared
to the United States

CHINA BOUND

A Guide to Academic Life

and Work in the PRC

Karen Turner-Gottschang
with
Linda A. Reed

for the Committee on Scholarly Communication
with the People's Republic of China

National Academy of Sciences
American Council of Learned Societies
Social Science Research Council

NATIONAL ACADEMY PRESS
Washington, D.C. 1987

NATIONAL ACADEMY PRESS 2101 Constitution Avenue, NW Washington, DC 20418

NOTICE: The project that is the subject of this publication was sponsored by the Committee on Scholarly Communication with the People's Republic of China. It is a completely revised edition of *China Bound: A Handbook for American Students, Researchers and Teachers*, published in 1981.

The Committee on Scholarly Communication with the People's Republic of China (CSCPRC) is jointly sponsored by the American Council of Learned Societies, the Social Science Research Council, and the National Academy of Sciences. The Academy provides an administrative base for the CSCPRC.

Since the normalization of diplomatic relations between the United States and China in 1979, the CSCPRC has developed programs with the Chinese Academy of Sciences (CAS), the Chinese Academy of Social Sciences (CASS), and the State Education Commission, in addition to those with the China Association for Science and Technology (CAST), with whom CSCPRC began exchanges in 1972. Current activities include a program for American graduate students and postdoctoral scholars to carry out long-term study or research in affiliation with Chinese universities and research institutes; a short-term reciprocal exchange of senior-level Chinese and American scholars; a bilateral conference program; and an exchange of joint working groups in selected fields.

This publication was supported in part by the CSCPRC Information Services Center, which is funded by the U.S. Information Agency and the National Science Foundation.

The accuracy of the information presented and the views expressed in this publication are the responsibility of the authors and not the sponsoring organizations.

Library of Congress Cataloging-in-Publication Data

Gottschang, Karen Turner.
  China bound.

  Bibliography: p.
  Includes index.
  1. Foreign study—China. 2. American students—China. 3. Teachers, Foreign—China. 4. China—Description and travel—1976– . I. Reed, Linda A. II. Title.
LB2376.3.C6G68   1987   370.19'6   87-11251
ISBN 0-309-03731-X

Printed in the United States of America

The calligraphy appearing on the cover and in the text was kindly prepared by Fu Shen, Curator of Chinese Art, Freer Gallery of Art of the Smithsonian Institution, Washington, D.C.

Acknowledgments

The authors wish to thank the following individuals for their contributions to the preparation of this manuscript:

BONNIE ACKERMAN, English Language Institute, China
HOWARD W. BARNES, Brigham Young University
WILLIS BARNSTONE, Indiana University
BEATRICE BARTLETT, Yale University
GEORGE BEASLEY, U.S. Embassy, Beijing
HALSEY BEEMER, Chinese University Development Project
BRUCE BORTHWICK, Albion College
J. RAY BOWEN II, University of Michigan
THOMAS BUOYE, University of Michigan
JANET CADY, Tufts University
RUSSELL CAMPBELL, University of California, Los Angeles
PATRICK J. CORCORAN, U.S. Embassy, Beijing
MARY ERNST, Council for International Exchange of Scholars
ROBERT M. FARNSWORTH, University of Missouri
ANDREA GAY, China Education Fund
ROBERT GEYER, Committee on Scholarly Communication with the
  People's Republic of China
THOMAS GOTTSCHANG, College of the Holy Cross
DIANE E. GRUENBERG, Edison State College
BOB CURTIS HAMM, Oklahoma State University
MAX HESS, China Educational Tours
PHILLIP IVES, U.S. Information Agency
STEPHEN KANTER, Lewis and Clark Law School
DONALD J. LEWIS, East-West Center

FUXIANG LI, Bank of China, New York
MARY P. MERVA, Rutgers University
JOHN R. MOORE, University of Southwestern Louisiana
CAROL E. NEUBAUER, Bradley University
OFFICIALS OF THE BUREAU OF FOREIGN AFFAIRS, State Education
  Commission of China
ROBERT PALMER, Columbia University
JESSE PARKER, Yale-China Association
MARGARET PEARSON, U.S. Information Agency
JOSEPH A. PERTEL, Yale-China Association
JACK POLAND, Centers for Disease Control
LISA ROFEL, Stanford University
BRUCE A. RONDA, Skidmore College
KYNA RUBIN, Committee on Scholarly Communication with the
  People's Republic of China
MELVIN SEIDEN, State University of New York, Binghamton
WERNER J. SEVERIN, University of Texas at Austin
BEATRICE SPADE, Harvard-Yenching Institute
BRUCE M. STAVE, University of Connecticut
GREGORY A. THOMAS, University of California, Berkeley
RUIZHONG WANG, Embassy of the People's Republic of China,
  Washington, D.C.
JOHN H. WELLS, JR., Monterey Institute of International Studies
BRUCE M. WILSON, St. Mary's College
RICHARD J. WILTGEN, DePaul University
MENG YANG, Embassy of the People's Republic of China,
  Washington, D.C.

Foreword

For most students and scholars in the China field, reasons to go to the People's Republic for study or research are obvious. Living in the culture and society they have studied in college and graduate school is the logical next step down a professional path that will be enhanced by and increasingly dependent on firsthand knowledge of contemporary China and what it has to offer in the way of library, archival, and human resources. For many people in China studies, the opening of the PRC eight years ago to foreign students, researchers, and teachers inaugurated a new chapter in their professional and personal lives by providing the opportunity to reevaluate and perhaps reframe the intellectual suppositions and premises of their work. Indeed, the students and scholars who have conducted research in China since 1979 are producing fresh, compelling approaches to China studies, and their voices are heard not just in academia, but in political and commercial sectors as well.

China attracts because it was closed to foreign observers for so long; the very process of its opening up is an important subject for study. In addition, the experimental, constantly changing nature of Chinese political, social, and economic reforms is an endless source of fascination and instruction.

But living and working in a land such as China, with customs and traditions so different from what we in the United States are accustomed to, can present innumerable difficulties as well as challenge and reward. Indeed, lack of familiarity with the minutiae of daily life may greatly affect the success of a visitor's study, research, or teaching experience. Today, American students, scholars, and teachers, with eight years of experience on which to draw, are going to China much better prepared than their predecessors, and their stays in the PRC are far more fruitful because of this.

China Bound: A Guide to Academic Life and Work in the PRC presents the latest information from academics recently returned from China about living and working in that country as a foreign student or scholar. What this book seeks to provide is information for those contemplating or already planning a trip to China—information that everyone who contributed to this project wishes they had known before their visit. As a person outside the realm of China studies who has only recently begun to discover the richness of that country as a site for my own research, I can personally attest to the usefulness of this handbook, and I offer it in the hope that it will enhance the China experience of all those who read it.

HERBERT SIMON, *Chairman*
Committee on Scholarly Communication
with the People's Republic of China

Preface

The numbers of travelers now bound for China, planning to go there in the future, or even hoping to make the trip some day have reached proportions never envisioned when the first edition of this book appeared in 1981. That handbook—which was produced and distributed by the U.S.-China Education Clearinghouse, a joint project of the Committee on Scholarly Communication with the People's Republic of China and the National Association for Foreign Student Affairs proved to be of great service to American academics traveling to China during the early years following normalization in 1979 and since. Today, however, so many changes are taking place in China, so many conditions are being altered in one way or another, that there is a pressing need for new and updated information. This revised edition responds to that need.

China Bound presents both general information applicable to all Americans planning to reside in China and specific information that should be particularly useful to students, research scholars, and teachers. It is recommended that readers carefully review both categories of material to gain a more complete understanding of the Chinese academic milieu, which is quite interwoven with and offers deep insights into day-to-day life and practices of the country and culture. For this reason, the information offered here is as helpful to those who are trying to decide whether to spend an extended period in the PRC as it is to those who already have been accepted into programs.

The information for this edition of *China Bound* was collected from a wide array of sources: from experiences of students and scholars who went to China on summer and year-long exchange programs arranged through both formal and informal agreements among U.S. and Chinese educational institutions and national organizations; from reports of teachers sent to China by the U.S. Information Agency under the Fulbright Program; and from Americans who have taught in China under private arrangements with Chinese universities.

For all those who hope to be bound for China but have not yet completed their plans, opportunities for study and for research and teaching positions in China are listed in the first chapter of this volume. Although limited facilities make it difficult to accommodate all who wish to study or work in the PRC, there are numerous and growing opportunities for American students, researchers, and teachers to go to China. A number of U.S. institutions have concluded formal exchange agreements with universities and research institutes in China, and many others have established informal ties.

To visit China, whether or not one is enrolled in a formal program, is to discover—or rediscover—the best of being a student. For no matter what preparation or plans one takes to China, there remains so much that is new to see and to learn at all levels that even the most experienced visitor is a student.

The authors and the Committee on Scholarly Communication with the People's Republic of China wish you *Yi lu shun feng*—a smooth journey.

KAREN TURNER-GOTTSCHANG
LINDA A. REED

January 1987

Contents

5. Teaching / 108

6. Services Available / 118

7. Leaving China / 135

Appendixes / 137

CHINA BOUND

1. Opportunities for Research, Study, and Teaching in China

To live and work in China* is a prospect that has intrigued Americans for more than a century, but opportunities to do so were foreclosed for nearly 30 years. Fortunately, the situation changed dramatically following normalization of relations between the United States and the People's Republic of China on January 1, 1979. Once again, Americans are able to study and teach in Chinese academic and research institutions. A small number of students and scholars are selected each year through national competitions administered by the Committee on Scholarly Communication with the People's Republic of China (CSCPRC). Many students, scholars, and teachers are placed through formal and informal exchange arrangements between individual institutions in the United States and China. Others are "recruited" by colleagues in China or apply to the State Education Commission of China (formerly the Ministry of Education), the Foreign Experts Bureau of the State Council, the Embassy of the People's Republic of China, or other organizations in the United States involved in the placement of students and scholars or in the recruitment of Americans to teach in China. Those interested in studying or teaching in China should explore each of these and other possibilities to ascertain which is most suitable for them. Those who have already been accepted by a Chinese institution should be aware that they will be in contact with people who have traveled to China by many different roads and under many different arrangements.

---

*The terms *China* and *Chinese*, as used in this book, apply only to the People's Republic of China and residents of the China mainland.

1

RESEARCH AND STUDY

The Committee on Scholarly Communication with the People's Republic of China administers the major nationwide student and scholarly exchange programs between the United States and China, including the National Program for Advanced Study and Research in China and the Visiting Scholar Exchange Program. For more information about these programs, write to:

Committee on Scholarly Communication with the
People's Republic of China
2101 Constitution Avenue, NW
Washington, DC 20418

A limited number of Fulbright awards also are available for study and research in China. For further information, contact:
International Education Program
U.S. Department of Education
Washington, DC 20202

Many U.S. colleges and universities have formal or informal exchange agreements with Chinese institutions for short- or long-term programs (see Appendix A). Many programs are limited to students and faculty at the signatory school, but questions of eligibility should be directed to the individual college or university.

In addition to exchange programs conducted under agreements between U.S. and Chinese institutions, there are a number of summer and/or semester or year-long Chinese-language programs, as well as other short-term programs, some with courses taught in English. These may be sponsored by individual U.S. institutions or by such organizations as:

Council on International Educational Exchange
205 East 42nd Street
New York, NY 10017

Information about these programs should be available in most study-abroad offices at U.S. academic institutions. Individual Chinese institutions also offer short-term courses; for information, see Appendix B.

Individuals wishing to study or conduct research in China also may apply directly to the State Education Commission of China. For procedures and other pertinent information, see Appendixes B, C, and D. A copy of "A List of Specialities in Chinese Universities and Colleges Open to Foreign Students" can be obtained for $2.50 postage and handling charges from:

National Association for Foreign Student Affairs
1860 19th Street, NW
Washington, DC 20009

TEACHING

For the first several years after normalization of relations between the United States and the People's Republic of China, the Chinese Foreign Experts Bureau (FEB) was responsible for overall recruitment policy and day-to-day administration for foreigners going to China to teach at institutions of higher education. In 1986 the Foreign Experts Bureau, which now reports directly to the State Council, continues to be responsible for overall policy concerning foreigners teaching in China, but recruiting and administration are now carried out by various agencies and institutions—depending on whether an individual is considered a "foreign expert" or a "foreign teacher." Detailed descriptions of the distinctions in qualifications, salaries, and benefits between foreign experts and foreign teachers are on pages 18–22. Information about the recruitment of foreign experts and foreign teachers is briefly described below.

FOREIGN EXPERTS   The Foreign Experts Bureau recruits foreign experts only for smaller universities not under the authorization of the State Education Commission. In addition, it recruits English-language specialists to train young interpreters and write articles for the *Xinhua News Agency*, *Beijing Review*, *China Reconstructs*, and other English-language publications produced in China. The Bureau of Foreign Affairs of the State Education Commission is responsible for recruiting foreign experts for all other universities and for overseeing the administration of their stay in China.

The regulations outlined in FEB's 1985 brochure, *Information on the Recruitment of Foreign Experts*, apply to all foreign experts traveling to China. Appendix E is a copy of the FEB brochure, which includes an application form, for teaching in China. (Also required is a health certificate, which is the same as the student health certificate in Appendix B, pp. 166–167.) Applications should be sent to:

Foreign Experts Bureau of the State Council
P.O. Box 300
Beijing, People's Republic of China

FOREIGN TEACHERS   Foreign teachers are recruited directly by Chinese institutions of higher learning, university departments, or local provincial or municipal departments or bureaus of education. Applications for such teaching positions should be sent directly to the interested agency.

FOREIGN LANGUAGE TEACHING   Each year there are approximately 700 positions available in the People's Republic of China for teachers of English, Japanese, German, and French. Of these 700 positions, 380 to 400 are filled by English teachers—80 percent by content teachers of English; 20 percent by teachers of English as a second language (ESL) teaching advanced methodology and pedagogy. Of the approximately 400 English teachers needed each year, 250 are classified as foreign experts and 150 as foreign teachers.

The English departments or departments of foreign languages at Chinese universities, colleges, or other institutions of higher learning where most Americans are placed offer a four-year course in English language, literature, and linguistics (including descriptive linguistics, sociolinguistics, and psycholinguistics). The basic aim of the Chinese in inviting native speakers of English to teach in China is to bring about a marked improvement in the English-language proficiency (listening, speaking, reading, and writing abilities) of Chinese undergraduates, postgraduates, and university instructors and to train them to teach the higher grades at tertiary-level institutions.

From past experience, the Chinese have learned that content teachers of English from senior high schools and universities in English-speaking countries can teach effectively in Chinese colleges and universities. They expect such teachers to have had experience in classroom English linguistics and literature or other subject matter, as well as experience in teaching English as a second language or English for specific purposes (ESP) at an advanced level. Content teachers of English in China generally teach literature (fiction, prose, poetry, and drama); major writers of modern and contemporary literature of English-speaking countries; writing (general writing skills, postgraduate essay writing, nonfiction or creative writing); rhetoric; analysis of spoken and written English, centering mainly on colloquial usage; and ESL or ESP at an advanced level.

There are specific requirements for both teachers and students in English-language courses in China. Teachers must—

• in cooperation with Chinese professors and senior lecturers, select reading materials of various styles in contemporary American, English, or Canadian literature and other subject matter to increase students' comprehension and to expose them to a variety of stylistic features so they can improve their writing styles;

• focus on advanced approaches and methods of teaching ESL;

• provide students with well-balanced information about and vocabulary in as many fields as possible (e.g., U.S. history, literature, and society);

• give lectures on points of grammar and rhetoric;

• provide background information about different styles of contemporary English writing.

Chinese postgraduate students must—

• perform drills, both oral and written, based on their reading and in combination with other oral and written work;
• use, both in and after class, taped materials (including educational films) demonstrating different styles of contemporary English writing; and, in addition to taking both practical and theoretical courses and completing class assignments, read within a six-month period at least four or five contemporary English novels selected for excellence of style and content.

AGENCIES IN THE UNITED STATES INVOLVED IN PLACING AMERICANS AS FOREIGN EXPERTS AND FOREIGN TEACHERS IN CHINA The agencies described below recruit both foreign experts and foreign teachers. When applying for teaching positions, you should inquire whether the position is that of a foreign expert or foreign teacher and what the conditions of employment are. Refer to pages 18–22 for more details.

Personnel at the Education Division of the Embassy of the People's Republic of China in Washington, D.C., recruit American educators and professionals to work in China. Specifically, they are interested in lecturers and professors to teach English, science and technology, finance, banking, business management, and law in Chinese institutions of higher education. They also recruit individuals for editing, translating, and publishing positions in the press, radio, and publishing houses. Personnel selected to teach in China are expected to perform the following assignments:

• upgrade the professional skills of Chinese foreign language teachers;
• teach both undergraduate and graduate students;
• counsel and guide Chinese teachers;
• offer advice on extracurricular language training activities and supervise graduate students in writing academic papers;
• compile and edit teaching and reference materials; and
• give lectures about the United States on such topics as culture, history, or other subjects as required.

Applicants must hold a master's or higher degree, demonstrate relatively high attainment in their own field, and have some teaching or work experience, preferably at least three years.

Persons who wish to apply for a teaching position in China should send an application and health certificate (see Appendix E), a detailed resume, and two letters of recommendation to:

Education Division
Embassy of the People's Republic of China
2300 Connecticut Avenue, NW
Washington, DC 20008

In addition to the Chinese Embassy, there are a number of other organizations and institutions in the United States that recruit individuals to teach in China. For example, a limited number of Fulbright awards are available for teaching in China. For further information, write to:

Council for International Exchange of Scholars
11 Dupont Circle, NW, Suite 300
Washington, DC 20036

In September 1980 the University of California at Los Angeles (UCLA) opened three training centers in China: one at Zhongshan University in Guangzhou under the sponsorship of the Ministry of Education (now the State Education Commission) and two in Beijing—one under the sponsorship of the Chinese Academy of Sciences and one for the Foreign Trade Institute (now the Institute of International Economics and Management). UCLA currently is recruiting individuals with teaching/research interests to work at these centers for periods of one year. Of particular interest to the recruiters are persons qualified to teach English for specific purposes; in addition, they prefer individuals who are currently in academic programs and who would use their experience in China to fulfill requirements for an academic degree (Americans going to one of the UCLA centers teach part time at the centers and have time to do pedagogical research in the classroom). If you are interested in this program, contact:

Russell Campbell
Coordinator, UCLA/PRC TESL Programs
1201 Campbell Hall
University of California at Los Angeles
Los Angeles, CA 90024

Americans who wish to teach in China should also contact the appropriate office at their institution to see whether a formal or informal agreement exists between their institution and one in China that includes the exchange of faculty. If individuals have personal friends at specific Chinese institutions or have met Chinese scholars visiting the United States, they can also write directly to those individuals/institutions requesting information about teaching opportunities.

2. Preparing for the Trip

Living in China is a challenging, unique experience, and it is prudent to prepare as thoroughly as possible for what must be regarded as a great adventure. No single source can provide complete advice; the pages that follow address common questions and offer tips gleaned from reports and conversations with individuals who have lived in China since the reopening of academic institutions to Americans in 1979. The observations and suggestions included here emphasize the mundane and difficult sides of life in China, but that is only because no special advice is needed to enhance the exhilaration of living there—the rewards of friendship, the benefits of travel, the satisfaction of professional achievement are part of every experience. And if life in China can be frustrating at times, it can also be great fun. It is hoped that the insights of others will help you avoid mistakes, minimize difficulties, and take maximum advantage of the opportunity to live and work in China.

ARRANGING TO LEAVE THE UNITED STATES

Sponsoring organizations in the United States or China generally provide detailed information on travel arrangements, visas, shipping procedures, methods of payment while abroad, and regulations and procedures governing specific cases. Because there is constant change in regulations, services, and procedures, you should seek specific information on these matters from your sponsor. The following requirements and procedures were in effect in the autumn of 1986; they should be read as a general guide of what to expect as a long-term resident rather than as a prescription relevant to every case.

7

PASSPORTS AND VISAS   Passports and visas are required for travel to China. U.S. citizens who do not hold a valid passport should apply for one through their local passport office, which is located in the post office in smaller cities. You should allow at least six weeks' turnaround time for receipt of your passport.

Visas may be obtained from the Embassy of the People's Republic of China in Washington, D.C., or from one of the Chinese Consulates in San Francisco, New York, Houston, and Chicago (addresses and telephone numbers are included below). You can ask your sponsor for a visa form; some large travel agencies keep them in stock as well. The application must be filled out in duplicate and mailed with the passport, two passport photos, and a $7 visa fee (for each applicant) to the nearest embassy or consulate. (If you want express mail service, include a self-addressed express mail label along with the proper postage.) If you have severe time constraints, ask the embassy or consulate for advice on expediting the process.

When you fill out the visa application, include the exact dates (if you know them) of your entry into and exit from China; if you do not know them, estimate as closely as you can. The visa will be stamped in the passport and returned, usually in 10 days to 2 weeks. Issuance of a visa hinges on your Chinese host unit's approval and its transmission of information to the appropriate consulate or to the embassy in the United States. Students' and researchers' visas are approved by the institution in China with which they will be affiliated. Teachers' visas are approved by the State Education Commission, the Foreign Experts Bureau, the ministry responsible for particular institutions, or the foreign affairs office of the provincial government—depending on the hiring unit.

When you apply for the visa, send as much supporting evidence as you can—including copies of contracts, letters of acceptance, or other documents—to prove that you are expected in China. Sometimes a visa approval is sent from China to a consulate other than the one to which the visa application was mailed; if delays occur, it is wise to check on this possibility. Be sure also to check the time span of your visa; if it expires while you are in China, it is your responsibility to have it renewed, with the help of your host unit. At the moment, only single-entry visas to China are issued; negotiations are under way, however, to issue multiple-entry visas to Americans going to China and to Chinese coming to the United States. There have been reports of visas issued at the point of entry into China, but relying on such a procedure seems risky for the long-term visitor. Visas also can be secured in Hong Kong through one of the larger travel agencies. (No transit visa for Hong Kong is needed if you plan to stop over there.)

If you plan to travel through Japan, you will not need a transit visa if your stay is less than 24 hours and is confined to Narita Airport. If you will be leaving Narita Airport, transit visas for 72 hours or less usually can be obtained at the airport, but the wait is generally long. The transit visa is good for up to two weeks in Japan. Before leaving the United States, it is wise to apply in advance for a Japanese tourist visa; they can be obtained at the nearest Japanese Consulate and are good for four years and multiple entries. You can also apply to the Japanese Embassy in Beijing for a visa should you want to visit Japan after your arrival in China. Many American residents in China travel to Japan for medical or dental care or for recreation, shopping, or research. For the addresses of the nearest Japanese Consulate, write or call:

Embassy of Japan
2514 Massachusetts Avenue, NW
Washington, DC 20005
(202-234-2266)

Listed below are the PRC government offices in the United States:

Embassy of the People's Republic of China
2300 Constitution Avenue, NW
Washington, DC 20008
Commercial: 202-328-2520
Visas: 202-328-2517
Telex: 440038 PRC UI
Commercial: 440673

Consulate General of the People's Republic of China
104 S. Michigan Avenue
Suite 1200
Chicago, IL 60603
Administration: 312-346-0287

Consulate General of the People's Republic of China
3417 Montrose Boulevard
Houston, TX 77006
Commercial: 713-524-4064
Visas: 713-524-4311
Telex: 762173 chinconsul hou

Consulate General of the People's Republic of China
520 12th Avenue
New York, NY 10036
Commercial: 212-564-1139
Visas: 212-279-0885
Telex: 429134 cgcny

Consulate General of the People's Republic of China
1450 Laguna Avenue
San Francisco, CA 94115
Commercial: 415-563-4858
Visas: 415-563-4857
Telex: 340515 chimission sfo

INVITING RELATIVES TO CHINA   The host unit or its parent organization (for example, the State Education Commission, the Chinese Academy of Social Sciences, or the Chinese Academy of Sciences) issues the approval for a visitor's visa. Because the host organization must clear the dates with the China Travel Service and then communicate its approval to issue the visa to the Chinese Embassy or Consulate in the United States, the process can be complicated and time consuming. Some Americans have secured Chinese tourist visas for individual travel in Hong Kong within a few days. See p. 41 for the address of the Hong Kong branch of the China Travel Service. If the wait for a visa seems unduly long, the invited party should call the Chinese Embassy in Washington, D.C. (202-328-2517).

Once your relative is in China, you are responsible for securing housing, which can be a problem, especially during the busy tourist season (from May through October). Some hotels will allow you to put up a cot or an extra bed for a small daily fee. Students in dormitories have also been able to make either formal or informal arrangements for housing guests for short periods. In addition to housing, you and your host institution will be responsible for arranging travel for your visitor within China. Arrangements for spouses and children planning to accompany researchers and teachers to China are discussed in detail in Chapter 3.

IMMUNIZATIONS   China currently does not require immunizations unless a traveler enters from an area known to have cholera or yellow fever. But recently, the Chinese press has carried articles stating that more attention will be paid to the health of those entering China and that an international health card with a record of basic immunizations is useful for those who plan to stay in China a year or longer. There are a number of immunizations that are recommended or that should be considered, in consultation with your personal physician, depending on your health history, the length of your stay in China, and where you will be living and traveling. Some of these are discussed below. Useful information about relevant immunizations, diseases, and prevention can be found in *Health Information for International Travel*, available for $4.50 from:

Superintendent of Documents
U.S. Government Printing Office
Washington, DC 20402
(202-783-3238)

(When ordering, refer to publication no. HHS 86-8280.) For information on health conditions in developing countries, contact:

International Travel Clinic
Johns Hopkins University Hampton House
624 N. Broadway
Baltimore, MD 21205
(301-955-8931)

Tetanus remains a problem in China, and physicians usually recommend the complete series of diphtheria, tetanus, and pertussis (DPT) vaccine and a booster dose (given every 10 years) for anyone over the age of 7. Children under seven should have the number of doses appropriate for their age. Typhoid vaccinations are recommended for travelers who will be living away from the usual tourist areas, in places where water or food sources may be contaminated and where typhoid is known to be endemic. In addition, because poliomyelitis is endemic in all developing countries, travelers who have completed the primary series of polio vaccinations should consult their physician for advice on supplementary doses. Measles, mumps, and rubella also are not controlled in developing countries. In particular, pregnant travelers should be immunized against rubella.

Viral hepatitis, type A, is widespread in China but does not present a particular threat to those who stay along the normal tourist routes. Nevertheless, you should consult your physician about the advisability of receiving immune globulin as prophylaxis for this type of hepatitis. Immune globulin is effective only for three to six months and is not available in China to renew your protection. Some long-term residents bring in the serum and arrange to store it in China. In deciding whether to obtain hepatitis A vaccine—and/or chloroquine medicine for malaria, which still occurs in some areas—you should discuss your lifestyle and the extent of your planned travels with your personal physician.

Vaccination against Japanese encephalitis is strongly advised although not required. The disease, which can cause serious brain damage and even death, is transmitted by mosquitoes and occurs mainly from June through September in rural Asian areas, although there have been cases in urban centers. There is no risk during the winter in temperate areas of China. All travelers to China, but especially those individuals who will be living or traveling for prolonged periods in rural areas, should take precautions against mosquito bites and consult their physicians regarding immunization. The Japanese encephalitis vaccine has been tested in the United States but is available only from specified Japanese encephalitis investigators. For a list of these individuals, see Appendix F, and for further information, contact:

> Division of Vector-Borne Viral Diseases
> Center for Infectious Diseases
> Centers for Disease Control
> P.O. Box 2087
> Ft. Collins, CO 80522
> (303-221-6428)

The U.S. Embassy in Beijing also provides immunizations through a series of three shots at nominal cost—Y15 each.

Although the official Chinese government regulations affecting foreign students, researchers, and teachers in China and the health certificate required from such persons have not yet been changed, the Chinese Embassy in Washington, D.C., reports that all Americans who will be in China for one year or longer are required to be tested for AIDS (acquired immune deficiency syndrome) prior to commencing their program in China. You may be tested in the United States within two months prior to departure for China and must take a medical certificate with you stating that you do not have AIDS. It is recommended that you have the test in the United States to facilitate your entry into China and the commencement of your academic program there. If you are planning to be in China less than one year, you do not need to be tested for AIDS. However, if you originally plan to be in China less than one year and then extend your stay beyond a year, you will have to be tested for AIDS in China.

Since no official regulations about the AIDS testing have yet been published in English, officials of the Chinese Embassy caution that the above are only general guidelines. You should check with the Chinese Embassy or Consulates about updated information on AIDS testing needed for China as you prepare for your trip.

MEDICAL INSURANCE   Travelers are strongly advised to retain their existing insurance policies; they should also discuss with their insurance companies how much coverage they will have abroad and how to apply for reimbursement of services rendered in China. Most Chinese health administrators will not be familiar with long, complicated insurance forms, and direct billing of insurance companies is unlikely. It is therefore a matter of some importance to clarify the procedures to be followed before you leave the United States.

Those who cannot maintain coverage through their home institutions should consider two insurance programs for which the National Association for Foreign Student Affairs acts as a policyholder.

Individuals under the age of 65 who meet the following criteria are eligible for coverage from Hinchcliff International, Inc.: (1) they must be engaged full time in international educational activities, (2) they must be temporarily outside their home country or country of regular domicile as a nonresident alien, and (3) they may not be applicants for permanent residency status in the country they are visiting. Eligible dependents with a similar visa or passport who accompany the major policyholder include spouses under the age of 65 and unmarried children under the age of 19 who are chiefly dependent on the major policyholder for support and maintenance. Further information and application forms can be obtained from:

Hinchcliff International, Inc.
120 S. Cayuga Street
Ithaca, NY 14850
(607-272-5057)

Full-time students under the age of 40 who are actively engaged in international educational activities outside their home country can write for information and applications to:

Marsh & McLennan Group Associates
Accident and Sickness Department
1211 Avenue of the Americas
New York, NY 10036
(212-997-8116)

MONEY, BANKING, AND CREDIT CARDS   Americans who will be paid by U.S. sources while in China can receive money directly in two ways:

1. Money can be deposited in a designated account in a U.S. bank that has an international division with correspondent relations with China (many major banks in large cities offer this service); funds can then be wired to a Chinese bank account as needed.
2. Money can be wired directly to a Chinese bank account.

Fund transfers to China for the most part are now routine, but before your departure you should clarify with the U.S. bank how these transactions are managed. Anyone who plans to stay in China longer than a few months should open a U.S. dollar bank account with the Bank of China.

Banking regulations vary from place to place, and policies change constantly. The following information is only a guide to a variety of current situations. Most long-term residents advise that you carry a good supply of traveler's checks. All the major brands are honored, but American Express traveler's checks can be purchased at designated branches of the Bank of China in 20 cities. In addition, the company has an office in Beijing (in the lobby of the Beijing-Toronto Hotel) and will arrange for reimbursement for lost checks within a few days in major cities. Traveler's checks offer a slightly higher rate of exchange than cash, and they can be converted at any Bank of China service desk located in airports, major hotels, and stores that serve foreigners. A 1 percent service fee is charged for cashing traveler's checks.

Because payroll and third-party checks cannot be cashed under any circumstances and personal or bank checks take at least one month to clear, obtaining cash in China can sometimes present problems. Residents of Beijing, Nanjing, and Shanghai report that by far the most useful method of obtaining cash is to write a personal check on a U.S. bank account and then guarantee it with an American Express card. According to American Express officials, at designated branches of the Bank of China in 42 cities, you may write a personal check for up to Y500 with an American Express green card and Y2,000 with a gold card. (The official exchange rate in January 1987 was Y3.71 to US$1.00.)

Residents of other cities, however, advise different arrangements, for example, international money orders. Unfortunately, there are no standard banking regulations in China, and what may be true in one city may not hold in another. For instance, a teacher in Jinan states that the American Express card cannot be used there and instead advises travelers to obtain money from home through international money orders, which can be cashed immediately. In other areas of China, however, international money orders may take a month to clear. And a teacher in Guangzhou reports that Visa is accepted there for cashing checks but that American Express is not.

Although American Express international offices in the United States report that regulations and services are constantly in flux as new agreements are signed with China, at this writing, within a 21-day period, you can cash up to a total of US$1,000 with an American Express green card and up to US$2,000 with a gold card. As cash, you must receive foreign exchange certificates, which can be reconverted to dollars at your point of exit if accompanied by all of your exchange memos. Also, Visa and MasterCard will provide cash advances of up to US$350 in major cities at designated Bank of China service counters (the service charge is 4 percent).

Credit cards can be used for some purchases, but policies are changing because of fraudulent use of the cards and it is unwise to count on using them for major payments. American Express advises that only major hotels, retail stores (such as Friendship Stores and other stores catering to foreigners), and restaurants authorized by the Bank of China will accept credit cards. It is safest to convert money at a Bank of China counter before making purchases.

To help you plan your finances, Appendix G includes sample prices for hotels, food, services, transportation, clothing, and medical care. For further information on currency and banking, see Chapter 6.

CUSTOMS REGULATIONS   On the final leg of your flight into China, you will be given a customs declaration form on which you must list any cameras, tape recorders, valuable jewelry, or typewriters being brought into the country and the amount of currency and traveler's checks on your person. The form will be checked at the customs desk—at the baggage claim area in most airports—and you will be given a copy, which must be presented each time you leave the country. If you cannot prove that you are taking out all that you declared upon entry, you will be assessed a fairly stiff fine. If you lose any of the declared items while in China, notify your host unit immediately.

Foreigners entering China may bring up to four bottles of liquor, 600 cigarettes, an unlimited supply of medicine for personal use (be sure that it is carried in its original labeled container), personal effects, and an unlimited amount of currency and traveler's checks. There are no restrictions on still cameras, 8mm cameras, or film, but professional film and video equipment may not be brought in or taken out of China without special permission. Appendix H lists items that can be taxed upon entry into China if they are not for personal use.

Americans going to Shanghai should note that the U.S. Consulate General there has received frequent complaints that Chinese customs officials in Shanghai routinely assess and collect unusually high customs duties, particularly for supplies forwarded as unaccompanied baggage or sent through the international mail. Shanghai customs has published a pamphlet that lists prohibited and restricted items and gives some ballpark duty figures. Although this information cannot be taken to be definitive, it does give prospective American residents an idea of potential customs hassles. If you are going to live in the Shanghai consular district, which includes the provinces of Jiangsu, Anhui, and Zhejiang, you should request a copy of this pamphlet from your Chinese host as you prepare to leave the United States.

According to the pamphlet,

● Articles prohibited entry include not only the usual firearms, wireless transmitters, drugs, plants, contaminated foodstuffs, and Chinese currency but also, and much more ambiguously, "publications, photographs, tapes, records and any other material harmful to Chinese politics, economy, culture or morals."

● Certain articles are allowed entry only in restricted quantity: wrist watches, pocket watches, and bicycles at one per person; cameras, radios, and sewing machines at one per family.

● Listed rates of duty are high: 20 percent for grains, flours, medical equipment, scientific instruments, and electronic calculators; 50 percent for medicines, home and office equipment, tape recorders, tools, televisions, sports equipment, and musical instruments; 100 percent or higher (150 or 200 percent) for all other items.

In addition, some advice for minimizing customs problems includes the following:

● Bring in as accompanied baggage as many personal supplies as possible since personally accompanied baggage usually receives the most favorable treatment by Chinese customs officials.

● Heavy books and other professional supplies are best shipped separately; your Chinese host institution should be requested to handle customs clearance as part of its support for your activities in China.

● You should be prepared to encounter what you might judge to be arbitrary and excessive customs duties levied on any packages sent by international mail.

Some Americans who will be in China for extended periods of time have requested information about bringing their pets. Personnel at the Chinese Embassy in Washington, D.C., have stated that although bringing animals into China is not prohibited, it is unwise to do so. Chinese customs officers are extremely strict about quarantining animals, and often this results in the animal being quarantined for about as long as the American remains in China.

When you leave the United States, be sure to register with U.S. customs officials any cameras or other equipment subject to duty that you are taking with you to China. Save the receipts to present upon reentry into the United States so that you are not taxed on items made in Asia that you bought prior to departure. A useful booklet, *Customs Hints for Returning U.S. Citizens: Know Before You Go*, is available free of charge from the:

U.S. Customs Service
1301 Constitution Avenue, NW
Washington, DC 20229

and from most travel agents. Travelers returning to the United States from China can bring back, duty free, purchases of up to US$400 per person; an additional US$1,000 worth of goods will be taxed at a rate of 10 percent. Regular duty charges, which are considerably higher, apply to purchases exceeding the initial US$1,400. Special rates and exemptions are given to Americans who live abroad for over one year. If you have a letter of invitation or appointment stating that you will be residing in China for one year or longer, be certain to show it to U.S. customs officials on your return to the United States.

BAGGAGE AND SHIPPING PROCEDURES   It is best to "travel light" if you wish to avoid excess baggage charges. Passengers flying to China are allowed two pieces of luggage, neither of which may exceed 62 inches (adding all three linear dimensions); both pieces together may not exceed 106 inches. The Civil Aviation Administration of China (CAAC), the Chinese national carrier, calculates limits by weight; economy-class passengers are allowed two bags, which may not exceed a total of 44 pounds (or 20 kilograms). In addition, travel agents advise that carry-on allowances are becoming stricter on all airlines.

Baggage allowances for traveling within Asia, including China, are also calculated by weight; the 44-pound limit applies in most countries. Thus, it is possible that if you travel within China, or if you stop in Hong Kong or Tokyo or Shanghai, for example, before going on to your final destination in China, you may be charged for excess baggage weight even though you stayed within the limit on your U.S. carrier. Excess baggage charges for groups are levied on the entire group.

For long-term stays, items may be shipped ahead by mail (allow two to three months for sea mail) in care of the foreign affairs office of your host institution. However, used clothing, even for personal use, cannot be sent through the mails. (See Appendix H for current regulations governing articles sent into China.) Of particular note are the special book rates that apply to China—check with your local post office for details. One returned scholar reports that the U.S. Postal Service will supply used post office bags that can be filled with boxed printed matter (15 pounds minimum, per bag 66 pounds maximum); the bags go by surface mail (six to eight weeks in transit) for 43 cents a pound. Several airlines will accept large parcels as air freight; check with the cargo division of the airlines for details. (It is best to schedule air shipments after your own arrival in China so you can pick them up and clear them through customs.)

INCOME TAXES WHILE ABROAD   In the summer of 1986, the tax agreement between the United States and the People's Republic of

China, which had been signed by President Ronald Reagan and Premier Zhao Ziyang in Beijing on April 30, 1984, was ratified by the U.S. Senate. According to this tax treaty, U.S. teachers and scholars in China are exempt from taxation by the Chinese government for three years—either consecutive or interrupted—on payment received for their teaching or research activities. However, if they do any paid free-lance work during their stay in China, they are subject to Chinese and U.S. taxes for the payment received for that work. The U.S. government gives a dollar-for-dollar tax credit under these circumstances; that is, if a U.S. citizen pays the Chinese government $65 in taxes and owes the U.S. government $100 in taxes, he or she will be required to pay the U.S. government only the remaining $35.

As U.S. citizens, Americans teaching or conducting research in China are subject to U.S. taxes, but there is a special exemption for the first $70,000 earned overseas if the individual is out of the United States for more than 11 months.

These laws apply whether the U.S. citizen receives payment from a Chinese or U.S. source because for tax purposes the U.S. government considers income to arise where services are performed. Thus, if a teacher or scholar is paid by a U.S. source for work performed in China, taxation is determined by the regulations of the tax treaty between the United States and China. Officials of the U.S. Treasury Department also indicated that if there are conflicting regulations between the new U.S. tax law, which went into effect January 1, 1987, and the tax treaty between the United States and China, the tax treaty will prevail.

TEACHERS: HIRING, INTERNATIONAL TRAVEL, FINANCES
As noted previously, the distinction between a "foreign teacher" and a "foreign expert" is extremely important because it affects all arrangements for a teaching assignment in China.

Foreign Experts   The number of foreign expert positions is determined each year by the State Council of the People's Republic of China. Funds for the positions are also provided by the State Council (i.e., the Chinese government) in two parts: salaries and benefits.

Salaries   As an invited expert in China, your salary is determined by the work you have accomplished and by professional ability, with due consideration of your record, experience, and education. Monthly salaries generally range from Y500 to Y1,500, but they are negotiable for well-known scholars, professors, and individuals with special skills.

Salaries are paid in local currency—*renminbi*—once a month. If your family (spouse and children under 12) has accompanied you to China, you are permitted to convert 30 percent of your salary into foreign currency. If you do not bring any family members, you may convert 50 percent of your salary. If your spouse has also been invited as a foreign expert and you have no children living with you in China, each of you may convert 50 percent of your salary into foreign currency. You will not receive U.S. dollars in foreign currency conversion. Rather, a portion of your salary can be remitted directly to your bank in the United States, or you can receive the converted salary as foreign exchange certificates, which can only be used in China. These certificates are widely accepted in Chinese stores that specifically cater to foreigners (such as Friendship Stores and hotel shops, which carry imported items such as cigarettes, liquor, soft drinks, and magazines). You can obtain the foreign currency allowance each month or all at once at the expiration of your contract.

Any foreign expert who has completed one calendar (or academic) year's service is given half a month's extra salary.

Benefits Following is a list of benefits that foreign experts will receive while in China.

• International Travel: If your term of service in China as a foreign expert is at least one calendar (or academic) year, you may take, with the host institution's consent in advance, your spouse and children under 12 years of age. The host institution will provide direct-route, tourist-class tickets to and from China on CAAC for you and your family. If you wish to purchase international air tickets to China on a different carrier, you will be reimbursed in nonconvertible *renminbi* for the cost of direct-route, economy-class airfares for yourself and any accompanying family members.

• Excess Baggage Allowance: The host organization will pay excess baggage charges, both to and from China, on no more than 24 kilograms per person and 72 kilograms for a family of more than three. The baggage must be shipped as unaccompanied air freight. If you prefer to send it by sea rather than air, the host organization will pay for the cost of 1 cubic meter of unaccompanied luggage per person but no more than 2 cubic meters for a family of more than two. The cost of incoming excess baggage will be reimbursed in nonconvertible *renminbi* upon the presentation of receipts.

• Housing: Housing includes furniture, bedding, a bathroom, a television set, a refrigerator, and facilities for heating and air conditioning. All are provided free of charge by the host organization for the expert and accompanying family members.

• Medical and Dental Care: While in China, you and your family will receive free medical service in accordance with China's medical system. Exceptions include expenses incurred for registration, doctor's home visits, fitting false teeth, teeth cleaning, cosmetic surgery, eyeglasses, meals in a hospital, and nonmedical tonics.

• Vacations: If you are a foreign expert who has worked one calendar (or academic) year, you are entitled, in addition to China's national holidays, to one month's paid vacation and an additional vacation allowance of Y800. If you have worked half a year (or two semesters in succession but less than one year), you are entitled to a two-week vacation and an allowance of Y400. If you have worked less than half a year, you are not entitled to any vacation time or allowance. Vacation allowances are paid either in one lump sum or in two payments, half at the end of each semester. They may not be converted into foreign currency. If you work in a college or university, your vacation must correspond with the Chinese academic vacation in those institutions. If you work in an information institute or a publishing house, you will not be entitled to a vacation until you have worked at least half a year.

See the FEB brochure, *Information on the Recruitment of Foreign Experts*, in Appendix E and the sample contract for teachers in Appendix I for more details about these arrangements.

Foreign Teachers   Foreign teachers are recruited directly by Chinese institutions of higher learning, by particular institution departments, or by local provincial or municipal departments or bureaus of education. Their positions are funded by the hiring institution.

The provisions under which teachers are hired by individual institutions are *not* standardized. If you have been invited to teach in China as a foreign teacher, you should request a contract from your host institution that specifies the details of your salary, housing, medical care, vacation time, excess baggage allowance, teaching load, and other requirements. A copy of this contract will be sent to the Bureau of Foreign Affairs of the State Education Commission. This agency has no influence in determining the contents of the contract, but it does keep the contract on file in case a foreign teacher has questions or problems with adherence to the provisions of the contract.

Salaries   The salaries of foreign teachers, which are paid in *renminbi*, are usually lower than those of foreign experts. And unlike the salary arrangements for foreign experts, some host institutions do not permit foreign teachers to convert any of their salaries to foreign currency (i.e., to foreign exchange certificates). As a foreign teacher, it is important for you to know before going to China whether your host institution permits such conversions because airline tickets for travel outside China—for example, your return tickets to the United States—can only be purchased with foreign exchange certificates. Foreigners also may be required to use foreign exchange certificates for airline travel within China.

Benefits Following is a list of benefits provided to foreign teachers in China.

• International Travel and Excess Baggage: Policies in this area vary with the hiring institution. In some instances, foreign teachers are required to pay their own international travel and excess baggage costs; in others, they are reimbursed for such expenses (usually in *renminbi*) by the host institution. To avoid difficulties, be certain to check with your host institution about what reimbursement, if any, you will receive for international travel and excess baggage expenses.

• Housing and Food: Housing, including utilities, is provided by the host institution. Sometimes a housekeeper also will be provided. Food for foreign teachers and their spouses is usually available free of charge at the institution's dining hall; also, for a small monthly fee, accompanying children may eat at the dining hall. (Generally, food is *not* provided for foreign experts who are spouses of foreign teachers; however, one gentleman who traveled to China as a foreign expert whose wife had been hired as a foreign teacher reported that food was also provided to *him* free of charge—but only after considerable negotiating on his part.)

• Medical and Dental Care: Adequate medical care is provided free by the host institution, although some foreign teachers have reported that they were sometimes requested to pay small charges for medical services. Dental care often is not provided. You should check with your host institution regarding its particular policies.

• Vacations: At any particular institution, vacation arrangements and allowances for foreign teachers may be similar to those for foreign experts; but again, it is wise to check on specifics with the host organization before signing a contract.

Notification/Contracts Americans going to China either as foreign experts or foreign teachers have had as long as eight months or as little as a few weeks to prepare for their assignments after being notified that they had been accepted for a specific position. In addition, a number of individuals have had only scanty concrete information before leaving the United States about salaries, living arrangements, and courses to be taught—and sometimes even these plans, particularly courses to be taught, have been changed after their arrival in China.

Most foreign experts receive a contract—or at least the draft of a contract—before they leave the United States, although some experts and foreign teachers report waiting as long as several months after their arrival in China before completing negotiations and signing a contract (see the sample contract in Appendix I). Most teachers have reported, however, that although they may have known few details beforehand about their situation in China and much had to be taken on faith, in general, arrangements were satisfactory. Overall, salaries have been more than adequate to cover expenses in China, and housing and living conditions have been acceptable. In some cases, teachers' salaries were even increased slightly or additional payments made to compensate for extra services such as grading college entrance examinations or writing textbooks and articles for local publications.

SUGGESTED READING   Americans who have adjusted to life and work in China without the benefit of a fairly comprehensive knowledge of modern Chinese history and thought recommend that individuals in a similar situation read as much background information as possible before beginning their work there. The references listed in Appendix L have been selected specifically for this audience. Also, you might find interesting the protocol for cooperation in educational exchanges that was signed by the United States and China in 1985 (see Appendix J).

WHAT TO TAKE FOR DAILY LIFE

The suggestions that follow are meant to serve only as a rough guide to help you prepare for life and work in China. Your choices will, of course, depend on personal preferences, how long you plan to stay in China, and where you will be living. If you are based in Beijing, if you like to shop, if you wear sizes that are not too different from Chinese sizes, and if you are lucky, you will be able to find almost any item you need—in time. But if you live in a smaller city or one that has fewer foreigners—and this includes even Shanghai—you should prepare more thoroughly. You should also take into account your plans for internal travel once you arrive in China.

Every Chinese city is dotted with neighborhood shopping areas complete with a hardware store (stocked with tools, pottery, and baskets), *Xinhua* (New China) bookstore, laundry, restaurants, bakery, barbershop, photography shop, bicycle repair shop, tailor, and a general store that carries everything from cooking items, toiletries, and clothing to bicycles and sewing machines. Clothing from Hong Kong and a variety of other items can now be found at the many free and night markets that have sprung up in Chinese cities in recent years. Imported specialty items, however, are available only in major hotels for foreigners and in Friendship Stores; the best buys tend to be luxury goods such as embroidered shirts and cashmere sweaters. Some hotel shops in Beijing and Shanghai carry quite an array of imported goods—from wines, candies, shampoos, and makeup to plastic kitchenware.

Despite an increasing abundance of consumer goods in China, it is still difficult to predict what will be available at any given time, even in the larger cities. If you plan to arrive during the coldest winter months, you should pack enough warm clothing to be comfortable while you survey the local stores. If you arrive in autumn, on the other hand, you will probably have ample time to accumulate all you need to get through the winter. Beijing residents report that down clothing is usually a bargain and the "down fair" held in the fall offers a good selection at reasonable prices. No matter what season you arrive in China, however, it is a good idea to plan to live out of a suitcase for the first hectic week or so.

In general, pack carefully; the less you take, the better because storage space is limited in hotels and dormitories. Excess baggage also is expensive to bring into China and even more cumbersome to take out; it can become a real burden if you move from place to place. A small footlocker or trunk with a lock is useful for storing and transporting goods.

CLOTHING   Dress is still very casual in China, but the Chinese are beginning to dress up more now and recent visitors observe that it is wise to take along a few dressy outfits for the most formal affairs. One senior scholar, who took seriously a suggestion to dress casually, writes back that he was surprised to be met at the airport in Beijing by four professors, all wearing white shirts, ties, and Western-cut suits. He asked his colleagues about dress codes, and they told him that there had been a major change in attire in the past year. New clothes received through government-issue programs or purchased with recent bonuses were all Western style. The American scholar also observed that in the parks in Beijing, young people wore Western formal attire (i.e., suits and ties, dresses) on their day off; the "Mao jacket," nearly universal in the countryside, was worn in cities only by older men and women. He concludes, "I think that some people were disappointed that I did not dress in more formal Western attire. They may have been looking for a role model." A female researcher's experience was similar—on a trip to Xinjiang she was asked to remove her Chinese army-style green overcoat for group photographs with Chinese colleagues, who were outspoken about their embarrassment at her "inappropriate" attire.

Other foreigners, especially students, have a different opinion—that the outsider will seem less foreign in more standard Chinese dress. As one teacher points out, "Foreigners can wear almost anything that is not obviously risqué, but the stranger (or more Western) your clothes, the more people stare at you." As Chinese clothing becomes ever more Western in design, the differences seem less apparent, and the question becomes not one of Chinese or Western wear but more one of what is appropriate for a given occasion and the status of the wearer. It is certainly no longer the case that living in China can be viewed, wardrobe-wise, as an extended camping trip.

The comments below—all from female teachers working in China—may be helpful in wardrobe planning.

Multi-purpose clothes that can be worn in layers are good for everyday wear. Chinese women are starting to dress up again, but in most places are still careful to dress modestly (Shanghai and Guangzhou being the exceptions), so women foreigners will feel less conspicuous if they avoid extremely tight-fitting, revealing, provocative, or bizarre clothing. It's not necessary to avoid bright colors and anything with frills or decoration. In fact, Chinese women enjoy seeing the contemporary fashion styles of their foreign colleagues. But, and this is very important, women should keep in mind that extremes in clothing (and, indeed, of all behavior) may offend Chinese people who have had little experience with Westerners.

Wear whatever you are comfortable wearing in front of groups of people. Modesty should be considered, but not to the extent of totally covering up. Chinese women generally don't wear sleeveless, low-neck clothing, but I always wore sleeveless clothes in the heat. Women can also wear shorts for sports and leisure activities, just not too short. Bright colors are fine. Earrings are also fine but not a lot of jewelry. Classrooms are not heated or air conditioned, so it is important to keep weather conditions in mind.

[I suggest] clothes that are easy-care, versatile, colorful, and somewhat professional for the classroom. Dresses are good for the summer. A larger pair of pants is necessary to put layers of long underwear on in the winter.

Male teachers recommend shirts, sweaters, and trousers for everyday wear with a tie and suit or sportcoat for special occasions. "Ties are not expected for regular classroom teaching, only at special banquets and official functions." Comfortable walking shoes are recommended for both men and women.

Most foreigners who have lived in China more than a few months put together their own unique wardrobe of Chinese and Western styles. Some make a hobby of having clothing made, seeking out fine-quality silk and woolen materials and the many good tailors to be found in Chinese cities. Providing a model is a relatively easy way to ensure proper fit and style, but it is not always foolproof; and tailoring can still be rather expensive (Y30 for a shirt, for example), time-consuming (it requires several fittings and about three weeks), and something of a gamble in the end. One woman's experience with a tailor, after she was unable to find interesting suitable clothes in the stores, was related in *The Boston Globe* last fall:

> Tailors, abundant in all the outdoor markets, and very cheap, seemed the obvious solution. I fancied navy wool and settled for a fine, thick black, with black silk for a lining. In a zipper, the closest I could get, though, was light blue. I presented the materials, with a model pair of pants borrowed from a French friend, to a tailor recommended by a colleague. Exactly the same, I instructed. She nodded. But weeks later, when I tried on the result, I found the crotch of my new pair of pants hanging halfway to my knees. The tailor explained of course I would need room for the two or three pairs of woolen underwear I would be wearing. Very dubiously, she agreed to take up the seam. (Marcia Yudkin, Special to the *Globe*)

Keeping clothing clean is a problem for any resident of China. Most Chinese cities are dusty, and air conditioning is rare in the summer; also, cycling is hard on clothes, and hot water is neither abundant nor constant. Because laundry must be done by hand or sent out, clothing should be washable and easy to care for. In a typical Beijing hotel these days, laundry costs about Y1 per piece—for an average of about Y25 a week—and takes from two days in hotels to one week in institutional and neighborhood laundries. Most people wash underwear and socks by hand and send out larger items such as sheets, shirts, and trousers. One researcher recommends that families buy a small washing machine (cost: Y380). Drycleaning is available, but it too is expensive and the results are not always predictable. (If you take Woolite, you can wash your own sweaters.) Reports indicate that the Jianguo Hotel in Beijing offers good drycleaning at relatively reasonable prices—Y7 for a padded jacket, for example. Chinese detergents are hard on clothes and hands, so be certain to take sturdy items in good condition and rubber gloves if harsh detergents irritate your hands. Repairs usually are not too difficult: sewing supplies are easily found in neighborhood shops, clothing repair shops are inexpensive and efficient, and shoe repairmen set up shop on the streets (their prices are quite reasonable).

To help you decide what to take and what to buy in China, Appendix G lists items that are generally available (with approximate prices) as well as goods that are not easily found. Clothing is stocked seasonally; try to make your purchases early in the season as stores run out of the best selections fairly quickly. Size is a factor in determining price: a large sweater costs slightly more than a smaller one because it uses more material. Also, large sizes are often difficult to find, especially in Chinese department stores. Men who wear extra-large clothing or shoes larger than size 10 should either take most of what they will need or plan to use a tailor. Long underwear, pajamas, and silk underwear generally may be good buys, but they are simply not available in larger sizes. Because Chinese sizes do not correspond exactly to American sizes, you should always try on clothing before you buy it—a sight, by the way, that often provides a great deal of amusement for Chinese onlookers because stores seldom have private fitting rooms.

Wardrobes should be planned for the city in which you will be located. For example, Beijing is bitterly cold in winter and hot and humid in summer. In general, except for the far south, you should be prepared for extreme variations in temperature. This advice, by the way, includes Shanghai, Nanjing, and Hangzhou; do not consider them "southern" cities when preparing for a stay that extends through the winter. Residents of these cities warn the newcomer that winters are cold and the heat is turned on late in the season (well into November)—and then only for a few hours a day. An American teacher writes: "Hangzhou appeared to me to be on a line with Jacksonville, Florida—I'm freezing!"

One reason to take warm clothing even for climates that appear to be moderate is that public buildings, libraries, offices, and laboratories are virtually unheated. The Chinese practice of dressing in layers that can be added or subtracted as conditions change makes a good deal of sense. Long underwear, woolen sweaters, down vests, woolen or insulated socks, heavy gloves, a warm, light overcoat or jacket, and sturdy shoes with heavy soles are essential for those who will spend long hours at work. "Many times I wear as much indoors as outdoors," an American teacher in Lanzhou writes. "Last winter I wore seven layers on top with thermal longies and Chinese wool long underwear under my trousers, and my feet froze with two pairs of socks on. You feel like a balloon and can't bend. And all this where the temperature never went below 16°F; sometimes I sat in my 'heated' office at temperatures between 45°–50°F and froze."

The following wardrobe (items marked with an asterisk are those best brought from home) would serve anyone living in a city with wide variations in temperature:

lightweight or cotton trousers*
sturdy walking shoes with thick
    soles for warmth*
long- and short-sleeved wash-
    and-wear shirts
turtleneck pullovers*
warm socks*
long underwear
cotton underwear
bathing suit and cap*
warm bathrobe

warm, sturdy slippers*
woolen sweaters
comfortable sandals for
    summer*
rain boots*
flannel and cotton pajamas
cold-weather parka
rain parka or all-weather coat
knitted cap
umbrella
walking shorts*

You should add to this list at least one or two dressy outfits for more formal occasions.

The median temperatures below give you some idea of what to expect, but you should know that indoor temperatures are often lower, and the cold more penetrating, than is suggested by average outdoor readings. Higher humidity in the south intensifies the cold. Most hotels and guest houses for tourists and researchers are heated and air conditioned; but most dormitories are not air conditioned and some (especially in the south) are heated only for a few hours each day in winter.

	Winter	Summer	Fall and Spring
Northeast (Harbin)	0°F	70°F	40°F
North China (Beijing)	23°F	78°F	55°F
Central China (Wuhan)	37°F	84°F	62°F
East China (Shanghai)	38°F	82°F	60°F
South China (Guangzhou)	57°F	83°F	73°F

MEDICATIONS AND TOILETRIES   While you are in China, managing your own health problems—as far as is reasonably possible—will relieve your Chinese hosts and save you time and energy. You should take with you any prescription drugs you might need, especially if you will be living outside major cities. It is useful to have the Latin names of medications because that is what Chinese medical personnel will recognize. People with a history of asthma, bronchitis, or tonsilitis should be prepared for frequent flare-ups, especially in cities that are becoming more and more polluted. For allergy sufferers, Peking Union Medical College, formerly the Capital Hospital, has a good allergy clinic. You can take allergy medicine with you, packed in dry ice, if necessary, and then have your prescription refilled at Beijing Union Medical College. One American with allergies—and small children—suggests that a vaporizer is a good item to carry into China. Almost every newcomer contracts a cold within a few weeks of arrival in China, and some foreigners are plagued with respiratory problems throughout their stay; so be certain to take plenty of cold remedies, cough drops, and throat lozenges if you are attached to particular brands. You can also ask your local clinic for help—Chinese remedies for colds are mild but quite effective.

Your personal first-aid kit might include vitamins, aspirin, Lomotil, Alka-Seltzer, cough drops, deodorant, sunscreen, Chapstick, first-aid spray, athlete's foot medicine, shaving cream, dental floss, insect repellent, and a thermometer and earplugs. Women are advised to take a good supply of sanitary napkins and tampons (available in some hotel shops in Beijing but sporadically) and remedies for gynecological infections. Contraceptives are not easily obtained in China and cannot be mailed from outside. Eyeglasses are quite inexpensive in China, but some residents have not been satisfied with the quality of the lenses. In any case, it is a good idea to take your prescription with you. Contact lenses and solutions are not available; also, contact lens wearers report problems with dust and advise that you take a pair of glasses with you as a fallback. A good pair of sunglasses will protect your eyes from dust and debris as well as glare.

Modern dental equipment is still scarce in China so be certain to have a thorough dental checkup before leaving the United States.

Chinese brands of soap, shampoos, face creams, and other necessities for personal care are quite good and inexpensive. Some hotels in Beijing now carry a few imported brands of shampoo and makeup, but if you have favorite brands and are unwilling to experiment with local products, you should take your own supplies.

FOOD AND COOKING SUPPLIES   Food in Chinese hotels and dormitories is usually nutritious, but it is almost always monotonous after a few weeks. (It is especially annoying to see a plentiful supply of fresh vegetables in the free markets outside your hotel and then find that they never seem to be available in the dining room!) Boredom and the incentive to beat increasingly high restaurant prices sometimes compel the foreign resident to prepare meals "at home." Hot plates are inexpensive but are illegal in most institutions because they are unsafe and drain already overtaxed electrical systems. Refrigerators for storage also are not usually accessible to foreign guests, although they are slowly becoming more available. Nonetheless, it is possible in Beijing to buy good bread and sweets, cheese, ham, and jams for sandwiches. If you like good coffee, take a supply with you, along with a cup-sized filter and filter paper. Instant coffee is available, but it is expensive and brands are limited. Instant soups, hot chocolate, presweetened powdered drinks (Tang can now be purchased in Beijing), popcorn, and other instant foods are easy and fun to cook, especially in winter. If you reside in a hotel, you will find that hot water, stored in thermos bottles changed at least twice a day, is something that you can count on in China. Note, however, that tap water is *not* potable—not even in the major cities or in the large joint-venture hotels.

If you plan to set up housekeeping in China, you might want to take rubber gloves, a good can opener, sponges, and a paring knife. Local hardware stores carry an adequate supply of pots and pans and tablewear. If you cook at home, however, the most important thing to remember is that vegetables and fruits usually have been grown in soil fertilized with human excrement, and they must be thoroughly washed.

(Most city dwellers are extremely hygiene-conscious, and you might wish to ask Chinese friends for food preparation suggestions and precautions.) There is also some debate about the wisdom of eating on the streets—which is now especially tempting in the free markets that sell the wonderfully spiced *Xinjiang*-style *shaslik* (lamb on skewers). Some of the Chinese will urge you to partake of these inexpensive delicacies; others will warn you that they are not safe to eat.

Available information about ration coupons is inconsistent. Some teachers report that they were issued coupons for oil and for flour and goods made with grain—bread and flour, for example. Others state that although they were given coupons by their host unit for use in the cafeteria and outside stores, they did not have to produce them consistently. No one reported that the coupons they received were insufficient for daily use. And the host unit will provide assistance if coupons are a problem.

ELECTRICAL APPLIANCES   Unlike U.S. power, electric current in China is 220 volts, 50 cycles, so be certain to take a transformer with enough capacity to handle tape recorders, radios, and any other appliances that need to be converted from standard American voltage. If your appliance can be operated using batteries or an AC/DC converter, you can save money on batteries by taking along a 110-volt converter with a transformer and battery recharger. Remember, however, that transformers do not convert cycles, only volts; even with a transformer, 60-cycle appliances with moving parts, such as tape recorders, will run more slowly in China than they do at home. As an alternative, you can have these items converted to 50 cycles in the United States; you also might want to purchase equipment that can be used on either 110 or 220 volts or buy electrical items in Hong Kong, which also operates on 220/50. Extension plugs and extender sockets can be purchased in Chinese general stores and at some Friendship Stores; in some cases Chinese clerks will even make extension cords and replace plugs—there is a daunting variety of electrical outlets in China, sometimes even within the same building. An international travel kit of plugs (one scientist writes that the Franzus kit is the best) is a useful item to take with you to China, especially since the "universal" plugs sold in the United States usually do not fit Chinese outlets.

Small electrical appliances are expensive in China. One of the most commonly sought is a small fan; a 9-inch model costs about Y80, and larger standing models are priced well over Y300. If you plan to buy a fan, you might consider buying it in Hong Kong. Used appliances can be resold at Friendship Stores and to certain other stores (ask your Chinese hosts) at about half the purchase price if they are accompanied by the original sales slip—and some stores will buy back Western-made appliances as well. Unfortunately, however, used appliances are not for sale to foreigners.

OFFICE SUPPLIES, TYPEWRITERS, PERSONAL COMPUTERS

For the most reliable, worry-free typing, you should take a standard manual typewriter with extra ribbons. High-quality, manual Chinese typewriters are expensive at Y300. Typewriter repair shops for manual models are relatively easy to find, and they also sell standard ribbons. Some Americans recommend battery-powered portable typewriters, but they caution that some brands require special paper that is not always available in China. A teacher recommends taking a typewriter with a carriage at least 105 characters wide for typing stencil blanks. And one researcher writes that he has been quite pleased with the operation of all his equipment; a battery-operated computer and printer that uses a battery-replacement transformer with a 220/110 Franzus 50-watt transformer (which, by the way, should not be left plugged in too long), as well as a 220-volt battery recharger that offers a constant electrical current. Zenith and Hewlett-Packard are popular models of battery-operated computers. Long-lasting alkaline batteries are not always available, though, and if you expect to rely on battery power, you should take a good supply with you.

Erratic supplies of electricity and servicing problems are two difficulties electric typewriter and computer owners frequently face. One scientist writes, "Microcomputers are adversely affected by the power supply problem, and their use requires considerable patience and effort. For example, a set of data may have to be entered several times since each time the electricity is interrupted, all information which has been entered but not yet stored is wiped out. Furthermore, computer hardware in general does not last as long as it does with normal usage in the United States since the large voltage fluctuations frequently burn or damage the computer circuits." Some teachers report, however, that an electric typewriter operated with a large Chinese-made transformer works quite well.

Despite the problems, Chinese organizations are using computers more and more, and foreigners also find them useful—albeit with the following cautions: (1) take a surge protector that you are certain can adjust to 220 volts; (2) take a transformer with the capacity to handle the voltage of a computer; and (3) take as many kinds of converter plugs as you can find—an international kit is a good idea. In the case of repairs, you should not count on help unless you live in a city with special repair shops or where representatives of your particular computer's company are in residence, although repair service may be fairly readily available if your Chinese host unit deals frequently with imported computers.

When asked what items they recommend for an academic visit to China, most respondents mention office supplies—correction fluid, carbon paper, manila file folders, tape, paper clips, a good pencil sharpener, book mailers for mailing small items home, colored pencils, magic markers, good-quality bond typing paper, lined notebook paper, and gluesticks. Manila envelopes, file cards, and boxes usually can be found at stationery stores in China. Desk lamps also are sold, but some travelers prefer to take their folding high-intensity lamps with them from home.

RADIOS AND TAPE RECORDERS   A small AM/FM shortwave transistor radio is useful for language practice and for news from outside China. Beijing Radio offers a special Chinese-English program (for schedules, see the *China Daily*); Voice of America (VOA) schedules, which change four times a year, can be obtained from the U.S. Embassy. *China Daily*, the English-language newspaper available in most major Chinese cities, offers useful information about television and radio broadcasts in Chinese.

If you buy a shortwave radio, be sure that the shortwave bands go at least to 23 KHz to tune in VOA and U.S. Armed Forces programs. Small transistor radios can be purchased in China and are adequate for local stations, but they are not powerful enough to bring in broadcasts from outside the country. Most foreign-made radios and tape recorders can now be repaired in Beijing and Shanghai. Imported and Chinese-made cassette recorders also can be purchased now in China, but they are expensive. Blank cassette tapes are easy to buy, but they are not of the best quality; taking a supply with you is worth the trouble, especially if you will be studying the language, since most language schools do not have good language laboratory facilities. In most cities you can purchase recorded music, mainly classical Chinese and Western selections, but Chinese pop music is available, too. Most foreigners take their favorite music with them, wish they had brought more, and find that these tapes make fine gifts for Chinese friends and teachers when they leave.

CAMERAS AND FILM   Color film is easier to buy in China now than it was a few years ago, but recent experience shows that it is still a good idea to take most film with you. Travelers to major tourist cities, like Xi'an, have been surprised to find that color film is unavailable even in tourist hotels. Both Kodak and Fuji film are available in major cities, but in general print film is easier to buy than slide film. Disk film is not yet for sale in most cities—although Guangzhou's Friendship Store does carry it. Some hotels even carry Polaroid film. Film prices in China are about the same as they are in the United States. Black-and-white film is easily purchased and processed, and many hotels now offer color film processing services. The Jianguo in Beijing has one-day service, and the Friendship Hotel develops film reasonably (Y14 for 24 color prints, Y21 for 36 color prints, and Y7.50 for 36 color slides). Be sure to tell the service personnel that you want your slides mounted. The quality of processing generally is reliable, and most long-term residents feel that it is safer to process exposed film than to carry it through airport inspections or to store it in extreme temperatures. Prepaid Kodachrome film cannot be developed in China, but it can be sent out to Hong Kong or Australia. Some post offices provide film mailers, and there have been few reported problems sending film out of China. Videocassettes are a special case, however, and cannot be taken in or out of the country without inspection and special permission. (See the earlier section on customs regulations for cameras and film.) If you go to Hong Kong during your stay in China to purchase photographic equipment, be sure to check with your host unit about customs regulations.

The U.S. Embassy issues the following advice about taking pictures: refrain from photographing airports, bridges, harbors, military facilities, soldiers, policemen, and wall posters. And always ask permission before taking a direct picture of an individual—taking pictures without asking permission is discourteous and has led to some incidents in which film has been confiscated. It should be noted, however, that Chinese parents seem very receptive to having their children photographed if you ask politely.

BICYCLES   If you are traveling to China by way of Hong Kong, you can purchase a bicycle there and take it with you. But if you decide to leave the bike in China when you depart, you will have to pay import duty. In China bicycles are still relatively expensive, and choices are limited to the heavy Huffy type. Opinions about the relative merits of different brands vary—ask your Chinese and foreign friends for advice before you buy. If you purchase your bicycle in a local shop, you will need a letter of permission from your host unit because bicycles are rationed. A new bicycle now costs from Y180 to Y200; prices for a used bicycle in good condition begin around Y80. All bicycles must be registered—again, ask your host unit for guidance. Although foreigners routinely sell bikes among themselves, this practice is illegal; bicycles in good condition should be resold only to the local Friendship Store for at least half the purchase price.

Used bicycle shops are fairly common in larger cities, and bicycle repair shops can be found in every neighborhood. Repairs are inexpensive: a complete overhaul may cost as little as Y10. Check any new or used bike carefully, however, before leaving the shop, and buy a bike light and reflecting tape for the front and back fenders for safety. Many riders carry repair kits with lockwashers of various sizes and other tools for repairs on the road. Theft is not uncommon in China; so you should keep your bike locked and park it in one of the many bicycle parking lots when shopping.

If your stay in China will be relatively short, you might want to rent a bicycle. In Beijing the rental shop is just opposite the Friendship Store; personnel at tourist hotels or local China International Travel Service offices can provide information on rentals in other areas.

I.D. PHOTOS   When you register with the local public security bureau, you must provide passport-sized photos for library cards, swimming passes, and diplomas. You can take along 10 or more extra copies of photos or have them done in China (the turnaround time is about two days).

READING MATERIAL   If you will be living in Beijing, you will find a good selection of reading matter in the stores catering to foreigners. Most of the paperback books are Penguin publications. Western newspapers and magazines are usually on sale within a week of publication; the *Asian Wall Street Journal, International Herald Tribune, Time, Newsweek, Reader's Digest,* and *Far Eastern Economic Review* are the most popular. There are also more Chinese novels and poetry in translation now than in years past. Some familiarity with Chinese classical and popular writing is both informative and educational; it also provides a rich source of conversation with Chinese colleagues and friends.

One important publication for the foreign community is the *China Daily,* which is published in English, distributed free in some hotels, and sold for Y0.10 in certain stores. Unlike most other publications in China, the *China Daily* notes restaurant specials and art exhibits; provides local entertainment schedules; reviews current theatre, opera, and films; lists Radio Beijing and TV programs; publishes daily exchange rates; and provides minimal coverage of Chinese and world news. The editorial section, in particular, is invaluable to the non-Chinese speaker because major pieces from the Chinese press are often translated there.

GAMES   Board games can be fun for relaxation with friends, both Chinese and foreign; and word games like Scrabble and Password provide novel ways of teaching English. Puzzles too can be useful for long winter Sundays—and they make thoughtful gifts for Chinese friends with families when you leave. If you are taking children with you, it is a good idea to pack their favorite toys and a few special decorations and treats for American holidays.

GIFTS Anticipating what kinds of gifts you should take is a problem for the prospective China traveler. Gifts to Chinese colleagues and friends, and to those who help out along the way—drivers, for example—must be chosen and given with care. Too lavish a gift will create embarrassment, and yet the days when a supply of ballpoint pens would suffice for any occasion are over. Chinese ballpoint pens now are quite inexpensive and of good quality. Many of your Chinese acquaintances will have been abroad and have accumulated some of the trinkets that were once deemed satisfactory gifts. As one student warns, beware of underestimating the sophistication of your Chinese friends. Well-chosen books and scholarly materials are always appropriate for advisers and academic colleagues. Scholars also appreciate Chinese calligraphy manuals, which are expensive in Chinese terms. Tapes of Western classical music are easier to buy in China now than they once were, but they are still a good gift. And art books and colorful calendars with scenes of U.S. life also are appropriate presents, as are English dictionaries and study guides and tapes for learning English.

One researcher took a beautifully printed greeting from the president of his university to his Chinese hosts, who enjoyed the calligraphy. Others have presented digital clocks, solar-powered calculators, and cooking aids (for example, can openers and potato peelers). If you are invited to a home for dinner, you might take along some imported candy or wine, or cookies in a decorative tin, all of which can be found in Friendship Stores and hotels. According to Chinese sources, it is appropriate to present gifts to the women and children of the family on these occasions. Selections of stamps and intricate jigsaw puzzles are popular gifts for children. You should not be surprised, however, if the recipient does not open the gift immediately; it is customary to wait until later.

A banquet is still an excellent way to repay hospitality—you might ask your colleagues to suggest favorite restaurants. (One American couple who favored a particular crispy duck restaurant in Beijing discovered from a close Chinese friend that such food was not considered proper banquet fare; they chose a seafood place instead.) Invite a few good friends and helpful colleagues, and try to encourage a relaxed atmosphere; the formal banquet is no longer considered an enjoyable means to meet with friends. Banquets can be expensive—Y50 or more per person in most good restaurants. An alternative might be to invite friends out for lunch—for example, to a local restaurant or the coffee shop of one of the hotels.

As "normal" relations with Chinese friends become ever more possible, traditional boundaries blur and reticence lessens. Today you can simply ask a trusted Chinese friend for advice about gifts. Your Chinese acquaintances, in turn, may well let you know directly what they want or need. But if some of the mystery has gone out of gift giving in China, courtesy demands that you remain sensitive nonetheless to the obligations and implications of a gift in that culture.

WHAT TO TAKE FOR PROFESSIONAL LIFE

BOOKS Most scholars with experience in China advise you to take any and all printed materials that are essential for your research and writing, including reference works. Even dictionaries published in China are sometimes hard to obtain, so be certain to take along the ones you need. Publishing is active in China, but new publications are often sold out soon after they reach the stores. It is also unwise to rely on library holdings or on access to them; even major secondary works in your field simply may not be available.

Experienced bibliophiles have discovered that you can now order directly from publishers based in China or visit their distribution centers to obtain books. And out-of-print books and back issues of journals sometimes can be found in used bookstores. Used bookstores in out-of-the-way spots may be virtual treasure troves. Bookstores in the newly renovated antique district in Beijing, Liulichang, often are a good source of books on early China. When you travel around the country, be sure to explore local bookstores; some cities such as Xi'an and Lanzhou, for example, have stores devoted to ancient history, stocking items that are hard to find in the larger cities. Ask your Chinese colleagues for advice, and offer to share your finds with them. Many scholars report that they have borrowed books from Chinese academics who have better private collections in their field than some libraries. In any case, if you see a book that you need, don't wait—buy it immediately.

Periodicals in Chinese may be ordered at the post office. A useful guide, arranged by subject, to newspapers and periodicals published in China is available from:

China International Book Trading Corporation (Guoji Shudian)
P.O. Box 2820
Beijing, China

(See also later sections on access to materials and the post office in Chapters 4 and 6, respectively, for the accepted wisdom about obtaining materials while in China.)

As you prepare for your journey, you should understand that in China you will almost certainly be asked to speak, either formally or informally, about the latest developments in your field. Take along any references that might be useful to you in answering what may well be quite wide-ranging questions. There is also a great deal of curiosity about U.S. life in general, and you must be prepared to talk knowledgeably about a variety of topics—from current slang and films to the intricate workings of the U.S. Congress. An almanac, according to one teacher, was "worth its weight in gold—we used ours every day"; a good paperback English dictionary and thesaurus are handy and make appropriate gifts for Chinese friends when you leave. In addition, the press and cultural section of the U.S. Embassy has a library that can be tapped, but its holdings are limited.

A standard survey of Chinese history, guidebooks that describe your particular city, and up-to-date tourist handbooks are all important references. Kaplan and Sobin's *Encyclopedia of China Today* is useful, as is *The China Guidebook* by Kaplan, Sobin, and de Keijzer. Brian Schwartz's *China Off the Beaten Track* is a favorite of adventurous types— likewise, *China—A Travel Survival Kit*, by Alan Samagalski and Michael Buckley. The more detailed and scholarly *Nagel's Encyclopedic Guide to China* offers historical information and is well worth the price ($65) in the opinion of some academic tourists. Many of these guidebooks are now on sale in hotels and Friendship Stores in Beijing; see also Appendix L for complete publishing details. The non-China specialist also might find that a subscription to the *China Daily* for a few months before departure will be good preparation for current events in China (both political and cultural); it can be ordered from:

China Daily
U.S. Distributor
15 Mercer Street
New York, NY 10013
(212-219-0130)

EQUIPMENT   Duplicating facilities are limited in China, and if gathering and copying materials is essential for your work, you may want to take a portable copier with a heavy-duty transformer. A tape recorder can be an important aid to research as well. Calculators are fairly easy to buy in China, but do not expect to find computers and software in your host institution. Instead, write ahead for information on what is available, and take your own software. Fortran is still the most common language. (See also the section above on office supplies and machines.)

Most returned scientists report that they took with them to China almost all of their basic equipment. For instance, a biologist writes: "Only basic research needs were offered for use . . . an office/laboratory was provided, but all necessary research equipment, including microscope, handling utensils, plastic petri dishes, vials, and cups, was brought with me as baggage. If unusual items were needed, requests were usually forthcoming but often not very promptly, and the delays sometimes outlasted the need." Another scientist warns colleagues preparing for a China trip that simple household materials such as Clorox necessary for research work are not available. It is critically important that you list all of your project needs well in advance when writing to your host unit and that you ask to be notified if specific items are not on hand. Be sure to specify the quantities you need; most Chinese scientists do not use disposable equipment and may not have adequate supplies—for instance, of laboratory glassware—in stock.

A geologist who needed detailed maps for his project found that some maps were not open to scrutiny by foreigners. He recommends that anyone who needs maps for a project find out not only what is available but also what can be used. A scientist who needed a particular chemical to perform an experiment had serious problems having it sent from his university lab in the United States to his Chinese unit. His experience suggests that prior arrangements for obtaining these items be made with your home institution before you leave. If you send equipment ahead, send it in care of your host unit's foreign affairs office. Some airlines offer nonstop parcel service between a few major U.S. cities and Beijing and Shanghai.

If you plan to use audiovisual equipment in China, write ahead to your hosts to let them know exactly what you need. Some organizations have overhead projectors, but you should bring your own transparencies and marking pens. Most also have slide projectors, although screens apparently are scarcer and quite often the projectors are not in working order. One returned scholar observed that the slide projectors in his relatively affluent Beijing institution "must have come with Marco Polo."

With equipment, then, as with all other aspects of life in China, you can only try to plan ahead—and then be patient when it fails to work and grateful when it does. In such matters, a sense of humor is always invaluable.

OTHER SCHOLARLY MATERIALS   You should be prepared to submit to your colleagues a detailed research proposal (ideally, in Chinese) soon after your arrival in China. Researchers and graduate students also suggest that you take an updated resumé, offprints of your publications and books, and copies of major papers.

If you plan to lecture, you might wish to prepare outlines or abstracts for handouts. If you will be working with interpreters, a dictionary that specializes in the technical terminology of your discipline can be of great use. Business cards printed, if possible, in both Chinese and English are also convenient; they can be made inexpensively in China or in Hong Kong.

TEACHING AIDS   The teachers surveyed for this handbook had taught a variety of subjects in China, and they all strongly urged prospective teachers to take with them as many books and materials as possible because there is a serious shortage of English-language textbooks in China. (Teachers of such courses as law and management in particular said there were few if any pertinent books available.) Even university libraries were not too useful, according to these teachers; many of the books in the libraries on the subject matter they taught were outdated and badly organized. Another drawback mentioned was the closed stack policy of most university libraries in China; students are not able to browse among the books to see what would be of interest. These teachers did find that some department libraries contained excellent books, but even in these there were sometimes problems in arranging access for the students. It is probably best to take some of the most highly used and regarded books in your field with you; you can then donate them to your Chinese host institution upon departure. If you will be teaching English, you should also obtain information about the Test of English as a Foreign Language (TOEFL) and take TOEFL books and tapes with you.

Because of the shortage of books, some teachers reported photocopying or dittoing articles from books they had brought to give to their students, but this is usually difficult. Duplicating facilities are limited at most institutions; some only have mimeograph machines, and photocopiers are scarcer still—a major university may have only one copier to serve an entire campus while smaller institutions may have none at all. Even if your institution has a copier you may have to pay for copying yourself. There is also no guarantee the copier will work reliably; repairing copiers is even more difficult in China than in the United States.

In sum, you should not count on duplicating large or even small volumes of materials in China. If you plan to use unbound materials, you should either take multiple copies with you or plan to have them copied at a hotel or neighborhood copy shop at a cost of from Y0.15 to Y0.50 per page.

If you plan to use audiovisual aids, be sure to read the preceding sections on equipment and review the customs regulations on videotapes and films. Some institutions do have overhead projectors, but teachers have found that at times their classes were so large, it was not practical to use transparencies as a teaching aid. Slide projectors are fairly common and teachers do recommend taking slides to use in classes. Also, reel-to-reel tape recorders are frequently available. Cassette recorders are becoming more and more common, but high-quality tapes are still not on the market. Some teachers found that they could arrange for films and videotapes to be shown, but if the department for which they work does not have the necessary equipment, it may be charged for the use of such equipment. Also, the equipment and rooms for viewing must be reserved in advance, and in some cases, tapes must be submitted to institution authorities one week in advance of the showing to be reviewed.

The following information on videocassette recorders (VCRs) in China and VCR tapes to be taken into China was received from the U.S. Embassy in Beijing. Multistandard VCRs are widely available but fre quently are standard play (fast speed) only. Persons taking NTSC extended or long play tapes to China may have difficulty. VHS is the most common format used, although many institutions also have ¾-inch U-matic or Beta formats. Equipment must be 200 volts, 50 cycles; 120-volt transformers are available in China but are expensive. The more serious consideration concerns cycles: electricity in China is 50 cycles as opposed to 60 cycles in the United States. Therefore, unless a player is rated 50 cycles, it will not operate properly. Americans planning to take videocassettes to China are advised to inform their institutions early on and to inquire what sort of equipment is available. Moreover, Chinese customs usually wants to examine all videotapes being taken into the country and may retain tapes at the port of entry. It is best not to take tapes into China that might be considered pornographic or politically sensitive.

Most returned teachers recommended that you write ahead to your host unit for details on their particular arrangements. In addition, you can talk with returned teachers and possibly even consider taking your own equipment, such as a slide projector with transformers, if you think it worth the effort. If you plan to donate equipment to your Chinese institution when you leave, be certain when you arrive to have your unit register it with Chinese customs officials as a duty-free educational item.

Teachers who have taught in China offer a number of ideas for providing students with course materials. (Books available in China can of course be used, but you will probably want to supplement them with U.S. materials.) You may apply to certain U.S. or community funding agencies that offer grants for books; or, if you have been awarded a Fulbright scholarship, you will be given a book allowance with which to purchase materials. Some teachers have typed course assignments on ditto masters and made direct transfer stencils of materials which were then duplicated in China. Duplicated articles about current events from *The New York Times, Newsweek, Foreign Affairs,* and other periodicals are avidly read by students and are a good form of language instruction because of their sophisticated vocabulary. You may also want to clip articles of current interest from magazines and newspapers to use as the basis for class discussions. Chinese students, however, are accustomed to the lack of textbooks; they take meticulous notes during class; and if lectures are concise and well constructed, they can manage quite well without textbooks, although they often use their own reference books in Chinese to supplement English lecture notes.

It is very likely that during your stay in China someone will ask you to give a talk about American culture. Consequently, you may want to bring slides and photographs showing various aspects of life in the United States—for example, shots of supermarkets, airports, subways, family life, holiday celebrations, city street scenes, farms, parks, schools, and the like can be of great interest to Chinese students who have had little opportunity to glimpse everyday life abroad. Returned teachers also stress balancing "the good and the bad" when discussing life in the United States.

Information about higher education in the United States is always welcome in China, and your hosts and students will appreciate any catalogs, course syllabi, or descriptive material that you can share with them. The U.S. government has placed collections of educational reference materials at 18 sites in China; the locations of these collections and the list of their materials are in Appendix K. U.S. colleges and universities have been requested to send their catalogs to these sites.

Finally, in terms of what books to take to China, returned teachers recommend the following: as many basic reference books as possible, several good dictionaries and encyclopedias, your favorite books at various levels on the subject matter you will be teaching, anthologies of American and British literature, *Bartlett's Quotations,* references on American culture, a copy of the U.S. Constitution, novels, a good atlas, standard grammar books, maps of the United States and the world in English, and a world almanac. As one teacher put it, "I can't think of anything *not* to take, except maybe pornographic literature. That is frowned upon, but the Chinese are remarkably open about what you bring for your own reading or for sharing with Chinese friends."

In addition to the guidebooks on China mentioned earlier, an excellent preparation specifically for teaching in China is a recently published book by two Americans, Tani Barlow and Donald Lowe, who taught literature and history in Shanghai from 1981 to 1982. Their thoughtful and detailed account, *Chinese Reflections: American Teaching in the People's Republic,* is well worth reading. (See Appendix L for publication information.)

3. Settling In

Life in China is a fascinating blend of common patterns with unique variations. Overall the experiences of academic visitors to China evince great similarity, but no two are completely alike. The shaping influences of personality, timing, context, and a myriad of other factors are as important in China as in any other country; so it would be unwise to assume that your experience will mirror those described here. Nonetheless, some common patterns have emerged during the seven years Americans have had the opportunity to live and work in China. Each returning "veteran" has a fund of anecdotes and insights, and it is the most exemplary and interesting of these that have been included in the observations that follow.

ARRIVING IN CHINA

You should plan to consult an experienced travel agent in the United States about the many methods to enter China. There are now direct flights to Shanghai and Beijing, but many travelers still prefer to stop in Hong Kong or Tokyo for a few days' rest before proceeding to their destination in China. In Hong Kong the China Travel Service can supply information and tickets; the address of the main branch is

77 Queens Road, Central District
Hong Kong Island
(phone: 5-259121)

The China International Travel Service, which serves non-Chinese visitors exclusively, has an office in:

South Sea Centre
Sixth Floor, Tower Two
Tsimshatsui East
Kowloon
(phone: 3-7215317)

*The China Guidebook** contains information on travel into China from Japan on cruise ships, overland by rail, and so on. The China National Tourist Office in New York (212-867-0271) also can be consulted.

It is the responsibility of the host institution to meet new arrivals and escort them to their residence. But the sheer volume of academic travelers to China has placed a strain on host organizations—which sometimes results in less than smooth arrangements for meeting and housing newcomers. To guard as much as possible against mix-ups at the airport, be sure to communicate your travel plans to your Chinese hosts clearly and early on; you can telephone or cable from Hong Kong if final plans are made there or cable from the United States. Whatever method you use, remember to notify *all* the organizations involved in hosting you. For example, if you are to be associated with a unit in the interior that has a parent organization in Beijing or Shanghai, you should not assume that the two organizations will communicate with each other. The local unit may send a representative to the city to meet you, or someone from the parent organization may be on hand. Or, in some unfortunate cases, weary travelers have found no one at the airport—although airport personnel usually are willing to find a taxi driver who will help locate temporary quarters. The experience of a non-Chinese-speaking scientist who arrived on a late evening flight and was not met is reassuring: "I arrived in Beijing at 10 p.m., but because my baggage did not make the connection in San Francisco I had to wait and eventually make the missing baggage report at midnight. By that time, the Academy person waiting for me had left and I was sent by the information desk person to the . . . Ritan Hotel, next to Ritan Park and the U.S. Embassy." This report does not indicate what happened to the bags; in most cases, they show up on the next flight. If they are clearly labeled with the address of your unit's foreign affairs office, they may be delivered there. But you might also want to return to the airport to check for your baggage. Whenever your bags arrive, you must be prepared to go through customs on your own because your hosts cannot meet you until you have picked up your bags and completed customs forms. The customs process is quite hectic in the Beijing airport; several flights usually arrive at once, baggage carousels are inadequate for the

---

*Unless otherwise noted in the text, Appendix L gives publication information for references cited in this chapter.

volume of traffic, and there are too few customs personnel. One word of warning: be sure not to lose your customs form in the mayhem. It is a good idea to have the phone number of your unit on hand so that you can call if you arrive during working hours. You should try to avoid a weekend arrival if possible. Most units are open on Saturday, but Sunday is almost universally a day of rest and offices will be closed.

If your flight is delayed en route, try to cable the unit so that personnel do not make unnecessary trips to the airport. In Beijing and Shanghai, these are long and time-consuming journeys. One American teacher tells how a conscientious Chinese cadre met every plane from abroad for two days searching for him because he had not been able to cable an abrupt change in travel plans. If after you arrive in China, you must make your own arrangements for travel to your final destination, ask for help at the reception desk of one of the larger hotels. Service workers should be able to direct you to the nearest office of the China Travel Service. At the Beijing and Shanghai airports, taxi service is available. Ask for help from airport service workers if necessary.

THE TENOR OF LIFE IN CHINA

THE DANWEI   Every foreigner who lives and works in China is assigned to a work unit, which in Chinese is called a *danwei*. For the foreign visitor, as well as for any working member of Chinese society, the *danwei* is the single most important frame of reference for all activities. Whether it be a commune, factory, research institute, or university, the work unit is a microcosm of Chinese society with its own political hierarchy, networks of personal and professional relationships, services, and, in many cases, living quarters. It is through the work unit that the Chinese government exerts its influence on the life of the individual, for it is the unit issuing the identification card that marks the bearer as a working member of Chinese society, entitled to medical care, ration coupons, and housing. And it is not only the necessities of daily life that are provided by the unit but also permission to marry, to bear the allotted number of children, and to travel. The unit acts as a go-between when its members must communicate with other organizations and screens outsiders who attempt to penetrate its boundaries. Lateral relations among *danwei*, even those engaged in similar activities, are cumbersome for permanent members as well as for foreign guests because of the autonomous nature of the units.

Temporary movement in and out of the *danwei* is common for Chinese intellectuals and administrators, especially since the advent of the new reforms, which stress the importance of self-improvement through education and specialized training. Permanent voluntary transfers are still rare, however, and it is not unusual for husbands and wives to work in *danwei* in different cities. There is some evidence of more job mobility for Chinese workers as a result of the economic reforms but usually only if the unit engaged in "headhunting" or the worker seeking new employment is willing to pay a stiff fee to compensate the original place of work. Thus, it is still true that, once they have been assigned to a work unit, most Chinese remain there for the rest of their working lives, in close quarters with friends and allies as well as with bitter enemies, especially since the Cultural Revolution.

These internal relationships are important and all too often unknown to the short-term visitor. But foreigners who have become integrated enough into a unit to be aware of its inner workings usually discover that surface cordiality among Chinese coworkers does not necessarily reflect deeper harmony. The presence of a foreigner, even if temporary, can create further imbalances, as such resources as office space and the use of assistants are redistributed to accommodate the newcomer. More importantly, as one veteran of two years in a Beijing research unit points out, the Chinese members of the *danwei* who associate most closely with the foreigner become both more visible and more vulnerable to their colleagues. It is wise then to refrain from showing too much favoritism publicly to Chinese friends and from betraying confidences that could create embarrassment or worse for those you come to know well.

In their informative study of a hospital work unit in Wuhan, Gail Henderson, a sociologist, and Myron Cohen, a physician, examine in detail the meaning and position of the work unit in Chinese society and in their own professional experience:

> *Danwei* are isolated from each other in relatively closed systems, dependent upon higher levels for the source of their power and authority over members. The *danwei* system is, of course, not the sole force affecting the lives of work unit members. Other factors include the family, relationships with people outside the *danwei*, membership in neighborhood organizations, the power of the professional within a bureaucratic organization, constraints on middle-level leaders, and the influence of the Communist Party and other national organizations. Nevertheless, the *danwei* has an extraordinary influence on its individual members and (in our case) on the formal and informal relations among the hospital administrator, doctors, nurses, and patients. This influence does not lessen the importance of the other doctors, but rather interacts with them and provides an additional layer of control with which Chinese citizens must cope in their daily lives. (pp. 7–8 in *The Chinese Hospital: A Socialist Work Unit*, by Gail Henderson and Myron Cohen. Copyright © 1984 Yale University, New Haven, Conn. Reprinted with permission)

If anything is predictable about a stay in China, it is that you will become a member (albeit perhaps a marginal one) of this highly structured society and can accomplish very little without learning to work within its boundaries. Although there may be a certain degree of security and simplicity inherent in such a setup—for example, you need not worry about the basic arrangements for daily life—most foreigners feel confined when they realize that most arrangements for daily and professional life must be channeled through the *waishi banshichu*—literally, "the office for outside business," but usually referred to simply as the foreign affairs office or *waiban*.

THE FOREIGN AFFAIRS OFFICE   Although the foreign affairs office looms large in the lives of foreigners, it does not exist simply to oversee the foreign guests within the unit. It is also the administrative office that handles all of the unit's external relationships, including arranging for its Chinese members to go abroad, receiving delegations, and negotiating exchange programs. Special *waiban* personnel, usually trained to some degree in foreign languages, look after the personal affairs of the foreigners in the unit and serve as their liaison with other units and with different departments within the unit itself. The foreign affairs office thus provides a mechanism that allows the foreigner to work within the unit without becoming integrated into its hierarchy. It is the duty of the foreign affairs cadre to interpret, negotiate, and supervise the implementation of the wishes of their foreign guests— and to take responsibility for the consequences.

Within this system the foreigner often feels a dismaying lack of control over the direction of academic work and the more mundane but equally important arrangements for daily living. In his description of his relationships in a rural commune that had never before hosted a foreigner, Steven Butler points out that the foreign affairs officials had little knowledge of or sympathy for his research goals; nonetheless, they were responsible for all of his onsite activities:

> The foreign affairs officials are responsible for ferrying foreigners in and out of the labyrinth of highly segmented work and residential units that make up Chinese society, and their main professional charge seems to be to make the foreigners comfortable and, as they say, to "promote friendship between the Chinese and American people." They do this mainly by arranging things so that foreigners do not have to lift a finger. For these persons, my visit to China was simply one more professional assignment, although the length and nature of my stay were new to them. (*The Social Sciences and Fieldwork in China: Views from the Field*, p. 103)

It is the burden of foreign affairs officials to show the best side of China to the outsider, a task complicated by their own marginality in Chinese academic society and their precarious role as interpreters for people whose cultures they know only secondhand. Very few foreign affairs personnel have the opportunity to spend any significant time abroad because they are not scholars and they are not highly placed in the administrative structure—and because their services cannot be spared in China.

It will take time and effort for you to figure out how your unit is organized, who has formal authority and who has actual power, how to couch requests, and what role the foreign affairs officials play. Advice about how best to deal with the foreign affairs office is difficult to offer because situations vary so much from unit to unit. Some China veterans suggest that you ignore the foreign affairs officials as much as possible and instead make arrangements through academic colleagues who often have more clout within the unit than functionaries and are likely to be more in sympathy with your academic goals. Others openly advise their successors that functionaries must be courted. One graduate student laments that he heeded warnings to avoid the foreign affairs office: "It has been my experience this year that if you get to know them well and have requests which are within their power to grant, they will be granted. This is not unlike bureaucrats and administrators in the West." He goes on to point out, however, that help from Chinese bureaucrats often hinges on personal feelings. Of one particularly powerful official, this student states: "If he does not like you, he will use every means to prevent you from achieving your goals." The traits that may help you to be perceived as a "friendly foreigner" include good cheer in the face of adversity, respect and understanding for the limitations of particular offices, and the ability to offer criticism constructively—which means, in the opinion of one researcher, that when frustrated you should not slander the socialist system or Chinese culture wholesale but rather focus on particular problems at hand.

It is helpful as well to understand your own role in the larger sense. Steven Butler achieved a rapport with the officials responsible for him, despite their constant scrutiny and attention, by displaying sensitivity to how his presence affected the balance for them. He compares the lavish hospitality accorded him to the treatment a populist-minded president might expect if he

> descended on a rural backwater to attend a town meeting. . . . To complain about such treatment makes you look like an ungrateful guest and makes people feel that they have been bad hosts. Rather than fight it, it is better to play along. It works out better for everyone. I became convinced toward the end of my stay that even ordinary Chinese peasants perceived of the way I was treated as role playing, in the fullest

sociological sense and part of an elaborate ritual. The status conferred on me was not intrinsic to myself, but derived from the role played in a situation that was really beyond anyone's control. When I played along, it put people at ease. They felt that they knew what they could expect from me and they could relax. (*The Social Sciences and Fieldwork in China: Views from the Field*, p. 119)

Experiences vary, and indeed some foreigners might envy Butler the solicitous attention he received. Your status, linguistic capabilities, prior contacts with the *danwei*, and outside networks, as well as the unit's own history and style of dealing with foreigners, all play a part in determining how to best approach the foreign affairs office. In addition, the number of foreigners in their care is a major factor influencing the way foreign affairs officials treat any individual. Butler was the only foreigner in his unit, and he enjoyed the status of a research scholar. A student in a university crowded with foreign students from all over the world can expect less help and even, at times, a disturbing lack of cooperation from overburdened officials. What students lack in comfort and attention, however, they are compensated for by a relative degree of freedom to make their own arrangements. Students can make their own travel plans, for example, and in doing so can determine the style and schedule of their trips far more easily than the honored foreign guest who tours with an entourage or is met along the way with interpreters and guides. Ironically, students also have the opportunity to understand the intricate workings of the bureaucracy because they often come face to face with it, and such experiences, although frustrating at times, also offer insights not always available to those sheltered by high status.

Sometimes busy foreign affairs personnel, who may not have been involved in placement negotiations at a higher level, are not quite certain of the status of their guests. One senior scholar, whose housing and travel arrangements were far from satisfactory because the *waiban* did not offer assistance, concludes that, in general, China does not have the physical facilities or student and faculty personnel to handle all those it would sincerely like to welcome. He goes on to say that the result of so many people coming in through the new "open door" is that "China seems to find it difficult at this stage to discriminate among her visitors with respect to their usefulness, seniority, etc. As a consequence, allocations of all kinds seem to be made literally on a first-come/first-served basis." It can be assumed generally, however, that when foreign affairs officials work on behalf of their foreign guests, it is to their own advantage rather than against their interests because they bear ultimate responsibility for the visit. As one young woman who works in the foreign affairs office of a large, prestigious Beijing unit remarked to a foreign couple about to embark unaccompanied on a long journey to western China, "If anything happens to you, I will pay for it!"

THE QUALITY OF LIFE   Every work unit is a minisociety with its own traditions, folklore, factions, history, and style of working with foreigners. Among university campuses the superficial aspects of life, such as dormitory accommodations, organizational structures, even the style of the buildings, might be uniform, but the flavor of daily life may be very different. The location of the city in which you live, the size and personality quirks of the foreign community there, the unit's experience or lack of it with foreigners, and its standing with other organizations all make a great difference. A small normal college that does not enjoy prestige within the educational system may be either more defensive and rigid with its foreign guests or more welcoming than a large key university; a research institute that has never hosted foreign guests may be eager to establish new ties or, alternatively, suspicious and unhelpful at first. As a result, generalizations about daily life must be made with caution. Nonetheless, recurring themes do emerge from reports and conversations with foreigners who have lived in China for any length of time.

One frequent observation is that there is little separation between personal and professional life, especially for those who live on the campus of their work unit. But no one, not even a hotel dweller in a far corner of the city, is immune to frequent visits from anxious colleagues, especially in the first few weeks when there is a genuine concern that newcomers become acclimated as soon as possible. There is reason for worry: most foreigners do in fact fall ill or at least feel out of sorts initially. But such attention sometimes only prolongs the adjustment process. As one American comments, "Some things are difficult to get used to—the absolute lack of privacy is one. There are people hovering about me from 6:30 a.m. until I retire. They are all well-intentioned, trying to make me comfortable and trying to help. But it's hard to adjust to and in many ways sets up a barrier between me and the society I am studying. I am gradually finding ways to get around this, but the key here is patience."

Indeed, the word "patience" comes up again and again as Americans offer advice for getting along in China: "Patience is the most valuable trait to take to China. The Chinese don't operate from the same premises as Americans do in terms of the appropriate way to get things done and a good measure of understanding is required to avoid considerable frustration." And from another: "Be sensitive to Chinese personality traits; they are much more patient than we, and a quick temper will get you nowhere. Never take yourself, or the Chinese, too seriously; they are extremely modest, a trait we Americans should learn to practice more assiduously."

Foreigners learn very quickly that there is a severe shortage of space in most Chinese organizations and that few of their Chinese colleagues enjoy the luxury of a private office—or for that matter, any office at all in some cases. Foreign visitors have admitted feeling ashamed at being so well-housed when their Chinese colleagues have to work without quiet space and to live in small and crowded quarters. As one researcher in a scientific unit put it, she felt guilty when she realized that her office had once accommodated six or eight of her colleagues, who now had to do without in order to supply her, the foreign guest, with adequate office space. Some scholars whose work takes them to the countryside discover that special quarters—with showers, kitchens, and personnel to staff the establishment—have been put together just for their use. Such luxurious accommodations place them embarrassingly far above the living standard of their Chinese neighbors.

On the other hand, some researchers and teachers have been dismayed at the conditions of laboratories, classrooms, and dormitories, which are not generally heated or well-maintained and are sometimes downright unsafe. One scientist, for example, discovered asbestos materials filtering through the heating system, and others have complained about inadequate fire escape outlets in dorms and hotels. But anyone who has visited a Chinese home, or is sensitive to the working conditions of colleagues, understands that in most cases foreigners enjoy conditions far superior to those of their Chinese counterparts, who are often quite frank about the problems generated by lack of space.

Because of the shortage of space and because many members of the *danwei* live on campus, business that is considered public and professional in the West is often conducted in the room of the foreign guest. It is not unusual for a foreign visitor's room to become the only place to hold language tutorials, conduct financial negotiations, arrange for travel, and so on. Although first meetings with Chinese colleagues may be very formal, once a relationship is established, friends and colleagues feel free to stop by, without phoning ahead, simply to visit; or they may make vague plans to meet, leaving you bound to your room for hours at a time waiting for a friend or student who promised to stop by "sometime in the afternoon, today or tomorrow." Sometimes Chinese colleagues and friends will appear without any notice at all at times when they are least expected—early on a Sunday morning, for instance. The only time that you can be relatively sure of privacy is during the *xiuxi* or rest period, from noon until 1:30 or 2 p.m. You, in turn, should not disturb Chinese friends at that time, which is not only a respite but for many an opportunity to run errands or do the day's marketing.

There is, in the words of one American scholar, a "different concept of privacy in China—people walking into one's room freely, inspecting personal items, reading mail, asking questions. An adjustment is needed." You will also find that the boundaries in China between acceptable questions and embarrassing intrusions are different, and you must be prepared to answer all sorts of questions that Americans generally consider taboo—about money earned and spent, where you have been that day, or where exactly you plan to go tomorrow. But rarely will Chinese colleagues and friends—especially the older generation—ask you about your personal life beyond a polite concern for health and family matters, nor will they offer details about theirs. Some foreigners have learned only by accident, for example, that a longstanding Chinese friend is divorced or about to marry. As one senior scholar observed, "It often took a genuine effort to establish a dialogue that moved beyond the superficial aspects of daily life, especially with my older Chinese colleagues."

Younger people are sometimes far more open. American students can expect a great deal of curiosity about U.S. life (from rock stars to romance), and they may, in turn, be offered insights into Chinese family life, courting behavior, and marriage expectations. Often the most intense encounters occur when you are traveling, for it is easier to talk frankly with people you will never see again.

PERSONAL RELATIONSHIPS   Barriers between outsiders and Chinese citizens are still formidable because they are the result not only of cultural differences but of official policies designed to mitigate the influence of foreign culture. Some of these barriers are obvious: Chinese guests often are required to register when visiting a foreigner in a hotel room; the Chinese are denied entrance to stores reserved for foreigners unless they have special permission. Other impediments are less clear and more troubling. Some Chinese intellectuals are cleared for contacts with foreigners while others must ask permission to visit a foreign friend. And some Chinese are obviously nervous about contact with foreigners for reasons an outsider may never be able to fathom. In addition to individual fears of the consequences of friendships with foreigners, your Chinese acquaintances may be responding to changes in government policies that affect their relationships with outsiders. Many times these shifts are known to foreigners only indirectly—for instance, when their relationships with Chinese friends subtly change without explanation or when the rules governing access to institutions or materials become more restricted—because policy shifts of this sort are rarely articulated publicly.

Over the past few years, vicissitudes in regulations affecting foreign students have created a good deal of confusion. Students report that at times they are free to invite Chinese friends into their dormitory for conversation, and then suddenly new registration procedures will be announced that limit visits to certain hours or prevent them altogether. These procedures are rationalized with explanations that make little sense—such as the common one that officials are only "protecting" their guests from the unsavory designs of certain "bad elements." Many Americans in China during the antispiritual pollution campaign in late 1983 described how they began to suspect a policy shift when all their Chinese friends suddenly became cool or were simply unavailable, and when libraries and reading rooms previously open were abruptly closed to them. Because as guests, as outsiders, foreigners operate so much in the dark, it seems best to let Chinese colleagues take the lead in determining the kind of relationship that can develop under circumstances that only they can fully comprehend. Some foreigners have expressed doubts about whether the Chinese even know fully the present or future consequences of contact with foreigners.

As Anne Thurston observes in her useful comments on the personal side of carrying out fieldwork in China ("Social Sciences and Fieldwork in China: An Overview," in *The Social Sciences and Fieldwork in China: Views from the Field*), antiforeign and anti-American feelings can be found at all levels of Chinese society. Suspicion of a foreigner's activities is most easily aroused when the outsider steps out of the bounds of the category in which he or she originally has been placed.

> Whether the foreigner is labeled a tourist, a foreign expert (a teacher), an undergraduate or graduate student, or a foreign scholar will have considerable bearing on what the foreigner is permitted to do. A tourist, after all, is expected to sightsee, a foreign expert to teach, a student to study, and a foreign scholar to conduct research. For a foreign expert to attempt to conduct research without official permission is to risk serious misunderstanding and potential jeopardy to Chinese friends who may have assisted in that research. (*The Social Sciences and Fieldwork in China: Views from the Field*, p. 24)

Those who travel to China to carry out serious work of any kind must have the sanction of officialdom at some level. Even with that sanction, they may well find it hard to balance the demands of a project with sensitivity to the situation of Chinese colleagues and friends.

The term *guanxi* comes up again and again when anyone, Chinese or foreign, tries to discover how to accomplish anything in China. It seems that the bureaucratic structure at times merely provides a framework for the more intangible workings of intricate webs of personal relations and favors. Chinese friends will tell you that personal relations (who you know, who owes you a favor, or who thinks you might be able to be of use in the future) are far more important to understand than the formal lines of authority. For example, Chinese friends that you have worked with and helped in the past may or may not have the power to assist you directly but will almost surely feel obligated to draw on their own *guanxi* to repay a debt to you; others might help you with the anticipation that you may repay the debt in the future—in the form of help to study abroad, more immediate access to scarce resources, practice with English, or entry to a store normally off limits to Chinese customers without special permission. The use of *guanxi* is one means to secure access to scarce resources in place of direct financial payment for services and material goods.

In *Chinese Reflections: Americans Teaching in the People's Republic*, Tani Barlow and Donald Lowe provide a sensitive, frank portrayal of the rich network of human relationships they both inherited—as a result of Donald Lowe's family connections in Shanghai—and developed—as foreign experts at Shanghai Teacher's University from 1981 to 1982. Barlow and Lowe offer a number of useful insights into the meaning of *guanxi* for them and for their extended Chinese family and friends. They point out the correlation between scarcity and the need to call upon *guanxi*, even when shopping for simple household needs:

> If you have no previous *guanxi* (perhaps you have neglected to give the clerk at your local grocery a piece of candy or new year calendar), your chances of getting what you want are pretty slim. When mothballs come on the market once a year, there is a frenzy of *guanxi* reaffirmations. People give cigarettes, generally in exchange for good cuts of meat. . . . The more powerful the recipient, the more expensive the gift. (pp. 104–105 in *Chinese Reflections: Americans Teaching in the People's Republic*, by Tani E. Barlow and Donald M. Lowe. Copyright © 1985 by Praeger Publishers. Reprinted by permission of Praeger Publishers)

After discussing the importance of family ties as a buffer against exploitation and manipulation, Barlow and Lowe define *guanxi:*

> The term *guanxi* describes social connections based on concrete, reciprocal exchange of favors and goods among family members and others. In a sense, *guanxi* is the way people organize relationships outside the *jia* (family), transforming strangers into kin by extending them favors and incurring obligations. All pseudo-family ties are cemented by this process. And ideally all relations between people should have a familist[ic] overtone. A Chinese doctor usually does not try to intimidate patients through a show of professionalism. Patients play on the familist[ic] ties between parent and child, making the doctor a parent through *guanxi*, usually giving the latter food or gifts. In return, the doctor is expected to treat the patient's entire being, including feelings and fears which Western doctors tend to consider "psychological" and hence not a part of their responsibility. This kind of relationship cannot develop unless both sides accept the obligation to give and receive concrete favors as tokens of the *guanxi*. (p. 104)

Outsiders cannot escape becoming enmeshed in this system even if they are unaware of the debts they pile up and the means at their disposal to settle them. Anyone who steps beyond the confines of his or her formal authority to ease your way will naturally expect to be repaid somehow. Social debts accrue in China just as they do anywhere. An invitation to a family dinner, always a precious opportunity for foreigners, may stem from a sincere desire to show you the personal side of life in China or to get to know you in more relaxed circumstances. Sometimes these meals quite obviously cost a great deal in time and effort, and you may feel inadequate in the face of such warm hospitality. One senior scholar remarks:

> When a friend insists on inviting you to a restaurant for dinner—inevitable, because so many people do not have big enough apartments to hold a dinner—along with a few other people, the evening may well cost him his month's salary (as well as a couple of hours spent holding the table until his guests arrive). A return banquet doesn't begin to make this up to him, so what do you do? This whole question has made me appreciate the function of the official welcoming banquet, which I tend to dislike because of its ritual nature. I now see that we should suffer such banquets gladly, because they allow some people at least to entertain us without bankrupting themselves.

Often the only way to repay hospitality is with a return banquet. But sometimes a great deal more eventually may be asked—help in getting a relative to the United States, for example—and in such instances the foreign guest is left wondering about the true motives behind the gestures of friendship. The problem of unrealistic expectations often affects relations between American and Chinese academics. For many Chinese intellectuals and bureaucrats alike, their greatest desire may be to boost a relative into the U.S. education system; but their understanding of the procedures and limits enforced by U.S. institutions may be very sketchy.

In his essay, "After Comradeship: Personal Relations in China Since the Cultural Revolution," Tom Gold emphasizes the pragmatic character of most human relationships there:

> The preeminent characteristic of personal relations in China today is instrumentalism. The principle that underlies it is *guanxi*, which means connectedness or particularistic ties, but is best left untranslated. *Guanxi* is based on reciprocity, the traditional concept of *bao*, where one does favors for others as "social investments," clearly expecting something in return. It is not a cold exchange, but is entertwined with *renging* (human feelings, empathy) which raises it to a higher plane. . . . *Guanxi* is a power relationship as one's control over a valued good or access to it gives power over others. . . . *Guanxi* is an informal, unofficial relationship utilized to get things done, from simple tasks to major life

choices. (pp. 659–661 in *The China Quarterly*, No. 104, December 1985. Reprinted by permission)

As Gold and other experienced foreigners agree, opportunism and corruption are inherent in such a system of relations. But friendship and *guanxi* relations are not necessarily incompatible in the Chinese view. The problem for the outsider is in determining just what mix of pragmatism and genuine affection make up relationships that are often formed in a very short time and in an unfamiliar context.

Despite the complexities of Chinese and foreigner interaction, in the past few years the climate has become so hospitable that you can count on a rich variety of human contacts in China. In part this is the result of familiarity. As more and more Chinese of all ages speak English, travel abroad, and become acquainted with Westerners and their films and literature, and as foreigners in turn become familiar firsthand with Chinese language and culture, the possibilities for genuinely meaningful friendships for both parties are enhanced. In part the new climate is also the result of the "open door" policy that has accompanied the economic reform program initiated in 1978. Efforts to understand Western languages and culture and to achieve access to a Western education can be justified not only as a means to personal advancement but also to aid in China's modernization.

Another factor encouraging more "normal" human relations is simply that foreigners are no longer the oddities they were 7 years ago following China's 30 years of isolation. In fact, many Chinese units in larger cities have had to scale down their ritual reception of foreign guests for reasons of economy and efficiency. For those who set great store by such rituals, this development may be disappointing. But it allows for more casual and natural social encounters—for example, in hotel dining rooms, in the homes of colleagues, or in coffee shops for lunch.

On the surface it seems at times that the boundaries governing human relations in China are internally monitored rather than externally imposed. But for many Chinese key individuals who choose to embark on a course of friendship with a foreigner, common interests and genuine affection may be only part of their motivation. Unease about the future direction of policies toward the West, the jealousy of colleagues, or the burden of a politically bad class background may all enter into their decision.

RITUAL   After two decades of closer and more extensive contact between China and the West, it is well known that ritual still structures professional and social encounters in China. Ritual plays the same role in contemporary China that it did in the past—it reaffirms boundaries, clarifies ranks, and teaches proper behavior by example. How and by whom you are greeted at the airport upon arrival, the order in which officials enter a room, the seating patterns at a welcoming banquet all place hosts and guests in their proper place in the hierarchy. In "A Shirtsleeves Guide to Corporate Etiquette" (*The China Business Review*, January–February 1983), Scott Seligman reiterates what other China hands have learned: that it is very much appreciated if a foreigner at least attempts to play by the rules and that you can learn a great deal in the process as well. Many academic visitors may not be accorded the elaborate treatment businessmen and official delegations receive, but they can derive the same benefit from knowing what to expect and the meaning of ritualistic signals.

There is security in knowing that some social patterns never change. Almost every major occasion in China (be it a welcome, departure, banquet, or formal meeting) opens with tea and a superficial exchange of pleasantries. Arrivals and departures are treated with great care. The host unit will, if at all possible, send a representative of suitable stature to the airport or train station to greet or—even more importantly—to see off an official guest. Chinese train stations and airports are equipped with special lounges expressly set aside for the rituals associated with meeting and departing—and to shield privileged travelers from the noise and bustle outside as they sip their tea.

Banquets are highly educational experiences. Sometimes the welcoming banquet offers the newcomers their first opportunity to discern the "pecking order" in the *danwei*. The host is always the highest-ranking person present and is almost always seated facing the door; the most honored guest sits to the right and the second-ranking host directly opposite or at a corresponding position if more than one table is used. Interpreters are situated for practical rather than ritually correct reasons. Banquets almost always last exactly two hours—say, from 6:30 to 8:30 p.m.—and are held in special rooms or screened portions of rooms in well-known Chinese restaurants or banquet rooms in the older foreign hotels. They start off with a cold plate and end with a soup and a simple dessert, usually fresh fruit; they may include sea slugs, if the guest is important enough, and they are punctuated with toasts of the fiery *maotai*, China's "white lightning." Beer and sweet red wine also are on the table, and according to recent reports, a drier white wine produced by a Sino-French joint venture is appearing fairly often as well. Those who do not drink alcoholic beverages can toast with the sweet soda *qishui*. Those who do not (or cannot) eat sea slugs and other delicacies are advised to move them politely around their plate without comment. It is correct to use a toothpick after dinner but not to fiddle with your chopsticks. Your hosts will use their serving chopsticks to place food on your plate. You can expect a great deal of bantering and good cheer.

No matter what the circumstances of a visit, a return banquet at the end of a stay can be a fine way to express appreciation. The best way to leave with good feelings and a good impression is to ask a Chinese friend or assistant to help plan the event. The great crispy duck restaurant with atmosphere that you frequent may not have the kind of food considered correct banquet fare. A good seafood restaurant is always safe. Be prepared to pay at least Y50 per person and be sure to find out what kind of drinks are included. Beer, *maotai*, sweet red wine, and soft drinks are standard. Remember to arrange for transportation for your guests and to pay for the drivers' meals. Open the dinner with a short toast of gratitude and expectations of continuing friendship, be sure to serve your guests with your serving chopsticks, and relax as everyone settles in to their ritual roles and the enjoyment of the food.

Recently Chinese units have been warned that the excessive time and money spent on banquets and other rituals must be reduced. Official visits during which high-level cadres were once received with great pomp are now to be simplified in the interests of economy and efficiency. This trend extends to the reception of foreign guests as well. The number of banquets for each visit has been cut down in many cases, or noontime dinners have taken the place of the evening meal out. In any event, these economizing measures should not be considered an insult to your status or importance but simply a practical response to the demands for efficiency.

Many China experts suggest that although it is always a plus when a foreigner understands the rituals well, attitude is more important than superficial correctness. The banquet table is not the place to discuss unpleasant business. It is a good idea to stick to safe subjects—comparative weather reports, your travels or plans for travel in China, and the food above all.

One researcher who had experienced more stalling than cooperation from his unit, which had never before hosted an American scholar, writes that although his welcoming banquet was finally held several months after his arrival in Beijing, he made it a point to be polite and positive on this public occasion. "My unit was very concerned that I would let my frustration show at my long-delayed welcoming banquet, and they were pleased to no end when I behaved like someone who understands China and can be a good guest." Steven Butler describes how he made use of a banquet to bolster the standing of the local officials responsible for the day-to-day implementation of his work with a visiting official from their parent organization in Beijing. After demonstrating through relaxed, genial behavior how well everyone got along and toasting the importance of individual cooperation, he reports:

The cadre from the Academy left for Peking [Beijing] feeling that he had been well entertained, that my project was proceeding well, that local cadres had been doing an excellent job helping me out, and, most important, that his own work arranging my field research had been successful. The local cadres, in turn, were pleased because I had made them look very good in the eyes of someone whom they regarded as influential. It is by taking advantage of opportunities like this that the researcher can find ways to reduce the heavy burden which he places on almost everyone with whom he comes into contact. (*The Social Sciences and Fieldwork in China: Views from the Field*, p. 121)

Of course ritual life is by no means confined to banquets. It is just as important to try to observe some of the proprieties on less grand occasions. When a Chinese guest comes to your dorm or hotel room, for instance, be sure to pour tea or a soft drink on a hot day, no matter how short the visit or how loud the protests. Having tins of cookies, fruit, or candies on hand for unexpected visits is always a good idea. When making appointments with Chinese friends or officials and teachers, avoid the rest period—it has been said that 10 a.m. and 3 p.m. are ideal times to schedule meetings. Remember that punctuality is essential.

If you are invited to a Chinese home, you should take a small gift with you. The guidelines presented earlier (see the section on gifts in Chapter 2) can give you some ideas. It is considered impolite to give gifts to individuals in front of others; either save it for a more private time, or, as Seligman suggests, give a gift that can be put easily into a pocket or bag. Do not press an individual to accept a gift when he or she seems genuinely embarrassed or frightened. Keep in mind that it is good form in China to refuse any offer, no matter how attractive, three times. Always give your Chinese friends a fourth chance to accept or decline whatever it is that you are attempting to give them.

One of the great advantages of the current openness in China is that you can ask Chinese friends for advice and help in negotiating the labyrinth of behavioral expectations. And most Americans agree that although the Chinese appreciate sincere attempts to respect Chinese culture by emulating some of the modes of behavior that ease potentially awkward situations, there is no need to lose your own identity in the process. As Seligman observes:

It's important to emphasize that no Chinese seriously expects a foreigner to behave appropriately in all of these situations. Allowances will be made for you whether you want them or not, and you will never be held to very stringent standards. But a small gesture which indicates an awareness of Chinese expectations will go a long way toward complimenting your host. Even in China, it is viewed as the most sincere form of flattery. ("A Shirtsleeves Guide to Corporate Etiquette," p. 13)

LAW   It requires both sensitivity and acute powers of observation to understand Chinese customs. As one American teacher expressed it, "There is less room for personal wishes in Chinese society than in the United States and considerable control over aspects of life we take for granted as being free from control; foreigners must have a sense of humor and patience and realize that they won't always know what is going on." Foreign residents are expected not only to respect China's customs but to conduct themselves in accordance with its laws, which unfortunately often seem as difficult to understand as the more subtle forms of control. Appendixes B and D contain the rules and regulations governing students and scholars in China. Of course these documents do not begin to cover all the situations that may arise. In general it is important to remember that foreigners are subject to Chinese laws and procedures and that once enmeshed in a criminal process, they are represented by a Chinese lawyer. In a recent article by Stanley B. Lubman and Gregory Wajnowski ("Criminal Justice and the Foreigner," *The China Business Review*, November–December 1985), the case of an American who was convicted, fined, and imprisoned for causing a fire in a hotel in Harbin that killed 10 people is used as an illustration of how the foreigner fits into the legal system in China. The authors point out that

> China's criminal code defines many crimes more vaguely than they are defined in the West, and it lacks specific standards of criminal responsibility. For example, negligence resulting in death, injury or destruction of property is a crime in China. Under United States law unintentional negligent conduct may result in criminal liability, but the defendant must first be found to have acted recklessly. China's criminal law provides no such standard for determining criminal culpability for unintentional conduct. (p. 27)

The authors also delineate the role of the U.S. Embassy when an American is apprehended:

> The initial, most important stage in China's formal criminal process is the provisional apprehension of a suspect by the PBS (Public Security Bureau). This is not a formal arrest. China's criminal law provides that the PBS must produce a warrant for the detention and notify the suspect's family or work unit within 24 hours. In the case of an American citizen, the Consular Convention between the United States and China provides that Chinese authorities must notify the U.S. Embassy within four days of the apprehension. (p. 27)

The article goes on to offer details of the case at hand and concludes that by Chinese standards, proper procedures were followed in the case. The authors do an excellent job of clarifying different concepts of guilt, procedure, and trial in China and the United States.

THE FOREIGN COMMUNITY   For better or for worse, more time than most China travelers can anticipate is spent adjusting to a multinational community, especially in larger universities. As one student put it, such universities constitute a mini-United Nations with each foreigner sometimes unwittingly serving as an unofficial representative. Many of the most obvious and disruptive clashes occur not between foreigners and Chinese residents but among foreigners who live in close quarters without a clear legal or ethical context to guide them in their interpersonal relations. Many Americans enjoy the opportunity to meet people from all over the world. And everyone understands the importance of maintaining a variety of networks in China—if only to know what is going on. Information is hard to come by, and whether it concerns events in the world outside China, the opening of a new temple to foreigners, or sudden changes in banking policies, news is passed along from person to person, taking on a variety of hues in the retelling.

Gossip flourishes in China, not only because of a very real information gap but because boredom plagues almost every foreigner at some point during his or her stay. An article in the November–December 1985 *China Business Review* ("The Quality of Life," by John Frankenstein, pp. 22–24) on the quality of life in Beijing concludes from surveys of long-term foreign residents that most feel the material side of life has improved in the past five years and that better housing, improved taxi service, and new and more Western-style restaurants have made life easier. But the big problem that plagues expatriates in particular is isolation:

> One of the most popular complaints among Americans living in Beijing is their sense of "isolation," the feeling of being far from Western-style sources of entertainment and recreation. Indeed, after a typically frustrating day at the office, the executive returns home to a very limited range of diversions. Close personal friendships with Chinese are rare, and hotel life rules out entertaining in the traditional sense. There is nothing wrong with reading, watching (and rewatching) old movies on the VCR, partying, and sports, but that just about exhausts the possibilities. (p. 23)

It is generally easier for the visiting academic to be assimilated into Chinese life than it is for business and diplomatic personnel, but the problem of isolation at some point is shared by nearly everyone who lives for more than a few months in China. Academics who have chosen to live in China to learn have an advantage, for even the most trying experiences are in the end educational. And the monotony of life is apt to be punctuated by professional breakthroughs that are usually unexpected: the sudden announcement that a famous Chinese writer who has been unavailable for months is suddenly free for a meeting—that afternoon; or that a long-awaited trip to the field is finally scheduled— for the next morning.

HOUSING

Foreigners who study or work in the Chinese educational system are categorized according to the type of program in which they participate. Each group is subject to different housing and financial arrangements.

Students almost always are assigned to a campus dormitory reserved for foreigners. Most colleges and universities do not allow Chinese and foreign students to room together, and the trend in the larger schools is to segregate foreign students in separate dormitories. How much students pay out of pocket is determined by the kind of program in which they enroll. Most U.S.-sponsored language programs charge a flat tuition, room, and board fee that covers all the essentials including meals; other programs include only partial payment to the Chinese organization for these services. Graduate students and undergraduates who make their own arrangements with a Chinese institution of higher learning will pay all expenses directly to that institution. In addition, there are a variety of agreements between Chinese and U.S. institutions for student exchanges that include remission of tuition or room-and-board costs.

"The Regulations Concerning the Admission of Foreign Students in Chinese Schools, 1986" (see Appendix B, items IV.A and IX.B) spell out the rules governing student housing. "Chinese schools have separate dining halls for foreign students. However, foreign students may, if they wish, have meals in the canteens for Chinese students. They should observe the regulations of the dining halls and canteens and maintain order in them. Chinese schools provide dormitories for their foreign students. In general, two students share one room. No special accommodations are available for married couples or for students' family members. Foreign students must abide by the school's regulations relating to housing." In some schools, if space permits, students can occupy a room alone—that is, if they pay for the unused bed. The 1986 regulations also set dorm rates: US$1.50 per bed per day for a double room, two students sharing a room. The cost of a single room is US$4.00 per day.

Scholars and academic visitors above the student level are considered guests; they usually are housed in hotels and guest houses and must pay tourist rates from their own funds. Because Chinese organizations usually have longstanding arrangements with one or two hotels to house their foreign guests, there is not much room for choice. Recently some foreigners who know the system well have been able to arrange their own housing but only if space is available. The high volume of tourists in China often negates the possibility of striking out alone to find housing—even if the host unit tolerates such initiative. Sometimes guest houses on smaller campuses will house students, scholars, and foreign teachers but at different rates depending on status and amenities.

Teachers are classified either as foreign experts (who are selected by the State Education Commission) or as foreign teachers (who make direct arrangements with the host unit). Provisions for teachers vary according to the organization, but generally either on-campus apartments or hotel suites are provided. As noted earlier, the regulations governing foreign experts state that the hiring party must provide housing and the following related items for the employee: furniture, bedding, a bathroom, a television set, a refrigerator, and the facilities for heating and air conditioning. However, returned experts caution their successors that while these material comforts are usually in place, problems with maintenance and electricity sometimes seriously reduce their efficiency.

There is a good deal of flexibility in this scheme. If space permits, some institutions allow researchers to live on campus in housing reserved for their own faculty or foreign experts. In such cases the rates are higher than for teachers but usually considerably lower than the cost of a hotel room. Similarly, in some units researchers and teachers have been able to live in student dormitories—but usually only after some negotiation and for a higher fee than students normally pay. Researchers who travel or who work in the countryside have been housed in a variety of accommodations—from dormitories (at about Y4 per night) to moderately priced hotels in larger cities (at Y80 and up).

HOTELS   Hotel accommodations in China range from the very expensive joint-venture hotels that offer Western amenities and service at Western prices to very modest establishments that house Chinese travelers as well as foreign guests. In most cases, if your Chinese hosts make arrangements, they will place you in medium-priced lodging, usually one of the older Chinese hotels. Typical suites include one or two rooms, a private bath, a very small closet or wardrobe, a bureau, a desk, a telephone, and a color television. The amount and type of furniture in each room is fixed by regulations, which allow for very little maneuvering within the system. Most long-term residents find ways to decorate their room with plants, prints, and extra furniture purchased outside. For a small daily charge, some hotels will set up a temporary cot for visitors, particularly relatives.

Kitchen facilities are rarely provided, but all hotels have a dining room and most offer both Chinese and Western food. Hotel fare is usually relatively expensive (about Y6 to Y8 for a simple lunch and Y15 for a dinner with several dishes) and almost always monotonous. To combat both high prices and the monotony, you can eat out frequently in neighborhood restaurants or other hotels or find creative ways to eat "at home" (see the section on food and cooking supplies in Chapter 2, "Preparing for the Trip").

Some residents have lunch at their work unit for a few *mao* per meal, eating only breakfast and dinner at the more expensive hotel restaurant. Some units strongly advise their foreign guests against eating in the canteen—sometimes to maintain the separation between foreigners and *danwei* personnel but sometimes because the food is genuinely of poor quality. One researcher who insisted on principle that he be allowed to take lunch at the workplace was told repeatedly by colleagues that the food was not up to minimal standards of cleanliness. When he finally won the right to eat at work, he became violently ill. Some reading rooms and offices close down for the noon *xiuxi*, and it is simply easier to return to your hotel for lunch and rest or to prepare for the afternoon's activities.

Hotel life in China is comfortable but confining. The academic visitor who goes to China to gain access to the culture often finds that social life there revolves too much around a community of foreigners, many of them cynical and disillusioned. There are far too few opportunities for casual, everyday contact with Chinese friends, who often cannot visit a foreigner without signing a slip at the hotel desk that identifies their unit and the room they are to visit. In some hotels Chinese visitors cannot even enter the grounds without a pass. The irony of hotel life is that it is hard to see Chinese friends naturally within its walls but even harder to maintain some privacy from the Chinese staff at the establishment. Keys are usually kept at the service desk on each floor, and service personnel are generally very responsible about protecting guests from outsiders. But because they consider the hotel their place of work rather than the living quarters of their guests, work schedules generally take priority over the individual needs of temporary residents. It is not unusual for five or six *fuwuyuan* (service personnel) to visit the room every day, each with a different task—from cleaning the bathroom to watering the plants. The hapless foreigner who spends any time at all in the hotel room must adjust to these elaborate routines because it is nearly impossible to have them altered. On the positive side, however, getting to know hotel personnel and to understand the nature of the hotel as a workplace offers another interesting perspective on Chinese life.

CAMPUS APARTMENTS   Campus housing is remarkably similar throughout China. Henderson and Cohen's description of the physical plant in their urban medical *danwei* represents a typical layout:

As one faces the hospital, the staff apartments are to the left, specialized or newly constructed facilities at the back, and the medical college on the right. Bricks lie in large and small piles in every empty lot, tangible evidence of the constantly changing physical environment. In the midst of the bricks, chickens scratch, children create makeshift platforms for table tennis, and construction teams are rarely absent. The apartment buildings are brick and cement. The older ones are one story high, with communal kitchens and baths for several families in individual three-room apartments. The newest buildings are four- and five-story cement structures housing one-hundred families. In addition to housing, the unit includes a dining hall, a day-care center, a bathhouse attached to the hospital boiler room, an administrative office, a garage for unit cars and jeeps, and shops for the maintenance and repair staff (plumbers, carpenters, electricians). (*The Chinese Hospital: A Socialist Work Unit*, p. 12)

Many teachers are housed in apartments on the campus of their host institution. Some of their comments about this housing appear below.

Foreign teachers at the college share an old brick house which is centrally located. It is a spacious, two-story structure, but attracts furry four legged friends (our cat ran away in frustration!). There are large, single rooms and bathrooms, with reversible heating/air conditioning units. Overall, it is very pleasant.

For a family of four, we had an apartment on campus in the Foreign Experts' Building. The apartment included two bedrooms, a good sized living room, Western bathroom with bath but no shower, a small kitchen with two gas burners and a refrigerator (which we moved from the living room to the kitchen). Hot water is generally plentiful at night and in the early morning. Radiator heat was available for several hours in winter evenings after December 1. The furniture provided was fine; esthetic improvements can be made inexpensively.

We're in a newly constructed guest house for foreign experts. The rooms are modern, spacious and relatively well appointed. There is a living room, two bedrooms, small kitchen (with no cooking appliances), and bathroom. The furniture is tasteful and abundant: four armchairs (no sofa), two end tables, two nightstands, two large desks, three single beds, a vanity, two bookcases, and a crib. However, the central heating is not adequate. We also have problems with our housemaid who thinks the apartment is hers, not ours. She lets herself in anytime she wants with her own key, gives advice loudly on all subjects and does not clean well at all.

There is a compound for foreign experts and Chinese professors and administrators. There are four apartments per building, which are brick, two story, circa 1950 vintage—with mice in the downstairs apartments. The apartments are either one or two bedroom, with a kitchen, living room, and bathroom. They are largely carpeted and have bookshelves, desks, chairs, beds, and almost everything needed. Bedding is provided. Each apartment has a propane stove, refrigerator, washing machine, color television, and air conditioner.

Our housing is adequate but cramped. We use the one large room as a bedroom, sitting room, and office for my spouse. The smaller room serves as my office and our dining room where we eat light meals. (There is no kitchen.) There is a separate room outside the apartment for our teenage son. The furniture, carpet, and wallpaper are pleasant. It is air conditioned, and we have a small refrigerator and a color television. However, there is insufficient drawer space, inadequate closet space, and hot water is only available for a couple hours in the morning and evening.

Overall, the most common housing problems included poor and leaky plumbing, insufficient heat, a lack of hot water, inadequate storage space, poor lighting, and erratic electricity. And there was one other commonly noted condition, to which most Americans (like the teacher whose comment follows) became resigned: "Be prepared to share room and board with local vermin. They are ubiquitous and bold but reasonably well-mannered and thrifty."

Foreigners in China, like the Chinese themselves, devise different ways of coping with food preparation. Henderson and Cohen present some of these:

> At noon, people pour out of the buildings and stop by the dining hall to purchase a square-shaped portion of rice or several squares for a family. . . . To avoid the ten or fifteen minute wait for lunch, some carry their rice home and cook vegetables in their own kitchens. Others, for convenience and to save home fuel, buy their lunch and either take it home or eat it at the dining hall. . . . Most agree that home cooking is better and a little cheaper, but the dining hall is chosen for convenience.

Foreign residents have the same range of choices, and most eat out, either in the dining hall or in local restaurants, for the same reasons that motivate their Chinese colleagues. Some returned teachers indicated that the food provided by their work units ranged from excellent to disastrous:

> The food at the cafeteria is inadequate, so I make my own breakfast and have an *ayi* (maid) who cooks dinner for me five nights a week at a cost of Y50 per month. There are a number of good restaurants close by also, and good vegetable markets abound in the area.

> The residence dining room serves Western breakfasts and Chinese lunches and dinners; three times a week, a Western lunch is also offered. The food is generally good, occasionally outstanding. I have a refrigerator in my apartment, so I can also shop and cook for myself.

We must eat in the foreigners' cafeteria where the food ranges from very poor to good. The atmosphere is reminiscent of a cross between an automat and a warehouse. The "window style" service means you have to wait in three different lines before getting all desired items; this means the cold food (supposedly hot) gets colder. In the section of the cafeteria served by a waitress, the food is somewhat better, but it's repetitive and disproportionately expensive.

There was a woman who cooked for the five foreign experts at the university. We paid a monthly fee for food (she'd do the buying and give us a bill at the end of each month). I usually ate one to two meals daily and my monthly bill averaged about Y35 each month (US$12.50). I also did some cooking for myself; my kitchen had cold running water, a one burner hot plate and small refrigerator (all supplied by the university), to which I added a small toaster oven purchased second hand from another foreign expert.

The food in the dining hall is fine, but the service is *very* slow and not at all well organized. However, there are many good local restaurants where the food is inexpensive.

STUDENT DORMITORIES   Whether located on the campus of a university, a research institute, or a medical college, dormitories are remarkably uniform in their outward appearance and furnishings. Almost all dormitory buildings are gray, three-story cement edifices with communal shower rooms, spartan laundry rooms equipped with washboards and clotheslines, communal bathrooms with Asian-style squatter toilets, a television lounge, and a reading or reception room. In many dormitories boiled water for drinking must be carried from a boiler room. Hot water for laundry or showers is usually available only a few hours each day, often right after the dinner hour. Not all dormitories are heated, and those that are usually have heat for a few hours in the morning and again in the evening. When the heat is on, the rooms are quite comfortable, but hallways and communal rooms can be cold and dark in the winter. Electricity is erratic, especially in the evenings. Many colleges and universities are building new dormitories with more Western-style facilities to house foreign guests.

Room sizes vary. Some (for example, in the Shaoyuan Lou Guesthouse at Beida) are small (3 meters × 4.5 meters); others are quite large, even by Western standards. No matter what their size, however, all rooms are furnished with a bed and desk for each occupant and at least one bookcase and wardrobe. Rooms are spartan: whitewashed cement walls, drab gray cement floors, and a stark fluorescent tube overhead. Every newcomer is routinely issued a thermos for storing potable water, mosquito netting, a padded cotton quilt, woolen blanket, two sheets, and a wash basin. This basic "survival kit" should be taken along whenever you move in China and should be turned in upon final departure.

Most students have found that with some imagination and effort rooms can be decorated and arranged to suit individual tastes. How a room might be made more livable is described by a CSCPRC-sponsored advanced graduate student who lived in Beijing from 1983 to 1985:

> During my second year at Peking [Beijing] University, I stayed in a west facing room on the fifth floor of the Shaoyuan foreigner and guest compound. The room has a small porch and a spectacular view of the West Hills to the northwest of the Summer Palace and the Yuquan Pagoda. It was warm enough in the winter after I winterized the windows and porch door by applying polyethylene sheeting and paper "storm windows." However, under the afternoon summer sun it was uncomfortably hot, even with a venetian blind to let the air through and keep the sun out.

This student and others mention frequently the importance of following the Golden Rule in finding ways to live harmoniously, in the absence of clear legal and disciplinary codes, with more than 500 foreigners from over 60 different countries expected just at Beida in 1986–1987.

Foreign students can eat at the foreign student dining hall for a few *yuan* a day, or they can eat at the Chinese students' canteen for even less. The latter are crowded and lively; there are usually no tables or chairs and students are responsible for bringing their own bowls and utensils. Most students complain that the food is monotonous and sometimes greasy and cold, but in fact an effort generally is made in most institutions to provide a nutritious diet at a nominal cost. Chinese and foreign students alike devise ways to cook in their rooms using hot plates and ingredients from local stores and markets. Most neighborhoods have at least a few good restaurants for eating out.

The dormitory community is a mixed one on most campuses. Foreigners of many nationalities, Chinese caretakers, teachers, and sometimes foreign teachers all live together. The dormitory is cared for by the *shifu*, the workers who answer phones, clean the hallways and common rooms, distribute newspapers and mail, and generally watch over dormitory residents and their guests. Mail comes in twice each day and is generally placed on a hall table or in mailboxes designated by nationality. Most dormitories have only one or two telephones for incoming and outgoing calls, and residents are notified of calls by loudspeaker. Some of the dorms that have been built recently have better telephone facilities. The Shaoyuan Guesthouse at Beida, for example, has a phone on each floor, and the apartment suites have their own telephone.

ARRANGEMENTS FOR ACCOMPANYING SPOUSES AND CHILDREN

Chinese regulations prohibit students from bringing spouses and children to China, but researchers and teachers may be accompanied by their families if prior permission has been received from the host institution. Not all institutions may accede to such requests, however; most have problems supplying housing for foreigners due to acute housing shortages. In addition, not all cities can provide adequate medical care, especially for small children. These factors may lead to a reluctance on the part of host institutions to accommodate families. Often those Americans who do take their families to China have been especially grateful to their Chinese colleagues for their efforts to help find adequate housing, to secure slots in overcrowded day-care centers, and to arrange for language tutorials for older children.

Spouses who accompany Americans going to China as "foreign experts" often are invited to teach English or other subjects in demand as a "foreign teacher"; their salaries usually are lower than those paid to foreign experts who may teach identical courses. But most spouses find work of any kind preferable to spending long hours alone in a hotel room or apartment. More important, the position offers them an entry into Chinese society and an opportunity to make a much-needed contribution.

Arrangements for children in China vary. The U.S. Embassy in Beijing reports that there are no English-language schools of any kind for dependent children of foreign experts or researchers working in China except for those operated by foreign diplomatic missions. One of these schools, the International School, was founded in Beijing in September 1980 by the embassies of Australia, Canada, New Zealand, the United Kingdom, and the United States. It is a coeducational day school for grades one through eight admitting foreign children 5 to 13 years old. The curriculum is based on but not limited to U.S. educational models. Space is extremely limited at the school, and priority is given to children of official personnel of the five sponsoring missions. Students of other diplomatic missions receive second priority; dependents of other nationals of the five cooperating countries such as businessmen, journalists, and foreign experts have the lowest admission priority. If you are interested in the school, you should submit an application as early as possible before your proposed arrival in China. Annual tuition is US$4,200 with no additional fees.

The U.S. Consulate General in Shenyang has established the American Academy, which is located on the consulate compound. Tuition is US$2,500 per semester. The curriculum consists of an accredited correspondence course administered by an American teacher. The school operates only if there are sufficient students and an available teacher. For information, write to:

Shenyang American Academy
c/o U.S. Consulate General—Shenyang
FPO San Francisco, CA 96659-0002

Several foreign experts and consulate staff members in Shenyang have placed their children in local schools. Tuition per semester is Y120 for middle school and Y90 for elementary school. There is no single school designated to accept foreign children; however, several schools have admitted them in the past.

The U.S. Consulate General in Shanghai also has established an American school in one of the consulate's buildings. In 1982, the tuition was US$5,000 per year. For updated information, contact:

U.S. Consulate General—Shanghai
1469 Huai Hai Zhong Lu
Shanghai, People's Republic of China

The American School of Guangzhou is located on the fourth floor of the Office Tower in the Garden Hotel. The school accommodates children of kindergarten age to the eighth grade. Tuition for the school year is US$8,200.

If there is no English-language school in the area in which you will be working, one alternative might be send your children to a Chinese school. For information about such possibilities in Beijing or in a city in which one of the U.S. Consulates is located, contact the U.S. mission in that city (see pages 120–121 for addresses). It might be possible for Chinese schools to accept foreign children, but, of course, classes in such schools will be in Chinese.

Americans who have taught in China and who have taken their children have worked out a variety of solutions for day care and schooling. A few examples are presented below.

Teachers located in Beijing who had a two-year-old child hired an *ayi* (maid) through the Foreign Experts Bureau. The *ayi* worked eight hours a day, six days a week, for a fee of Y50 per month. For an extra Y5 per month, the *ayi* washed the child's clothes and diapers. Another couple in Beijing whose son was in the ninth grade arranged for him to take correspondence courses from the University of Nebraska School of Continuing Education. He spent eight hours a day studying eight subjects and had a tutor for French and Chinese. The parents noted that there were no other teenagers in the area, a circumstance they regretted, but they hoped the experience of being in China would be compensation for the lack of peers.

A couple in Tianjin with two children sent their five-year-old daughter to a Chinese nursery school six days a week from 8 a.m. to 5 p.m. Their 12-year-old son attended a Chinese music academy from 8 a.m. to 12 p.m. and then returned by bicycle to their hotel where his mother taught him his American curriculum in the afternoon. Neither child spoke any Chinese on arrival nor were there any English-speaking staff at their schools, but the parents felt that their children did remarkably well and that children of other foreign experts in the area also seemed to adjust rather easily.

Teachers in Shanghai commented that American preschool children seemed to thrive in Chinese kindergartens but that older children had some trouble adjusting to Chinese schools—which in turn had difficulty accommodating foreign children. The American school at the U.S. Consulate has received plaudits from parents in the past, but unfortunately the school now has stopped Chinese-language training. It also has become rather expensive to arrange transportation for children from institutions at some distance from the school because the city of Shanghai has abandoned its former policy of allowing foreign teachers to pay Chinese rates for taxis and some institutions are reluctant to provide cars.

During their first year in China, a couple in Lanzhou with children aged 11 and 13 sent them to a Chinese school three afternoons a week for art, music, and physical education. During their second year, the local school system was reorganized and the arrangement was no longer possible. So the children's mother taught them their American curriculum at home, with advice from the children's teachers in the United States. A teacher from the university's primary school taught them Chinese for three hours a week, and another university teacher gave them Chinese painting lessons once a week.

As there is no foreign language school in Nanjing, a couple there with children sent them to the university's Chinese preschool in the morning through lunchtime. In the afternoon, their seven-year-old child did his American second-grade work at home. The arrangement worked out well, and the children gradually learned some Chinese. One note of warning was added to this report, however. The parents had given strict instructions to the children's school not to give them any medications or vaccinations without prior parental approval. They were glad they had made this request because there was a serious health incident at the school when the wrong medication was mistakenly given to a large number of children. The parents believed this was probably an isolated incident that would not be repeated, but they wanted to recommend caution about such school medical treatments to other Americans taking children to China.

In Wuhan, Americans with children there reported that at the local primary school "foreign children are extended every courtesy and the teachers are warm, helpful, considerate, and very flexible." Their children attended the school when they wished and also had an English-speaking tutor. The parents also reported that the children liked the school so much that they went even when they were not required to attend.

The son of a couple in Xuzhou who was a sophomore in high school studied by correspondence with the American School in Chicago and the University of Wisconsin extension. His parents commented that the latter is superlative and has high academic standards.

One last piece of advice: some of the teachers offering comments urged parents who plan to take children to China to find out about arrangements for housing and meals *before* they go—or they may receive a large bill at the end of their visit for their children.

THE ACADEMIC CALENDAR

The academic year in China revolves around the Spring Festival or Lunar New Year (*chunjie*), a celebration that theoretically marks the end of winter. The month-long holiday after *chunjie*, which usually falls during the last week of January or the first of February, marks the end of the academic term that begins in late August or early September. The second term begins around the end of February—depending on the date of *chunjie*—and runs through late June. The pace in most work units slows considerably during these holidays because staff often travel to visit relatives or for sightseeing. Most foreigners in recent years have found these holidays especially enjoyable when celebrated with Chinese friends and colleagues. If your research plans require meetings with specific scholars or continuation of work during one of these holidays, be sure to make arrangements as far in advance as possible, recognizing that your plans could force your coworkers to give up their vacation time.

Foreigners are given time off to observe Chinese holidays, and many institutions schedule trips or other activities during semester breaks. Shorter holidays, such as National Day (October 1) and May Day (May 1), may offer opportunities for two or three days of travel. Foreigners are not entitled to time off for their own national or religious holidays, but it has been possible in some units to arrange for celebrations of Christmas, Hanukkah, and other holidays. Chinese guests appreciate joining in these festivities.

4. Research and Study

Educational reform in China has been given the same priority as modernization. And the pragmatic spirit that characterizes reforms in these sectors has also affected China's universities and research institutes, which have been given increased responsibility for their own economic well-being as well as freedom to implement internal changes and establish links with other institutions and enterprises, both within China and abroad. To date, Chinese institutions of higher learning have developed formal exchange agreements with more than 180 U.S. colleges and universities. In addition, countless individual arrangements are being made between U.S. academics and their Chinese counterparts.

On the Chinese side, these exchanges are motivated in large part by a genuine desire to use foreign materials and methodologies to improve the quality of the nation's academic programs. But many, quite frankly, are aimed at generating revenue as well. American academics who work in China now find themselves more intimately involved in Chinese intellectual life then they did five years ago, but they are also being drawn into a cash nexus as scholarship and study become increasingly more contractual and formalized. What this means in practical terms is that prices for services are going up and contractual relations are replacing informal agreements. A scientist who worked in China in 1985 and returned in 1986 calculates that he paid almost 7 percent more for his latest research trip even though it involved far less assistance. Internal inflation and the devaluation of the *yuan* are frequently cited to explain increases in prices. Some researchers who have worked in China in previous years through informal personal arrangements have returned to their *danwei* only to find themselves faced with the task of drawing up a contract for their proposed project—complete with agree-

71

ments about payment for services. Recently, researchers have been asked to pay a flat research fee—$300 per month—if they are unaffiliated with a formal exchange program. Especially thorny is the problem of how to pay research assistants. Some American scholars have been disgruntled when asked to pay assistants who already are compensated by their *danwei*; others meanwhile have been thwarted when they attempted to reward assistants for extra services. Non-Chinese-speaking scientists have reported considerable frustration when they have been unable to enter into the process of negotiations for payment.

Foreign students too are being charged more for room and board and tuition, sometimes without warning. In one case, students were presented with a midsemester increase and the explanation that the order had come from a higher authority. When they asked to see written proof of the increase, the local foreign affairs office backed down.

It seems clear that policies are interpreted locally; that negotiation is warranted if demands seem unreasonable or unclear; and that, however personal are your relations with Chinese colleagues, interaction with the academic institution will be much more contractual than in the past.

THE UNIVERSITIES AND COLLEGES

As part of the reforms in education, universities have been granted virtual autonomy in deciding matters of curriculum, personnel management, and relations with other organizations. To oversee this vast network, the State Education Commission (SEC) was created in June 1985 and placed directly under the State Council with status equal to that of the State Economic Commission and the State Science and Technology Commission. The SEC replaces the Ministry of Education and is charged with formulating and implementing educational policies and with coordinating the distribution of resources.

The reforms have affected the universities in significant areas. For example, there is more scope for economic and academic activities on an institutional level as well as individually. Although still primarily teaching institutions, universities are encouraging faculty to pursue their own research topics and to meet with colleagues at conferences both inside and outside China. Moonlighting is tolerated to an extent so that intellectuals who are still underpaid and less free than workers or peasants to take advantage of the economic opportunities made possible by the reforms can supplement their salaries. Faculty can also pursue on their own opportunities to teach and study abroad. But with this new latitude has come more responsibility for faculty. Now that some universities once again can confer master's and doctoral degrees, professors are busy with graduate students. And in line with improvements in undergraduate education, senior professors are now assigned to teach basic subjects in addition to advanced courses, which adds to their teaching burden. Because of the Cultural Revolution and the relatively low status of teachers in China generally, there is a shortage of well-trained personnel, and teacher training has become a priority in higher education. But until these newly trained teachers are ready to assume their duties, it is the middle-aged educators trained before the Cultural Revolution who will bear the major responsibility for teaching.

New departments are being added to universities and existing departments are being revitalized. The international politics program, for example, is being upgraded at Beijing and Fudan Universities. Multidisciplinary study is being encouraged with the establishment of research centers such as the American Studies Center at Beijing University, which will oversee an interdisciplinary M.A. program. At Qinghua University, which has traditionally focused on engineering, multidisciplinary studies have been set up to integrate the study of science and technology in such fields as environmental engineering, biophysics, and genetic engineering. Also at Qinghua, a school of continuing education has been approved, and an accelerated program for gifted students has been added. The impact and structure of the new social sciences department at Qinghua is described by a graduate student who studied Chinese Communist Party history there: "While I was at Qinghua, the department sponsored a one-week seminar on the curriculum for revolutionary history, which was attended by 100 teachers from all over China. They came to hear lectures given by the Qinghua staff and to look at materials developed for teaching" (China Exchange News, June 1986, p. 17).

Decisions to establish new departments and to expand the curriculum, as well as personnel policies, are now determined internally at each particular university. The general trend has been to replace older scholars who dominated university departments and administration in the late 1970s with younger, more active staff. Many of these new administrators were educated in China or in the Soviet Union in the early 1950s and are less familiar with Western methodologies and languages than the older generation, some of whom received their advanced education in the West.

Students too are deeply influenced by the new educational policies. In China all students must pass extremely competitive examinations before they can enter university programs. They finance their education in one of three ways: securing funding from the state, which then has the right to assign a student to a particular job after graduation; contracting with an employer who pays the student's bills and then hires him or her after graduation; or paying for oneself, which, of the three methods, is the only one that carries no obligation after graduation.

The trend seems to be that the financial burden of an education is shifting more and more to students except for those in critical disciplines who have severe financial hardships and unusual academic ability. Students have new opportunities to earn their own way through part-time work-study programs on their campuses and in jobs off campus during vacations. This trend clearly has advantages, but the urge to make money in some cases may begin to outweigh academic motivation—one American professor noted that some students cut classes to knit and sell homemade sweaters on the free market. There are numerous reports of corruption and "backdoorism" in the universities as students use personal *guanxi* to get better grades and good jobs and some faculty engage in questionable outside activities. These practices generally have been dealt with severely when they are discovered, but in the competitive atmosphere that prevails in China, they probably will continue at some levels.

The reforms announced at Beijing University in the spring of 1985 are reflected in other institutions. Students now have more flexibility in determining a major and in choosing courses and scheduling classes. Summer school is now offered for credit, class hours have been shortened to allow more time for outside study, and in some cases electives are now allowed and the number of required courses has been reduced. As yet, these structural changes have not visibly changed attitudes toward study. Rote memorization and passive learning within rigid disciplinary bounds still prevail. And the quality of student life still warrants improvement. Students have continued the tradition of activism that is a part of student culture in China, and demonstrations can be stimulated by mundane concerns, such as bad food and the increased cost of textbooks, or by far more serious political issues, as recent reports suggest. Finally, although education in one of China's prestigious universities is still coveted, study abroad has become an important means to advancement. If they are not being financed by the government, students can make their own arrangements for study abroad, although rumor has it that new regulations are being formulated to restrict the numbers and categories of self-sponsored students going to other countries.

How do these changes affect the foreigners who work and study in China's universities? For one, outsiders enter into a far more lively academic atmosphere than was possible five years ago when the universities were still recovering from the Cultural Revolution and were trying above all to rebuild a faculty. Improvements in campus facilities are immediately noticeable. Deserted and ramshackle buildings have been removed or repaired, and on many campuses special dormitories and classrooms have been erected for foreigners. This segregation, however, is often viewed by foreigners as a negative rather than a positive move because isolation from the university community becomes the price of better living conditions.

Recent visitors have found their Chinese colleagues more overwhelmed with institutional commitments than in the past when teaching duties were light or at times nonexistent. The increased pressure on Chinese academics results in their having less time for work with foreign colleagues. The foreign scholar will be far more successful in China if he or she contributes—whether through lectures, tutorials, or informal English classes—to the modernization effort. Patricia Beaver, an anthropologist who studied women's roles as an exchange professor at Northeast University of Technology in Shenyang, describes the importance of her own efforts and her husband's participation in teaching as a means of entering the community:

> My husband and I, as teachers and occasional lecturers at a Friday night English lecture series, were able to participate more fully in the day to day life of the university. Placed in a foreign compound, we could have easily bypassed entirely the flow of Chinese community life. However, our roles as teachers and colleagues gave us the opportunity to interact with students and colleagues and develop friendships, which enhanced both the research process and our living experience. (*China Exchange News*, December 1984, p. 13)

But even with the best possible rapport with the institution and warm relationships with a few colleagues, most American academics are never fully integrated into university life. Many report being routinely excluded from departmental meetings and functions. Lynn Struve's research, for example, was facilitated by Nanjing University's history department, but she was not able to take full advantage of its intellectual life: "Everyone was very kind, but I never was invited to any departmental social functions or colloquia. I was introduced to only one graduate student in the very last week of my stay, and I met no other members of the departmental faculty besides the two who were formally appointed to assist me" (*China Exchange News*, December 1984, p. 18).

Foreign students have found themselves part of a rapidly growing community on most campuses. Beijing University, for example, hosted over 200 self-paying language students from abroad last summer; similar situations exist on other campuses. These large numbers of students place considerable strain on the human and material resources of the universities and at times lower the overall quality of academic work. The segment of the university that pays the heaviest price for all of this activity—and reaps few benefits—is the foreign affairs office. On some campuses, the *waiban* oversees all activities relating to outsiders: on others with large student populations, these duties fall to the *liuxue-*

sheng bangongshi or *liuban*, the office for overseeing foreign students. The *liuban* plays a key role in the lives of foreign residents on any college or university campus.

Liuban personnel are responsible for overseeing the myriad details of everyday student life. They assign housing and, if appropriate, roommates, arrange travel permits, issue ration coupons, and upon departure see their charges through customs. The *liuban* shares the responsibility for the scholarly needs of its constituents with the academic departments, managing such activities as arranging for library and photocopying privileges, helping to gather materials, providing language tutors, and finding a suitable academic adviser.

It is possible to cross departmental lines and establish informal networks within the university, but generally speaking as a foreigner you will be expected to work through departmental offices when making formal requests (for example, for permission to attend a conference or to meet with scholars in other units). You will be identified with a unit, and within that unit, with a particular department; but you should not expect to become a fully integrated member of either. American researchers and students have at times expressed deep disappointment about their exclusion from departmental activities and their limited contact with faculty and students.

Whether channeling requests through *liuban* personnel is helpful or restrictive depends on how such individuals perceive their duties, how much authority they have been given, and how tightly the unit is organized. Students and researchers at one university, for example, may find *liuban* officials supportive of their research goals and helpful in arranging housing, attitudes that reflect the university's commitment to international exchanges. In other units, *liuban* officials may be less willing to push the limits of their narrowly prescribed authority on behalf of foreigners. Barriers among institutions are formidable, and Chinese officials often are hesitant to cross them. Officials will on occasion tell you that they cannot help fulfill a particular request because the power to decide resides in another jurisdiction. It should be recognized that this is a very real problem for *liuban* personnel.

Other problems sometimes arise because cadres often work with unclear directives as to what they can and cannot do. As a foreigner, one of your best options is to try to understand cadres' viewpoints and the limits of their authority while you seek workable channels to achieve important goals. It takes considerable sensitivity and some time in China to know when to press your requests and when to give up and try another route. As one seasoned researcher comments, the indirect approach often yields far more than a "frontal assault on all the things that are not ideal."

Unfortunately, there are some bureaucratic restraints that cannot be overcome. For example, permission to visit a site not open to foreigners may be repeatedly denied, no matter how important it is to your project or how supportive your colleagues try to be. You should bear in mind that research opportunities in China are still developing, and part of your role involves laying the groundwork for colleagues and fellow students who will follow you.

THE RESEARCH INSTITUTES

Scholars hosted by a research institute have found that the character of their association with a particular unit is often determined by the kind of work to be done and where that work is to be conducted. Those working in the countryside may have little contact with their urban-based host institution beyond a welcoming banquet and a few visits to the research site. A collaborator from the institute may be assigned to the project, but access to materials and other resources is controlled by the local foreign affairs office. Because local offices often provide interpreters and assistants, the research team is sometimes composed of members from more than one unit; but in such cases, the researcher remains effectively "unitless" and must negotiate directly with bureaucratic organizations as the need arises.

Researchers who have worked within the confines of an institute have been assigned a counterpart and a team of assistants from the unit who are responsible for making living and working arrangements on behalf of their foreign colleague. If travel is essential to the project, Chinese coworkers take care of the details and at least part of the team accompanies the foreigner to negotiate with other organizations during the trip.

Constant assistance from supportive collaborators not only frees the researcher, often working under a strict deadline, to concentrate on the work at hand but, in the opinion of one returned scientist, is "critical for the success of the project. Without them I would not have been able to complete my work." He advises others to write to their prospective units as soon as an assignment is made with a detailed outline of the research plan, the kind of materials and equipment needed, and the estimated time necessary to complete the project. It is essential that potential problems be identified and resolved early in the process; misunderstandings encountered once the work has begun can be particularly difficult to unravel in a situation in which the researcher is dependent on a small group of people with whom he or she must interact on a daily basis.

Scholars engaged in research in China generally find their hosts willing to help in the professional as well as the personal realm, but they stress that effective collaboration and the success of the research project are impossible unless Chinese colleagues understand fully the objective and requirements of the work. Without such an understanding, colleagues and the sponsoring unit will be unable to meet the researcher's professional needs. Most of the problems that have arisen derive less from antipathy or incompetence than from a failure to understand precisely what is needed by the foreign scholar. Certain problems are, however, endemic to the kind of bureaucratic structure that exists in China. You must always be sensitive to the difficulties and requirements of working within such a system and remember that it is important to avoid statements or actions that might jeopardize future requests.

In most cases the foreigner's arrangements for activities outside the *danwei*, such as travel and housing, are taken care of by the foreign affairs office of the parent organization. For example, a researcher working in one of the institutes under the aegis of the Chinese Academy of Social Sciences (CASS) would negotiate with the academy's foreign affairs officials for most matters of daily and work life. At times, when the foreign affairs office is either unable or unwilling to meet certain demands, it may be possible to ask colleagues within the institute to intervene—but you should resort to this selectively. The relationship between the institutes and their umbrella organization is often an uneasy one.

The Chinese research institutes have been affected by the country's push toward modernization in several ways. Although some receive funds from the parent academy, most are being encouraged to become self-sufficient. Competition for funds is fierce, and to make up for gaps in funding, many institutes are linking up with industry and other organizations. Some have allowed their personnel to engage in work as consultants. And some institutes have lost their most talented researchers to the recently established high-level think tanks that advise government organizations on policy. Like the universities, research institutes have actively pursued links with the outside and have participated in exchanges. But unlike the universities, the institutes are somewhat less free to engage in their own activities because they still are part of a hierarchy and because they have limited resources for foreigners' research projects. The physical plant of most of the institutes is an indication of the relative poverty of the research units. Even the highest-level institutes under CASS are still housed in poorly maintained buildings. Personnel complain bitterly about poor-quality food in the canteens, lack of living space, and inadequate housing.

Many of the younger research unit personnel have not been formally educated because of the Cultural Revolution and attend special staff schools. Their potential for study abroad is hindered by lack of prior training, but the institutes are able to send some of the more talented researchers abroad, integrating them, on their return, to the best advantage of the organization.

THE RESEARCHER'S EXPERIENCE

AN OVERVIEW OF THE RESEARCH CLIMATE   Research scholars who have worked in Chinese institutions have learned early on in their stay that no arrangement is predictable, permanent, or self-executing. For example, even though the research proposals of all students and scholars selected by the Committee on Advanced Study in China were approved by the appropriate Chinese organization and placements were carefully negotiated with host institutions, most researchers soon discovered that the actual implementation of these carefully laid plans required continuous negotiation with their host unit. Some scholars adjusted the scope or character of their project in light of available materials and resources. In the end, the project's success depended in large measure on the researcher's ability to balance relations with Chinese colleagues and with officials intent on safeguarding bureaucratic boundaries and the demands of the project. For such efforts, personal qualities are important—a flexible outlook and a reputation for dedication, trustworthiness, and competence are essential for gaining the respect of colleagues. Experience has demonstrated that the willingness of the host institution to support a particular project is largely determined by how the work fits into China's national priorities and the current research program of the unit. Severe shortages of equipment, work space, and trained personnel dictate the allocation of available resources to projects that are relevant to national priorities. This is true of the humanities and social sciences as well as the natural sciences.

The foreign scholar is often perceived as the representative of a particular institution—a unit, as it were—in the U.S. educational system. As such, he or she brings a certain amount of prestige to the host institution and at the same time incurs a "responsibility" to enable people from the host institution to work or study at the researcher's home campus. This positive aspect is balanced by certain negative ones. For example, supporting a foreigner whose project depends on sensitive data or threatens bureaucratic integrity may be seen as setting a precedent for future unwanted intrusions.

American scientists working on projects in earthquake prediction, cancer research, and nuclear science—all fields that have held a high priority in China despite institutional disruption during the Cultural Revolution—have been well received by Chinese colleagues eager to make their own work known to the West. Because of these priorities, some Americans have had to tailor their work to fit pre-existing agendas, but they have also been aided by cooperative and knowledgeable Chinese colleagues and by the high prestige enjoyed by their units.

In the fields listed above, Chinese scientists have shared data generously with the expectation that the work will lead to publication in both Chinese and American journals. Researchers in these and other fields have lectured and participated in seminars at the host institute and elsewhere and have found such meetings to be important forums for exchanging information with a wide variety of people in all parts of the country. In addition, field trips with Chinese colleagues have helped bridge gaps between specialists engaged in similar research but with little knowledge of work outside their own unit. For foreign researchers who are necessarily working with limited time, the lack of centralized data has been the most serious constraint; equipment problems in some cases also have caused delays.

Scientists performing experimental work in institutes in which Chinese researchers have not been able to keep up to date and in which analytical techniques and facilities are inadequate have found their colleagues willing to help but substantially hindered by a lack of basic equipment and by unfamiliarity with the latest developments in their fields. Language also can pose formidable problems to effective research cooperation. One researcher spent the first week in his unit working with his colleagues to compile a glossary of technical terms so they could sustain conversations related to the project. In this situation the scientist's unanticipated tasks included not only teaching basic English vocabulary but also helping with methodology. Despite the extra time and work involved, the scientist in question felt that the effort was worthwhile—not only because he was given access to valuable materials and the project was ultimately successful but also because by helping his colleagues raise the quality of their work, he had contributed to future scientific collaboration.

Reports from researchers in China indicate that the success of a project depends on whether or not it addresses a problem of current interest to China; that is, whether or not it is central to China's drive for rapid modernization. Thus, projects in the field of agricultural economics, plant studies, and architectural engineering, for example, have been enthusiastically received. Success also depends on how well one's Chinese colleagues understand why certain materials and work in the field are necessary to solve the key problem. Important data have been collected and trips to the field effectively organized and profitable, but according to one researcher, his colleagues' enthusiasm for gathering material was directly related to their understanding of why it was necessary.

Research in the social sciences and humanities is carried out in research institutes organized under CASS and in university departments.

In the 1979–1980 academic year, Americans who worked in these in-stitutions were acutely aware that most of their units' efforts were aimed simply at rehabilitating personnel who were victims of the Cul-tural Revolution and rebuilding their faculty. Some departments were so understaffed that they could not accommodate graduate students, and the presence of foreign scholars added another drain on depart-mental resources. It was important, therefore, that projects that con-tributed to faculty improvement or the departments as a whole received more support than those that were incompatible with ongoing priori-ties. Even today, projects that enhance the intellectual community are received with enthusiasm. And despite the impact of the new opening to the West, many Americans have found themselves the first foreign scholar to be hosted by a unit, and have encountered colleagues who are eager to learn of Western methodologies and topics.

In the social sciences and humanities, research in many universities focuses on events and personalities of local importance. (For example, projects on the Boxers conducted at Shandong University, on the 1911 Revolution at Wuhan University, and on the economic history of the Tianjin region at Nankai University, have been warmly received and actively supported.) One researcher points out the advantage of working in a university that is located strategically for a particular topic:

> The Nanjing University history department seems to wield a great deal of influence nationally and especially in the Jiangnan region. The chief advantage of affiliation with this unit for me was the ease with which I could obtain letters of introduction from my adviser-professor to his former students, old classmates, and colleagues who are now in posi-tions of responsibility in museums, libraries, scholarly publishing houses, and other universities all over the south. (*China Exchange News*, De-cember 1984, p. 18)

The success of a project often hinges on the willingness of individuals to use their connections to help the foreign scholar.

Some university departments may be oriented toward a particular historical era rather than toward local interests. Beijing University (Beida) has aided scholars working in Shang and Qin-Han history be-cause its departments are strong in those areas; Beida is also strong on May Fourth literature. Recent experience has shown that working on a widely admired text or literary work can generate enthusiasm from Chinese colleagues. One researcher describes the positive reaction to his project on *Hongloumeng* (The Dream of the Red Chamber):

> The research climate surrounding any work on *Hongloumeng* is quite open and healthy. The topic commands considerable respect and in-terest on the part of both eminent scholars of the older generation and

among younger teachers and students as well. The amount of new materials being researched and published these days is a veritable flood, one which contains much very good scholarship. Virtually all the scholars I worked with seemed genuinely interested and receptive to the special concerns and approaches of an outsider working on their own literary heritage. (*China Exchange News*, June 1986, p. 10)

Gaining access to contemporary writers is more difficult, but as a graduate student studying satire in contemporary Chinese fiction points out in *China Exchange News*, it is possible for the foreign scholar, by virtue of his or her unique status. Reflecting on an analogous situation, the student asks her readers to "Imagine a graduate student from China arriving at the English department at Yale or the University of Chicago and announcing to a professor that she would like to interview several American writers, beginning with Saul Bellow, Kurt Vonnegut, Joseph Heller, and Norman Mailer. I wonder what that professor's reaction would be and what, if anything, would come of the request" (*China Exchange News*, June 1986, p. 11).

Yet in China such a request is not seen as extravagant. An American student explains why: "To understand this difference, we must consider such factors as the role of the Chinese writer as public spokesman, Chinese notions of literary criticism and research, the writer's own interest in reaching a world audience, and the privileged status granted to an American doing research in China. The last is a matter of politics and economics; this special status is a political courtesy easy for us to take for granted, yet quite susceptible to change, as history has shown us. It is worth reminding ourselves of this from time to time" (*Ibid.*, p. 11).

For a foreign researcher, selecting a suitable department at a Chinese university can be difficult because often there is little concrete information about faculty and current research efforts. In the first few years of exchanges, historians found literature and philosophy departments better organized than history departments, which were understaffed and still fearful of tackling sensitive historical issues. Recently, however, that trend has changed, and some universities have even formed study groups or centers that approach topics across disciplines.

In the late 1970s and early 1980s, American anthropologists and sociologists faced particularly difficult challenges in conducting research because their fields had not been active in China for almost 30 years. Moreover, senior Chinese scholars accorded higher priority to rebuilding institutions and training a new generation of scholars than to carrying on research. The CASS Institute of Sociology was established in 1979, and university sociology departments have been set up since then. A major turning point in the renewal of the discipline came when sociology was recognized as a key area of research that should be included in the Sixth Five-Year Plan adopted in 1982. Thus, a more definite institutional structure and clear-cut economic support have enhanced the possibilities for Americans to conduct research in this discipline. Similar changes have affected the field of anthropology. A sense of history is already possible when describing the research environment in China. In 1979–1980, after 30 years of broken contracts, American researchers channeled a great deal of energy into simply finding scholars active in their fields. Chinese scholars themselves did not have a clear picture of their intellectual and academic world, for they had lost touch with their own colleagues in the Cultural Revolution years. Recently, however, numerous conferences and less-formal gatherings have brought scholars together. Not all foreigners have been lucky enough to attend many of these gatherings. For example, an intellectual historian whose topic, heroes and sages in Chinese history, on the surface seems tame enough nonetheless had problems gaining access to conferences. He notes that there still are conservative party bureaucrats who fear scholarly interaction, especially among social science researchers. Scientists on the other hand are welcomed because they possess technological information critical to China's modernization.

Those who have managed to attend conferences are immeasurably helped by them. One scholar reports how a conference opened new research avenues for him, but his comments are even more important as a testimonial to the crucial importance of personal contact with Chinese scholars:

> . . . without a doubt, the most useful and rewarding aspect of my sojourn to China so far has been the friends and contacts I have made here and elsewhere in the People's Republic. Most of these acquaintances are scholars I met at the Song History symposium held in Hangzhou in May 1985. As far as my research work is concerned, the main benefit I have derived from these friends has been information on scholarly activities related to my research project. Here is just one example: a friend provided me access to a document that listed virtually all of the major research projects currently being undertaken which relate to Song studies (and many other areas as well). As a result of this opportunity, I was able to contact two scholars working on selected aspects of Fan Chengda's travel diaries. Other Song specialists whom I have come to know have provided me with three separate bibliographies, all of which are devoted solely to the Song. I even managed, with the help of a colleague, to get hold of all the papers presented at the "Conference on Song Literature," which was held in Chengdu in September 1985. I should also add that the many conversations and dinners I have shared with the Song scholars at Hangda [Hangzhou University] have benefited my research work in no small way.

The most significant single change in the research environment has been the revitalization of the Chinese intellectual community and the increased openness with which Chinese scholars interact with their counterparts from abroad. Progress is slow and setbacks are still to be expected, but the groundwork for a genuinely international scholarly community is firmly in place.

MEETINGS WITH COLLEAGUES   Soon after the foreign researcher arrives at a Chinese unit, a series of meetings will be arranged to discuss the project in detail. These talks are important for setting the tone of the collaborative effort and for clarifying expectations on both sides. They give the researcher a sense of how the unit views the project and how well it conforms to ongoing research efforts and existing resources. The Chinese side, in turn, forms an impression of the researcher's knowledge of the topic and ability to carry out the project. Veteran researchers urge their successors to be prepared for these discussions with a well-formulated plan—in Chinese if possible. The host institution may have received an abstract of the original proposal, but they will want to work out a detailed plan that includes the kind of assistance and travel needed and the costs of the project. Researchers emphasize that when drawing up a plan it is important to state clearly the relationship between the problem and the data and travel needed to address it. They add that once agreements have been made, the foreign scholar should not make arbitrary changes, especially if resources and personnel have already been allotted to carry out the work. By the same token, it is important to clarify what services will be provided and at what cost so that the Chinese side has no room for arbitrary changes. Such matters as how travel will be arranged and paid for, how assistants will help, and how they will be paid should all be agreed upon in advance. In addition, if the work will lead to publication, details regarding authorship and where the results will be published should be discussed at the initial meeting with officials.

You should also ask about regulations affecting data that will be taken out of the country. One scientist reports that four days before he left China, he was informed that he could not take his data with him unless it was all copied—and the unit's only copy machine was broken. Fortunately, just as he despaired of carrying home his hard-won materials, the machine was fixed. Others have had problems with plant and animal specimens and with videotapes.

Some scientists have been introduced to their host institute through a series of lectures, and scientists and social scientists alike have been asked to lecture to institute colleagues. These talks can prove useful for both sides: they enable the foreigner to establish his or her credentials and research interests while bringing Chinese colleagues up to date on methodology and the state of the discipline in the West. Chinese scholars are eager for information, and this often prompts them to urge their foreign guests to lecture and present seminars throughout their stay. Both scientists and social scientists have discovered that a great deal is expected of them—lectures, seminars, conference papers, and help with language, technical vocabulary, and methodology—all of which can cut drastically into work time. Most Americans agree that you should help whenever possible but that it is important to stress a serious commitment to the completion of the project.

WORK SCHEDULES   A project work schedule will be agreed upon in the meetings mentioned above, and when you set up a daily schedule or travel plans, be sure to take into consideration the holidays and the personal and work commitments of colleagues. Insisting on working over a holiday, for example, may deprive Chinese coworkers of their only chance for a rest. And many returned researchers comment on the toll on work schedules taken by ill health; it is not at all uncommon for an assistant or coworker on whom you have come to depend to lose time due to illness. Also, the pace of work varies; some foreigners, particularly scientists on short-term visits, have felt overworked while others find the easygoing pace frustrating. As one researcher points out, you must learn to use waiting time creatively.

In the institutes, most researchers put in a full 8-hour day (although in some instances it may be as long as 10 hours because of transportation to and from the workplace), five to six days a week. Most researchers are given an office or laboratory, which is shared with their coworkers. Lunch is usually followed by a rest period, and many researchers are encouraged to return to their hotel for lunch and rest. Others remain at the unit, thereby saving time and expense.

The organization of the research team varies, but usually a member of the host unit directs the activity of assistants. Virtually every American conducting research in China has expressed gratitude for the competence and cooperative spirit of his or her Chinese colleagues. Of the problems that have arisen, most involved interpreters who were not familiar with technical vocabulary.

As mentioned earlier, the responsibilities of assistants should be agreed upon by all those involved in the project. Some assistants are assigned mainly to improve their English or to learn from the foreign researcher; often they are extremely willing to help but sometimes lack the experience, stature, or connections to accomplish all they might like to. Be sure to find out how long the assistant will be available. One scientist was surprised to learn that his assistant was accompanying him only part of the way on a research trip; the scientist found this out when the assistant was suddenly sent back to Beijing—at the scientist's expense!

Work schedules tend to be less structured in universities. There you might meet with an adviser once or twice a week or with a group of colleagues for a few hours each day. Most universities do not provide office space, but foreigners who live off campus may be allowed to use a room in the foreign students' dormitory for rest. Some universities set up special reading rooms where foreigners can study and read materials that cannot be removed.

WORK-RELATED TRAVEL   Many foreign researchers have been able to visit units in other parts of the country to talk with colleagues, exchange information, or attend formally organized seminars and workshops. Some have traveled to the countryside to gather data. To arrange such work-related trips, you must apply to the host unit and state clearly the purpose of your proposed travel; if it is approved, the unit will arrange transportation, lodging, and meetings. A member of the research team usually will accompany you, especially if you do not speak Chinese, but many foreigners also travel alone to conferences and workshops. Experience suggests that the success of the trip depends largely on the host unit's influence with other organizations as well as on who makes the arrangements. One scientist contrasts a very informative trip arranged by a colleague from his unit, who used personal connections to set up meetings, to a far less fruitful visit arranged by unit officials. Association with a unit that has little bureaucratic influence can result in difficulties for Chinese coworkers whose authority may carry little weight with officials in other areas.

Work-related travel that takes the foreigner to out-of-the-way places (for instance, remote Buddhist caves or mountaintops) might meet with some resistance; Chinese colleagues often worry about foreigners having to deal with inadequate accommodations, dangerous transportation, and possible illness in such locations. Most serious scholars manage to convince their hosts that their dedication outweighs their caution, but obviously it is important not to complain about facilities (or the lack of them) when you have been warned. One resourceful scientist, armed with a good guidebook to "traveling on the cheap," was able to persuade her hosts that she really did want to save money and that she could tolerate anything. As a result she saved a significant amount by staying in dormitories most of the time.

Procedures for covering travel expenses vary, but in most cases the foreigner pays all personal transportation and lodging costs. Travel is increasingly expensive. One researcher reported that in March 1985 his expenses totaled about Y150 a day, excluding car rentals and other special expenses. Some units will negotiate a per diem charge while others allow payment in stages. If your spouse accompanies you, most likely he or she will be charged full tourist rates for transportation but will be allowed to stay in your hotel room without charge since room rates in China are not calculated according to the number of occupants. Food costs for spouses can usually be negotiated.

If you travel without someone from the unit accompanying you for the entire trip, be prepared for some gaps in communication. One disgruntled scientist reports that he was not met at the train at one of his stops and had to lug heavy equipment onto a pedicab to find a hotel. One way to avoid these problems is to ask your local hosts at each stop to telephone ahead to the next host and if possible give you a brief letter of introduction to be used in case of mix-ups.

SHORT-TERM ACADEMIC VISITS

If patience is the critical character trait for a successful long-term stay in China, stamina and flexibility must rank as equally important for the short-term academic traveler. Reading through the reports of CSCPRC-sponsored distinguished scholars and consultants for the Chinese University Development Project, and judging from the experiences of American scholars who have offered short courses for other academic organizations, it seems that the intense pace characterizing the final month of a long-term stay in China often is replicated in shorter visits. Although the short-term visitor does not have the opportunity to develop firsthand experience with the inner workings of professional and personal life in China, many scholars report that precisely because they are not permanent fixtures, Chinese colleagues are more open to frank conversation and serious collaborative work—and more willing to help with logistical arrangements. But even with the best intentions on the Chinese side, and elaborate planning and scheduling by the American sponsor, these scholarly visits almost always are marked by last-minute changes, unexpected developments, and missed opportunities.

Timing is essential and usually not under your control as an American visitor. For example, the intellectual climate is affected not only by internal rivalries and competition among organizations engaged in similar activities but also by shifts in political attitudes; all of these can have an impact on your reception. A specialist in history of science noted that just before his arrival in China, Premier Zhao Ziyang called for sweeping reforms of the management of science and technology, which were endorsed by the Central Committee. This sequence of events in turn "electrified" the academic communities the scholar encountered, and his visit was noticeably enhanced by such a fortunate convergence of events. Alternatively, a negative official attitude toward a particular discipline can have a significant dampening effect.

In addition, the time of year is important to consider if you are planning a short-term academic visit. Work tends to slow down in the hottest summer months and in the dead of winter. Some Americans have observed that summer is not a good time for academic business because major Chinese cities are overrun with other foreigners, who strain the resources of Chinese hosting organizations, and are virtually devoid of Chinese scholars, who use the vacation months to travel abroad. A recent visitor, disappointed that many of the Chinese scholars he hoped to meet were out of town, observed:

> The intellectual dimension of Deng's open door policy means that it has become much more difficult to meet Chinese in China. If no one travels, no one ever meets anyone from a different place. If everyone travels, however, no one also ever meets anyone from a different place except at conferences and in chance encounters at airports.

Internal travel in the heavy tourist season (May through October) creates headaches for Chinese hosts and guests alike. Several scholars complained that they were not met at airports nor informed ahead of time about schedules, hotel accommodations, or local travel arrangements. Long delays in airports due to weather, mechanical failures, or overbooking of flights also are not uncommon. The most serene reports come from individuals who manage to combine a Taoist philosophy that everything will eventually work itself out with low-key but persistent negotiations with Chinese hosts and traveling companions to ensure that an appropriate blend of academic work and tourism can be maintained.

PREPARATIONS   In general, the most successful short-term visits are the result of careful arrangements with the hosting organization combined with communications with individual Chinese scholars. Itineraries, requests for meetings with colleagues, lecture formats, and collaborative arrangements must be worked out well in advance. Goals for the project, as well as meeting and site visit requests, must be presented clearly. If you are going to be lecturing, it is a good idea to ask your host unit for advance information about topics, the probable size and composition of classes, what students or colleagues expect to learn from the lectures, and what kind of interpretation will be provided. If special equipment is necessary, be sure to inform your hosts; past experience, however, indicates that you should never expect audiovisual equipment to work.

Visits to other organizations in China are too difficult to arrange once the hosting organization assumes responsibility, and they are too complex to arrange informally in a short time. Returned scholars therefore urge you to write ahead of time to arrange to meet organizations and individual scholars not associated with the hosting unit. In the words of a recent grantee: "If I had it to do over again, I would invest a lot more time than I did before going to China in specifying exactly what I wanted on my schedule and, most importantly, corresponding directly with those institutions and individuals I wanted to visit, thus avoiding some of the lateral communications problems which existed despite the good intentions of my host."

Even with elaborate advance preparations, some fine-tuning of the schedule usually occurs the first working day after your arrival, in consultation with colleagues from the host unit and the foreign affairs officer in charge of your visit. This is the time to point out any potential problems—the most common being that too much tourism and not enough substantive academic content has been planned. If you are going to be lecturing, this is a good time to distribute abstracts or outlines, if this has not been done earlier, and to confer with interpreters.

SCHEDULES   Most scholars returning from short-term visits have remarked that their schedules in China were demanding by any standard. According to reports from a number of lecturers, a month-long stay probably would include a minimum of seven or eight lectures and several informal seminars. The Chinese workday begins around 8 a.m. and ends around 5 or 6 p.m., with a two-hour break from 12 to 2 p.m., although there is word that the noon *xiuxi* is being phased out in some units. Saturday is a workday in China, and Sunday is usually saved for arranged touring or shopping with colleagues or guides.

A typical weekly schedule for a short-term academic visit might look like this:

DAY 1: Introduction to work unit and discussion of agenda; evening banquet with colleagues and foreign affairs officers

DAY 2: Sightseeing with colleagues or interpreter/guide; informal meal in evening

DAY 3: Lecture in morning; discussions with colleagues or students in afternoon; preparation of lecture or work with interpreter on translation in evening

DAY 4: Lecture in morning; lunch with a few colleagues; meeting in afternoon to discuss exchanges; informal dinner with colleagues in evening

DAY 5: Lecture in morning; seminar in afternoon

DAY 6: Sightseeing in morning; shopping in afternoon; appreciation banquet for hosts in evening

DAY 7: Depart for in-country travel, accompanied by a representative of the hosting organization

Travel schedules are typically lighter on academic time and heavier on touring, although the wear and tear of travel takes its toll. Some scholars have complained that during their visit they had little free time to meet people informally or simply to rest; others suffered from the lack of cultural stimulation. One scientist remarked, "I had little opportunity to develop any sense of the Chinese people or their daily lives. This was all the more frustrating because I was aware that an incredible number of interesting opportunities existed beyond the walls of the hotel, but since I did not speak Chinese, I was reluctant to strike out on my own without a guide or interpreter." Another scholar who does speak Chinese remarked that his visit was so intense and so richly rewarding personally and professionally that he lost 15 pounds, in spite of too many banquets, and returned home exhausted and elated. Most travelers report that at some point they politely declined to see one more site and instead took a day off to rest, write up notes, or prepare a lecture.

LECTURES AND SEMINARS   Most foreigners who go to China to give lectures or hold seminars will be assisted by an interpreter. Often, however, interpreters are not professionals in the field and are not familiar with the concepts and vocabulary of the visiting scholar's discipline. Sometimes it is all too obvious that they have been assigned to the foreign scholar for more practice in English and an exposure to methodology. Reports from returned scholars indicate that some interpreters were not at all functional in English, a difficult situation for all concerned. In one instance an interpreter solved this problem by ad-libbing—the lecturer suddenly noticed that the interpretation was about India when he was in fact talking about Australia! Even if the interpreter knows English, valuable time is often spent explaining the meanings of particular concepts on the spot—sometimes with help from the audience—which disrupts the smooth, integrated flow of information. In one case, the audience finally requested that the lecture be delivered in English—without the "aid" of an interpreter. If you do find yourself lecturing directly in English, speak slowly and clearly; if possible, supplement the talk with outlines and handouts.

According to reports, the best interpreters (that is, if they are willing to take the time and can be spared from other duties) are students who have studied abroad and are familiar with vocabulary and American approaches to their discipline. One scholar reported working in collaboration with a Chinese-American scientist who served as interpreter, guide, and colleague; this evidently was an extremely fortunate and successful combination.

If your interpreter acts as a guide as well, it will soon be evident that a good rapport between the two of you is essential for carrying out daily business. Flexibility, understanding, and patience on your part are crucial; remember that although interpreters/guides may not understand their roles initially, they often grow into them quite successfully in time.

Lectures usually last two to three hours with the final half-hour reserved for questions and discussion. The comments of lecturers on audience participation in China vary. Most lecturers report that responses from a Chinese audience are less lively than those from a similar audience in the United States. And one senior scholar was quite disheartened that his lecture series for graduate students was not well attended; apparently, students were busy with other activities and had no time for a course that was not given for credit. If the school hosting the lecture or seminar wants the course to be graded, you should consult carefully with other teachers, assistants, and interpreters to be certain that any tests are comprehensible to students. For example, one lecturer learned through hard experience that multiple-choice tests are alien to most Chinese students.

If lectures are aimed at colleagues and students are present, the students may be reluctant to ask questions. One scholar suggests that time be allotted for informal discussions with students, who often are eager to talk when they are not inhibited by the presence of senior scholars and officials. Because of unwillingness to express an opinion publicly, or simply out of shyness or respect for the speaker, questions from a Chinese audience often come in writing. Once an exchange has begun, audiences may relax and talk more freely. But, according to one source, asking too many questions of a speaker implies that the lecturer is not competent. Nevertheless, some Americans report that they never found a way to really "break the ice" in the formal lecture setting.

Audience size can vary from fewer than 10 close colleagues to over 400 people, some of whom may have traveled long distances for the event. Seminars are sometimes arranged around a seminar table in a classroom or with the speaker and audience seated in overstuffed chairs in a reception room sipping tea. One senior scholar found that what was billed as an informal dinner turned out to be a seminar in which he was expected to present an informal talk on the state of his discipline in the United States. Indeed, curiosity about the state of your field is the most predictable trait your Chinese colleagues will display. A literature specialist states that he felt many times as if he were being given a comprehensive predoctoral exam, so intense were the questioners and so wide-ranging the topics. Experience indicates that you should go to China prepared to speak generally about current debates, methodology, and new research in your field.

Formal U.S.-China scholarly exchange has now operated for more than seven years, but American academics still find their Chinese colleagues eager for new information and materials. The best gifts for Chinese friends are materials, new books, and periodicals. Some scholars send a boxful of things ahead; others wait until they know what their Chinese counterparts need and send them later.

EQUIPMENT   Problems with equipment are noted in nearly all reports, so you would be well advised not to rely too heavily on visual aids to make a point. One returned scholar remarked that the projectors in his relatively affluent Beijing institute must have come with Marco Polo, and another scholar tells of a projector without a plug that nonetheless became usable after his Chinese colleagues plugged the three bare wires in a socket and secured them with toothpicks. According to various reports, slides have been mangled or lost in the insides of these ancient machines. As with all other aspects of work in China, you can only plan ahead, reiterate the importance of the equipment in time for preparations to be made, be patient when the equipment fails to work, and be grateful when it does work.

STUDENT LIFE

For most foreign students, daily life revolves around a small community of Chinese and foreign friends and classmates, a few *liuban* personnel, and teachers—a rather limited world in the opinion of some Americans. Adjusting to this life-style can involve some degree of culture shock. Beverly Hooper, a former exchange student from Australia, aptly describes a typical student reaction to the first sight of a Chinese dormitory: "Many an Australian's face has dropped on arrival at the Beijing Languages Institute, when the mystery and vastness of China have suddenly been reduced to a small, concrete-floored room to be shared with either a foreign or Chinese student in a somewhat forbidding, barracks-type gray brick building" ("The Australian-China Student Exchange Scheme: Could It Be More Effective?" *The Australian Journal of Chinese Affairs*, No. 1, p. 116).

As Hooper points out, however, it is not the Spartan material conditions that most students find hard to accept, but the psychological pressures. Even though most *liuban* cadre and teachers are accustomed to the eccentricities of their foreign charges, they still expect, understandably, a certain conformity to the highly regimented Chinese student life. Foreign students chafe at rules regarding living quarters, class attendance, travel, and relationships with Chinese friends. Almost every campus requires that Chinese visitors to foreign dormitories register at the door, giving their name and *danwei*, a practice that the Chinese authorities sometimes maintain is a protection for foreigners but that many foreigners believe is aimed at spotting those who frequent foreigners' residences too often. Some schools sporadically attempt to impose limited visiting hours for Chinese guests. A student at Fudan University comments on the effect of the rule that Chinese teachers and students could visit the dorm only between 4 and 7 p.m.: "This rule is in effect for all schools in Shanghai with foreign students and is sometimes accompanied by very rude treatment on the part of building attendants. This is unfortunate for most Chinese are very loath to visit here."

Ironically, serious students sometimes find it less difficult to adjust to Chinese customs than to the habits of other foreigners, many of whom are younger and considerably more carefree than the average American exchange student. One student eloquently describes life in the Shaoyuan Guesthouse at Beijing University, which houses between 250 and 300 foreign students and several foreign experts, researchers, and visitors: "Living in small rooms close together and sharing communal facilities means interaction with neighbors who are from all parts of the world. Among the notable customs are the long and involved food preparations frequently beginning with live poultry and animals. Late parties are a multinational phenomenon." He goes on to indicate that foreigners live in a near legal vacuum; *liuban* and dormitory personnel do not intervene actively in problems between foreign students unless requested to do so when the dispute becomes violent. As this student puts it, "Personal foresight and presence of mind together with the Golden Rule are what we effectively depend upon for survival." But he concludes that, fortunately, reason and good will usually prevail, and you can learn a great deal from other foreigners.

Other students comment that living with too many foreigners at times slows progress in adapting to Chinese life-styles:

> When there is a congenial and stimulating group of friends, with a more or less common set of cultural assumptions readily available, getting out regularly, particularly getting out alone can require conscious effort, especially after the original excitement of being in China wears off and is replaced by the frustrations of being there.

This student goes on to point out that she and her colleagues must find creative ways to take advantage of living in China—"buying a television, going to performances, movies, and plays with Chinese friends, and most of all travel are enjoyable ways to partake of Chinese culture in China."

Conditions for study are less than ideal, partly because of inadequate space in libraries and dormitories and partly because of the disruptions created by spontaneous loud gatherings of foreign students in the evenings. However difficult the problems created by close quarters, most foreigners realize early on that their living situation is far better than that of the Chinese students, who live six to eight to a room and at many institutions draw lots each evening for seats in the library. Because most academic institutions are located in the suburbs, tending to the details of everyday life can cut into work and study time substantially. A trip downtown by bicycle or bus for banking and other business can take an entire afternoon. Those accustomed to using the telephone to make appointments, ask questions, or conduct business will learn quickly that in China it is you, not your fingers, that must do the walking. Face-to-face contact is almost always an essential part of any transaction.

Students usually must do their own negotiating with the university bureaucracy and make their own arrangements for research, study, and travel. This can be a frustrating exercise, but it is also a useful one. Students often gain insights into Chinese life that allow them to understand the frustrations of their Chinese friends better than foreigners who are protected from the bureaucracy by their status. Although students may be poorer than other foreigners in material amenities, most consider themselves incomparably richer for the daily opportunity of living within a Chinese environment and mingling naturally and casually with Chinese people. Most American students who have lived with Chinese roommates or have made friends on campus feel that they have been allowed glimpses into intimate corners of Chinese life that would never have been possible without the sustained contact and shared experience of student life. Many American students agree that simply coping with daily life may well be the most frustrating, but in the end, the most valuable part of their experience. Once you have lived in China as a student, you can return again and again; and you will know how to get around on your own and how to negotiate for yourself if the need arises—an invaluable legacy of your student days.

Students choose to study in China for different reasons. Some advanced students carry on research or combine research with language work; many others study only the language. According to He Dongchang, vice minister of the State Education Commission, currently there are 2,500 foreign students studying in China, and he predicts enrollments will double by 1990. Since 1949 a total of 15,000 foreign students have attended universities and institutes; since 1978, an additional 13,000 have enrolled in short-term courses.

Student exchanges have a long history, and Chinese bureaucrats and educators have developed well-defined procedures and attitudes regarding foreign students. Until 1978 most students were undergraduates from Third World countries who spent up to five years in academic programs—generally, one year in Chinese-language studies followed by specialized technical programs. Their numbers were supplemented by a small contingent of students from Second World countries (most of the European countries fall into this category) who spent one or two years in language study and/or attended the small number of university courses open to foreigners. A relatively high attrition rate plagued these early programs. The discontent of foreign students then and now is usually manifested by students quietly dropping out of the academic life of the college or university. Absenteeism among foreign students remains high; a class of 13 or so often dwindles to 1 or 2 within a month of the end of term, demoralizing teachers and squelching any inclination to regard foreign students as serious scholars. Inadequate language skills have made university-level classes intellectually unavailable to many students. But many others become so disenchanted with classes that they believe they can learn more outside the classroom.

It was problems like these that conditioned the response of the "system" and individual teachers to the new waves of American students who entered China after normalization of relations with the United States. These students have confronted the Chinese educational system with a wide range of demands and expectations as well as with unprecedented numbers. American students have been fortunate. Their arrival coincided with, and indeed resulted from, a new intellectual climate in China that paved the way for their warm reception. At the same time, that climate precipitated an upgrading of academic standards and new policies for the educational system as a whole. The new, livelier academic climate has benefited Americans in many ways. Along with the new openness, however, came a more rigid articulation of the regulations governing foreign students (see Appendix B).

Foreign students can now earn master's and doctoral degrees in some Chinese institutions. But most will fall into one of three other categories: (1) undergraduates (*liuxuesheng*)—those whose purpose is to obtain a degree from a Chinese university and who will remain in China for four to six years; (2) general advanced students (*jinxiusheng*)—students who intend to pursue coursework in a special field while in China and who have finished at least two years of undergraduate study in that field; and (3) senior advanced students (*gaoji jinxiusheng*)—those who have at least the equivalent of a Chinese master's degree or are candidates for doctorates in their home country and who will study independently under the direction of Chinese tutors for a period of one year. All students except those in the senior advanced category are expected to attend classes; only those in the senior advanced category can expect to be assigned tutors.

The opening of several institutions and disciplines to foreign students in 1979 was coupled in many units with a more rigid application of rules governing attendance, examinations, and travel. These policies were designed to raise standards and correct a laissez-faire attitude toward academic work, but they were not compatible with the needs of advanced graduate students more intent on pursuing dissertation-level research than on gaining basic knowledge in the classroom. Moreover, in 1979–1980, Chinese universities were not equipped to provide graduate-level training for many of their own students, much less for foreigners. Now more than 70 colleges admit foreign students and student researchers, and many of these are upgrading their graduate studies. The environment also is more conducive to research, and students have accomplished a great deal that has directly enhanced their graduate work. But frustrations abound, for students cannot be assured of anything and must find their own means to impress their hosts. Many students still combine some classroom work with independent research and fieldwork. As the level of teaching improves generally in universities and colleges, and as younger, more dynamic scholars are brought into positions of prominence in Chinese education, foreigners will continue to reap the benefits.

Changes in Chinese attitudes toward foreign students are difficult to measure. Students who study overseas, whether in Western Europe or Asia, often are not seen as genuinely part of the academic community. China is no different, and many recent reports from graduate students mention the problems of being taken seriously by Chinese advisers. One woman states that the teachers at Beida (Beijing University) regard students in general as "difficult and immature." She elaborates:

> My adviser told me with remarkable candor that when there was a foreign student attending one of his classes in fiction, he would talk to the student and ask him or her to read one of the stories required for the course. If at the end of the semester the student could repeat the basic plot for him, he gave a passing grade. This lack of enthusiasm and respect for foreign students is one that a student with more serious purpose and specific goals to accomplish should be prepared to work against. Older Chinese scholars on the other hand, whose memories reach back to days of cooperative scholarship or study abroad, will often accept a foreign student with more eagerness and less reserve than he would show toward his own colleagues. Thus a foreign student needs to be prepared to accept that she is far more what she represents than who she is while in China.

Another woman points out that the female student faces more barriers in developing a student-mentor relationship with a male professor than does a male counterpart. She reports that her hosts usually took great pains to produce female companions or assistants to serve as intermediaries or chaperones. "At first I resented the intrusion," she writes, "but now I think it was unrealistic for me to expect to have a direct adviser-advisee relationship given the present social conventions so I tried to develop better relationships with the woman who had been dragooned into 'helping' me." She adds that the pattern has been repeated in other academic settings in other Asian countries where women have little visible power in the academic establishment.

Diligence usually pays off, however. Another female student who specializes in literature had to contend with the attitude that foreigners, particularly Westerners, can never truly appreciate in depth the Chinese literary tradition. But, she adds, for all the differences in approach, the bond that develops between scholars working on similar ancient texts— the shared sense that only a few scholars in the modern world care about these works—creates an environment conducive to communication: "Older professors, if skeptical of our competence, are openly moved by the devotion they perceive in one who has acquired their language and then traveled so far to join them in their studies. Thus, they may go to great lengths to encourage and facilitate research."

Despite difficulties and stalemates, American students in the past seven years have had remarkable success in their research. Students have worked on archeological digs, traced the footpaths of the ancient poets, joined opera troops, lived with minority peoples, labored in silk factories, mined the Ming-Qing archives, recorded Taoist performances on site, and presented papers at conferences; but most importantly, many have forged lasting ties with Chinese advisers and fellow students. If one important lesson has been learned from the student experience, it is that no matter what the regulations or how they change, individual students must build a personal reputation for perseverance and proficiency before they can hope to receive active institutional support. As one very successful graduate student in anthropology observed in retrospect: "The first semester was a period of 'feeling out' how to go about getting my research done—including interviews at factories and trips to libraries. For my Chinese counterparts, the first half of the year was a time to find out whether they could trust me."

Students do not enter the Chinese professional world blessed with a status that guarantees respect. Their gains are worked out on a case-by-case basis that does not ensure that similar privileges will be extended to future students. Attitudes change slowly in China, and foreign students' successes will probably continue to be determined by their own ability to work through the system, by the kind of unit in which they must work, and by the nature of their demands.

INITIAL MEETINGS WITH TEACHERS AND ADVISERS   Soon after arriving on campus, foreign students receive a general introduction to their institution and its rules and regulations. They then usually meet individually with *liuban* and departmental representatives to discuss class schedules and specific requests. Some graduate students have been asked to submit an outline of their dissertation proposal in Chinese before an adviser is assigned. Others have worked with a tutor for a time before handing in a detailed proposal. Experienced students and researchers stress that when drafting a proposal it is essential to state clearly the relationship between the topic and any requests you may be making for materials, tutorials, and travel. Because foreign students must depend on teachers to help gather materials and facilitate research, it is important that they present their research plan thoughtfully in these initial meetings. It is a good idea to take copies of your own published work, major papers, and bibliographies to establish credibility and define the level at which you hope to proceed. If you prepare a plan early in your stay and insist on beginning library work and other scholarly activities from the beginning, your advisers can hardly fail to be impressed with your seriousness of purpose. As one student at Beijing University states, "You may be one of over 200 foreign students in your department and you must distinguish yourself as worthy of help."

Establishing yourself is only the beginning of the process of developing a productive working rapport with an adviser. Language problems generally loom large and can assume even greater dimensions when the teachers speak a dialect. And there are other, less easily defined issues as well. A student of classical literature reports:

> There is more to communication than speaking a common language. A second, more subtle and persistent problem was that of establishing my credibility as a student of Chinese literature. During the initial stage of our discussions I was anxious to convey my own approach to the text, while my advisers had not yet been convinced of my grounding in the rudiments of the field. In fact, my struggle to describe ideas quite alien to them only served to obscure their perception of what I actually understood. Even worse, it provided no common ground of discussion by which I might benefit from their knowledge. (*China Exchange News*, June 1986, p. 2)

This student switched to asking more direct specific questions related to the texts themselves and began to make progress. Once a working vocabulary was established, topics of common interest began to emerge. Other students mention the difficulties of finding common ground for their work with advisers. Many have found that focusing on broad topics and bibliography rather than on methodology is a compromise that can make the most of time spent with an adviser. And searching for a common range of interests yields better results than trying to mold sessions using a preconceived notion of what should transpire. Students remind their successors to be sensitive also to teachers' work schedules and holidays and to expect that schedules may be interrupted by travel or ill health. In fact, many student reports mention the ill health of their Chinese colleagues as a factor in losing work time.

COURSEWORK   There is no formal registration process for foreign students attending Chinese institutions. Ideally, new students are informed of offerings by *liuban* or departmental personnel who handle any necessary paperwork, but sometimes students complain that they are not informed of the full range of courses available. There are few Western-style college catalogs in China, and many students learn of course offerings only through the student grapevine. Check the bulletin board in your department to see what courses are listed, and ask your Chinese friends what is being offered in a given term. Be aware too that not all courses are open to foreigners. Most universities allow foreign students to move between departments when choosing courses, but they do not encourage them to change their departmental affiliation once a commitment to a particular discipline has been made. It is important to have some prior knowledge, if possible, of the best department for your topic. An anthropologist, for example, found no anthropology counterparts in her university; she affiliated instead with an economics department—with some success.

The fall semester in China begins in early September in most universities, and the spring term begins in late February or early March after the month-long spring holiday that follows *Chunjie* (Lunar New Year). Most classes are scheduled in two-hour segments beginning at 7:30 a.m. and meet two or three times a week. Some graduate courses meet once a week for two to three hours in much the same fashion as a seminar. But the content of many courses, even those for graduate students, is often not advanced enough for the taste of many American students. One graduate student reports that the professor read from textbooks and assigned no outside reading, allowing questions only during the 5- to 10-minute break in the middle of the class. Grades depend on either a long research paper or, in some cases, a final examination (exams are sometimes handed out ahead of time). Some professors test foreign students orally or not at all. Faithful attendance is mandatory if you want to establish a good relationship with a professor, because teachers in China view cutting class as a personal affront. Once you make a commitment to a class, you should fulfill it.

Classes are usually conducted in "rapid unadulterated Mandarin" or in a dialect unintelligible even to some Chinese students. Few concessions are made for foreign participants beyond the occasional repetition of terms or use of the blackboard. One American graduate student who considers himself fluent in Chinese described note-taking as a "harrowing experience." Some courses have textbooks; others do not. Students have varying opinions about the worth of their texts. Archeologists, for example, have discovered that the informally produced mimeo notes for class often contain valuable new information that is a long way from being published. A common complaint of students is that Chinese professors are either unfamiliar with Western literature or woefully out of date; thus, courses are not "on target" for their particular interests. Most American students avoid the classes for foreigners only because they are aimed at foreigners studying for undergraduate degrees in China who have little background in Chinese studies. But the classes that professors design for their own students offer interesting insights into how particular disciplines are studied in China, as well as the chance to become acquainted with Chinese professors and graduate students.

FIELDWORK AND TRAVEL   Relatively few American students have been able to conduct genuine fieldwork, but many have traveled extensively, establishing informal contacts along the way. Some students have been given permission to travel to out-of-the-way places, either alone or accompanied by Chinese students or advisers; and some have been successful in collecting data—for example, on folk music and Taoist liturgical practices. Some also have traveled with their Chinese classmates on school trips. Others, however—an economist, for example—found the constant presence of an overbearing and jealous adviser a real hindrance. Some students astutely observed that they had far more freedom and resources to travel than many of their Chinese teachers could hope for.

Student travel is generally much less expensive than tourist travel, especially on school-arranged trips for which hard-class train accommodations and student dormitories are used. Whenever possible, buses are used, but if a project demands a journey that is inaccessible by public transport, a car and driver sometimes will be hired. Occasionally illness mars these trips. In one case a student was warned that conditions would be less than comfortable and insisted on going on a school trip—only to become seriously ill with dysentery along the way.

In a number of instances, students have been able to travel widely, sometimes to areas not normally open to foreigners; these travels have been accomplished with the help of—or, occasionally, in spite of—their foreign student office. A student who traveled to the sites important in the poetry of the famous Tang poet Li Bai received extraordinary cooperation and reports an unforgettable trip:

In both Anhui and Zhejiang, each town provided me with at least one well-prepared local expert, either an historian, gazeteer researcher, or member of the local "cultural station." In cases where transportation to a given site was difficult, a jeep or a boat was put at my disposal for the trip. The flexibility of my hosts made it possible to take advantage of opportunities for impromptu interviews with villagers who would recount (and sometimes debate) their versions of Li Bai's life as it was lived in their village.

Not all students are so fortunate to have a topic that captures the imagination of such a wide variety of people. But the possibilities for this kind of informal contact are far greater for students than for other foreigners and are one of the most enjoyable aspects of the student status.

LANGUAGE STUDY   Some advanced students elect to take language classes at the university; others opt for making their own arrangements with a tutor or trade English lessons for practice in Chinese. Complaints about language classes are common. Many students are disappointed in the lack of rigor, the prevalence of lecturing rather than drilling, and in general the paucity of opportunities to practice the language creatively. As one student notes, teachers often do not take their foreign charges seriously enough to correct their mistakes.

Many students have noticed that upper-level translation classes are usually better than lower-level conversation classes. If you plan to work with a tutor, it is a good idea to take some texts and tapes along to help structure the class. Your tutor may have no training in teaching the language but may be quite willing to follow a plan and to use materials suitable for your interests. One student practiced reading handwritten Chinese and writing business letters as well as developing her reading comprehension in her own field. Reading a classical text line by line with a tutor who knows the literature can be a very rewarding experience.

Some students trade English lessons for Chinese lessons, a less than ideal situation but sometimes the only way to practice informal conversational Chinese. As in work with a tutor, you must be prepared to organize your time with your language partner. Watching a television program or movie and then using the new vocabulary and theme as a focus for language practice is one method of mixing class time with leisure time. A word of caution, however: be sure that you receive as much time in Chinese language training as you give in English. Chinese who are trying to learn English are remarkably persistent when they have a native speaker with whom to practice.

Many Americans lament that immersion in Chinese is hard to manage at universities with large numbers of foreigners. As one student puts it: "Oddly enough, coming to China may not be the optimal method for improving Chinese language skills. Not only is one subjected to periodic unannounced arrivals of unknown Chinese students or teachers who need help filling out U.S. university application forms, but the language predominately used in the foreign student dorm and cafeteria is almost invariably English. Even the Russians are more eager to speak English than Chinese." This observation illustrates a common dilemma for foreigners, many of whom are approached to teach English in part-time schools and the like. You must find a happy compromise—between demonstrating sympathy for and a desire to help Chinese people in their quest for better English-language skills and fulfilling your own purpose for living in China.

According to Chinese educators, language students make up the bulk of foreign students in China, and efforts are being made to increase enrollments in Chinese-language courses. Several Chinese universities accept students directly and others set up programs in cooperation with an American college or university. Choosing a suitable program for your particular goals will involve some investigation; check with the foreign study adviser or Asian studies faculty at your home institution. A useful guide to language study in China has been compiled by Jesse Parker and Janet Rodgers for the Yale-China Association (*A Guide to Living, Studying and Working in the People's Republic of China and Hong Kong*, rev. ed., New Haven, Conn.: Yale-China Association, January 1986). Parker and Rodgers point out that there are positive and negative aspects of both types of programs.

The student who elects to study language in a program administered by the Chinese must secure applications from the Chinese Embassy and then send the application directly to the particular Chinese school. Experience indicates that students are not necessarily guaranteed a place in the institution they have selected. These programs have the advantage of being much less costly than the U.S.-Chinese cosponsored programs, but because there is no intermediary U.S. administrator to consult, you will have to negotiate for yourself on most issues. Many students find this situation frustrating, especially those who have not yet acquired the language skills to function independently. But students who have arranged their own study find that they mingle more naturally with the Chinese community and that their confrontations and successes with the bureaucracy are valuable learning experiences.

Cosponsored programs are more costly, but they offer students the advantage of applying through a U.S. institution and working with an American resident director in China. It is difficult to evaluate these programs because they are constantly in flux as Chinese teachers come and go and U.S. administrators move in and out of the organization. Some programs have maintained good reputations consistently while others do not live up to the promises in their brochures. It is a good idea to talk with other students who have studied in China, to seek advice from your Chinese-language teacher if possible, and to call the program director for specific information. Be sure to ask about travel arrangements to and from China, whether a trip within the country is included in the fees, how credits are granted and transferred, and whether a content course taught by an American professor is planned. Some cosponsored programs have managed to develop a language curriculum suited to the needs of American students, but the degree to which any outside force can influence the Chinese philosophy of teaching is limited. Eventually, students must adjust to Chinese methods of language teaching if they are to make the most of their studies in China.

Some difficulties arise because Chinese language teachers believe foreign students should acquire all the skills of language learning—speaking, writing, reading, and aural comprehension—simultaneously. Language classes are organized to include reading (*hanyu* or *yuedu*), conversation practice (*huihua* or *kouyu*), listening comprehension (*tingli*), and composition exercises (*xiezuo*). Regular examinations cover progress in all four skills (*sihui*). Most American students have not been as adequately prepared in speaking as in writing and reading, and the most commonly voiced complaint centers on their frustration at not learning practical, everyday vocabulary fast enough to become functional in Chinese while in China. Teaching Chinese to foreigners is a new field in China that is only slowly gaining legitimacy. Many Chinese are not trained to teach the language, and most are unfamiliar with the drilling, creative conversation, pattern drills, and language labs that make up an American program. Often the materials used in China do not mesh with those students have used in the United States, and most language programs must incorporate students with widely varying backgrounds, a serious problem for many Chinese teachers.

Most intensive programs schedule between 16 and 24 class hours each week, usually in the mornings from 8 a.m. to noon. Afternoons are used for excursions in and outside of the city, for study, and for special coaching (*fudao*). Classes usually concentrate on a set text, which the teacher and the students read repeatedly and then memorize and analyze. Many Americans have observed that students are expected to play a rather passive role in the teacher-student relationship. Creative use of language is not encouraged nor is genuine dialog between teacher and students. Materials often are not adequate, but a good teacher will respond to students' suggestions and make an effort to find relevant, interesting materials. Students should remember, however, that their teachers work within a fairly rigid bureaucracy and that their power to implement change is very limited. Teachers usually work as part of a team and are expected to use only approved materials; they also work under the close supervision of departmental authorities. Examinations are often prepared by a committee of teachers who work at the same level—all first-year teachers are part of a team, for example—and are designed to test progress in absorbing materials presented in the basic texts.

Chinese teachers complain that American students are often casual about cutting classes and that a single class usually brings together students with very different skills and motivation. Many teachers have little experience with the methodology and materials used in the United States and become as frustrated as their students at the difficulties of adjusting time-honored methods to the needs and backgrounds of American students. On the other hand, most Chinese teachers feel responsible for all aspects of their students' lives and visit them in the dormitory, worry when they are unhappy or ill, and offer extra help for those having problems in class. Some Americans find this attention suffocating, but most feel genuine affection and respect for their dedicated, hardworking Chinese instructors.

ACCESS TO MATERIALS

Policies in China governing access to libraries and archives vary as do individual experiences with certain libraries. Your status, work unit, research topic, and approach to problems all determine the limits to access as much as do the particular policies of the library you hope to use. There are more than 200,000 libraries in China, including the national library in Beijing: 1,732 public libraries; 700 college and university libraries; 100,000 middle school and elementary school libraries; 1,000 scientific and specialized libraries; and 110,000 trade union libraries. Detailed descriptions in Chinese and English of Chinese and foreign books and periodicals along with addresses of important libraries can be found in the *Directory of Chinese Libraries* (Beijing: China Academic Publishers, 1982). (This information comes from a very useful article by Chi Wang of the Library of Congress, "An Overview of Libraries in the People's Republic of China," *China Exchange News,* September 1984.)

Foreign scholars probably will use only a few of these libraries; yet reports indicate that gaining entry to heretofore untested libraries is continuing. A few guidelines for library use follow. They have been gleaned from reports, published and unpublished, of scholars who have conducted research in Chinese libraries and archives.

One conclusion that applies generally is that library work is time-consuming in China. Advance preparation can be of great help in cutting down some of the time lost in bureaucratic maneuvering once you are on site. One researcher remarks that a search for a book that would take 20 minutes in the United States can take up to two weeks in a Chinese library. He advises that you read all the secondary literature available before going to China. Many Chinese libraries do not have workable catalogs or do not make them available to foreign scholars so you must be prepared to ask for particular holdings. Fortunately, there is a growing literature on the kinds of materials available and reference guides for further information, all of which can be of great use in preparing to work in China.

Researchers have also found it useful to have on hand a summary of their topic in Chinese and the kinds of materials needed for its investigation. The summary can be presented to library staffs or helpful colleagues in China. One successful researcher gave a talk about his work and the materials he needed to a group of scholars who then offered to help him informally by lending their own collections. Good personal relations with colleagues are as important in gaining access to materials as in other aspects of scholarly life. And by no means are important written resources confined to libraries. Americans have discovered that the rich mine of unpublished material relevant to their field can be tapped only through personal contacts with Chinese colleagues. A linguist remarks: "There is simply no substitute for direct personal contacts with one's academic colleagues in China. In my field there exists a vast quantity of unpublished field material on dialects of every corner of China and the only way to obtain access to this valuable storehouse of data is through personal contacts."

A reputation for seriousness and diligence also pays off with library personnel who may be bound by regulations but often are willing to bend them for the deserving individual. A researcher who worked in the National Library in Beijing found that his initial request for materials relevant to his topic was quickly accepted. He goes on to add, however, that he met with reluctance when he stepped outside these initial limits:

> Only when I began to ask for more and more materials not directly connected with my original topic did the hold-ups begin. Since the materials in my field do not involve much in the way of sensitive or controversial topics, any difficulties I had did not amount to much more than bureaucratic inertia of the kind not totally unknown in our own institutions. I managed to overcome these difficulties in the Beijing library through the sheer passage of time, as the library staff gradually became convinced that I was no troublemaker, and began gradually to regard me as a daily fixture in their domain. (*China Exchange News*, June 1986, p. 9)

Two additional points are made in this account: (1) scholars in a hurry will be frustrated by the slow pace in which newcomers are accepted and books delivered, and (2) requests for books outside the original list presented may create problems. Most scholars have discovered important materials only after working for some time in a facility, and most have also had to convince library personnel that these were indeed genuinely relevant to the project at hand. Chinese categories for arranging knowledge are sometimes quite different from those accepted in the West. Again, advance information, not only about the materials in a library but about their classification, can be of great use in presenting requests.

Your work in a library may be slowed down by several factors. Often, collections and reading rooms are separated, sometimes in different parts of a city. In some cases, books or periodicals must be ordered as much as a week in advance. Photocopying facilities, if available, usually are limited. At the Beijing University Library, for example, only 30 sheets at one time can be copied, and the turnaround time is at least two days. String-bound books and most pre-1800 materials may not be photocopied, although in some libraries they may be microfilmed. Usually, however, microfilm readers must be reserved in advance. Research assistants to help with transcribing materials by hand may not be admitted in many facilities. Many libraries are being renovated and books cataloged in an effort to improve facilities that were at best neglected and at worst actively destroyed in the Cultural Revolution years. Some libraries will not be usable for years, and you should check ahead before planning a research visit whose success hinges entirely on using particular collections. Also, some libraries do not allow their old books to circulate during the hottest months of the summer.

Many scholars associated with universities have found departmental libraries useful, especially for periodicals and secondary works, although other treasures may be found in them—a fine collection of stele rubbings exists in the history departmental library at Nanjing University, for example. Catalogs in these smaller collections usually are orderly and complete.

Access to materials is determined by the host *danwei*, which secures privileges within its own boundaries and negotiates with other *danwei*. Scholars who have been affiliated with nonacademic units have at times had difficulty obtaining permission to work in libraries. Foreigners placed in a university or research unit are issued library cards that must be presented when requesting books. Only certain books—nonsensitive secondary works, for example—may be taken out, and then the quantity is usually limited. Rare books are handled with care and generally may be read only in certain areas of the library. Those foreigners affiliated with CASS may have little trouble gaining access to the libraries of the various CASS research institutes. But someone in a university might have more trouble using CASS libraries simply because the necessary connection for use must be made between autonomous *danwei*. Similarly, in some cases students and research scholars in universities have been able to use municipal libraries after producing a letter of introduction from the foreign affairs office of their host unit; others have had to be personally introduced to library staff. In some cases these bureaucratic barriers simply could not be crossed. Museum and factory libraries also have presented problems for some scholars.

The use of archives, such as the No. 1 Archive in Beijing housing the documents of the Qing dynasty, is a special art. Strict rules that are given to the newcomer govern the use of these facilities, which have only gradually opened to foreigners. A graduate student who successfully used the No. 1 Archive proves that status is not the only determinant of access. He advises researchers to do the following: cultivate a relationship with the primary person assigned as a go-between, refrain from asking for complete collections, make it clear that any microfilmed materials are for personal use only, and keep any special privileges that have been allotted to yourself.

The primary expert on the No. 1 Archive, Prof. Beatrice Bartlett at Yale University, has written extensively on its history and materials. She points out that the history of the Qing archives has taken a different turn from that of many earlier finds of documents, which are now housed outside China: "The Ch'ing archives were saved for the Chinese, to be developed by the administrative vision and genius of Chinese curators. Foreigners are welcome, but as readers, not owners of the documents" (*Times Literary Supplement*, July 4, 1986, p. 734). In another essay, Prof. Bartlett offers advice about using this unique library that could well apply to any situation in China. After noting that map files are closed from view, she observes:

> The situation is constantly changing, however, and frequently one is gratified when a curator's generosity is employed to prevail over a narrow interpretation of the rules. In view of the fact that the materials in all Chinese archives are magnificent, offering much to the scholar willing to search, patient submission to the rules while at the same time quietly attempting to negotiate improved terms is a worthwhile posture, likely eventually to produce desired results. ("Archive Materials in China on United States History," pp. 504–506 in *Guide to the Study of United States History Outside the U.S., 1945–1980*, vol. 1, ed. by Lewis Hanke, White Plains, N.Y.: Kraus International Publications, 1985)

5. Teaching

As discussed earlier, foreigners are hired to teach in China either as "foreign experts" or "foreign teachers." The distinction is important because it determines many aspects of the treatment an individual receives in China. Americans who have taught in China, however, report that no matter what their official designation, Chinese host institutions try to ensure the comfort and well-being of their foreign guests. Indeed, some American teachers feel too protected and isolated even though "all is meant in the best spirit and intention." In return, much is expected of teachers: "It is important to be as generous as possible with your time and energy. If [you've been hired to teach English and] you're weak in English grammar, become an expert soon; the Chinese want to learn from experts, not novices." "The prime directive is: be well-prepared and trained in the field you will teach." Since 1979 the Chinese government has sought to hire well-qualified foreign teachers rather than merely "friends of China."

To date, most American teachers in China have taught English language and literature, but the range of subjects is growing to include American studies, American society and culture, U.S. history, economics, business management, international trade and investment, marketing, U.S. law (constitutional, criminal, and criminal procedure), environmental and natural resources law, library management, and journalism. American teachers also have worked in a wide variety of institutions and in all parts of China. And no matter what their particular situation, they have been made to feel that their contribution to China's modernization effort is deeply appreciated. Some advice offered by Americans who have taught in China to individuals planning to have this experience include the following:

These personal qualities are needed: flexibility, human warmth and sociability, an ability to relax and "flow with the current" and good health and physical stamina. Persons with the following qualities should *not* go: workaholics, schedule and time-oriented people, people hooked on creature comforts, people concerned with efficiency and order and people who must have things neat, clean and tidy.

If you remember that you have gone to China to learn, to share knowledge and ideas and to enjoy the Chinese people and their culture, you will have an easier time "rolling with the punches." No one is going to change China during a year's teaching visit! Perhaps the most valuable characteristic a foreign expert can have is a healthy sense of humor.

THE BUREAUCRATIC STRUCTURE

The work unit or *danwei*, as explained earlier, is all-important in China. Americans have been employed by universities, trade institutes, finance and economics institutes, agricultural schools, normal schools, scientific and technical institutes, medical colleges, foreign language institutions, and others. Despite some important differences, these and other units do have many of the same characteristics described earlier in the section on the bureaucratic structure of universities and research institutes (pages 72–79). Perhaps even more than other foreigners, teachers are almost entirely dependent on their unit; it pays their salary, arranges their lodging, issues their ration tickets for cloth and food stuffs, helps arrange schooling for their children, obtains the permits needed for travel outside their city of residence, and generally acts on their behalf with all other bureaucratic offices in China.

Within the work unit, there is a specific office or department to which the foreign expert or teacher is responsible. China's complex bureaucracy can be very confusing. Many teachers do not know prior to arrival to whom they will be responsible; others don't know this even after their arrival. Because this information is crucial to your survival, it is important to clarify things as soon as possible. However, as many Americans have commented, to learn how to get things done within the system requires effort and patience. One teacher noted, "It took us almost two full months before we knew to whom to talk about what."

The two major components of the work unit with which a foreign expert or teacher will have contact are the foreign affairs office (*waiban*) and the academic department. Although the duties of and relationships between these two components vary from unit to unit—some have excellent communication, others have little or no contact with each other—the basic functions of each seem to be as follows. The foreign affairs office handles administrative details, that is, hiring, conditions of employment, signing of the contract, daily living concerns, issuance of necessary documents such as the university identification card, expert privileges card, alien residence card and library card, assisting with travel arrangements, and the like. The academic department is responsible for teaching matters, that is, curriculum, course assignments, teaching schedules, class size, room assignments, class materials, and so forth.

Some teachers have found the staff of the foreign affairs office to be extremely supportive; others feel that they are only helpful in overcoming obstacles they themselves have set; and still others report that they will only respond to specific questions. Relations with department personnel also vary considerably. It is therefore important to learn as quickly as possible what will work best in your situation. For example, one American teacher learned never to confront directly the director of the department about conditions of employment, as the answer would always be "no." But if he gathered all the official information about the situation and wrote a memo to the director outlining the regulations and stating his specific request, he always received an affirmative answer.

Many American teachers speak little, if any, Chinese when they arrive in China, and official discussions between them and their departmental or institutional sponsors are in English (through an interpreter, if needed). It has been noted by a number of teachers that their departmental colleagues often speak far better English than do administrative cadres. However, they also indicate that language is not a key problem. Although some find that speaking Chinese is extremely helpful, others have commented that foreign teachers who speak Chinese are considered too independent.

The problems, as noted by American teachers, are cultural and social organization. "Americans are used to a high degree of independence and self direction. The Chinese are not. There are a lot of banquets and other displays of friendship which cover up some very hard bargaining. One needs to go along with all the formalities and rituals and still be very assertive concerning one's own interests." Another teacher recommended that two important cultural characteristics be kept in mind:

> (1) Chinese work through intermediaries. Americans like to talk things out face-to-face. This means that rather than talking over problems or concerns with the head of the department directly, you may have to work through a third person who will carry messages back and forth.
> (2) Compromise. Chinese do a lot of horse-trading, bargaining and exchange of favors. In regard to classes, teaching loads and academic responsibilities, this is an ongoing process. Nothing is ever etched in stone. The whole year is a game of musical chairs.

WORK LOADS

Work loads often vary substantially from one institution or program to another, but all teachers report that they are expected to do far more than teach assigned classes. Additional activities include work on special projects, such as helping to write or edit textbooks and dictionaries, editing university publications in English, giving informal English lessons to colleagues, conducting oral exams, overseeing thesis projects, and assisting students with writing papers. Teachers also may lecture to their unit and to other units about specific academic topics or about cultural and social aspects of the United States. Or they might be asked to record tapes and help students and faculty write applications to colleges and universities in the United States. One teacher warns that although it is important to be as helpful as possible, "how much work you do will depend on how much resistance you put up—you must not become chronically fatigued to the point of illness."

As a foreign teacher, the actual number of hours you spend in classroom teaching can vary from as little as 6 per week to as many as 20. Additionally, you will probably spend several hours weekly holding "office hours," perhaps 5 to 6 hours cutting tapes, and numerous hours preparing materials for class, correcting papers, having unscheduled or scheduled meetings with students and teachers, and conducting editorial work. As one teacher pointed out, "No matter how many hours you are scheduled for, your actual work week will average between 45 and 50 hours." Another commented, "The work week is 6 days, and teachers can count on being busy almost all that time."

Class sizes also vary radically. Although Chinese universities appear to have huge faculties, making "the student-teacher ratio sound like a dream," the numbers are deceptive. Many Chinese professors actually are studying abroad. There are also a large number of professors now in their late 30s and 40s who have no academic qualifications and who are given no teaching assignments. You might therefore teach a seminar of only 3 or 4 students or give a lecture course to 75 students; from reports, however, it seems as though the average class size is between 20 and 35 students.

As more and more teachers are going to China to teach courses other than English, new concerns are surfacing. Some teachers are told they will be teaching certain courses prior to their departure for China and on arrival are told they will teach something totally different. Others find that their host institution is not clear about what subject matter should be covered in a course or, alternatively, the institution is not only clear but adamant that what the American considers to be proper course content is not what the Chinese want at all. Still others may discover they have been assigned to the wrong department to teach the wrong subject (for example, an economics professor being assigned to teach a course in international trade law), perhaps the result of different nomenclature used by Chinese and Americans in titling courses. Finally, many teachers find that their students do not have the necessary background to comprehend the subject matter they were planning to teach; as a result they are forced to simplify presentations greatly.

The English-language skills of students also sometimes cause problems. If there is no interpreter, for instance, in a course such as economics, and the students' English ability is not good, it may be impossible to teach the course properly. Or a teacher may find that instead of teaching history, he or she must first teach English, or, before teaching journalism, must first teach basic grammar. Where interpreters have been provided, both good and bad experiences have resulted. One American law professor reports that he has a regular interpreter through whom he does all his teaching, including dialogues with his students. He says he encourages his students to speak English as much as possible; however, without a good interpreter, he would find it impossible to teach the course.

Others have not been as lucky. Some teachers find themselves with an interpreter who speaks less English than some of the students and who sometimes challenges the American's teaching even though the interpreter knows little about the subject. Another issue that arises when courses must be taught completely through an interpreter is the grading of exams; because the exams are written in Chinese, the teacher must accept the word of the interpreter about what the students write. Teachers have handled such problems in various ways. One began using an interpreter who proved less than satisfactory and tried teaching the course without the interpreter. Although comprehension was sometimes difficult, he found that both he and his students were happier. In this case the students discussed particularly difficult topics in Chinese and then reiterated to the teacher in English their understanding. Other teachers have tried using simpler materials—switching from complicated texts to short articles. Others provided outlines of lectures that could be followed while the lecture was being given—a time-consuming effort but one that had worthwhile effects. And some found it essential to spend nonclass time with the students to give them enough exposure to a foreigner speaking and to overcome "typical" language problems such as lack of confidence, shyness, misuse of verb tenses, and omission of pronouns and articles. The teachers found that once the students gained confidence, their learning curves increased dramatically.

Teachers of English in China find that their pupils' proficiency varies considerably. In general, however, aural and spoken skills are weakest because most students have had few opportunities to practice with native speakers of English. Reading skills often are better but are usually limited to a rather narrow spectrum of materials. The students' command of writing skills varies widely, but most teachers find that their students are particularly good at grammar.

Chinese students in general lack a wide-ranging knowledge of the outside world, and this has presented special problems for teachers of literature, particularly modern contemporary literature. Standard texts and novels are scarce in China; many of those that are available are hopelessly out of date—one teacher discovered that the text being used in a literature course introduced Rudyard Kipling as a contemporary author!

Problems of a different sort arise from cultural differences and opposing attitudes regarding the "correct" process of learning. American teachers note repeatedly that their Chinese students prefer lectures to discussions and are often reluctant to engage in genuine dialogues about course material. Chinese teachers taking courses seem to some Americans to be even more resistant to discussing ideas than are regular students and more apt to expect a rigid, structured presentation and curriculum than most American teachers are accustomed to presenting. Americans therefore tend to use a variety of teaching methods including lecturing, asking questions of the students, conducting structured discussions, and introducing case method analysis. They have found that it is difficult to prompt students to answer questions but believe it is important to insist persistently and politely to motivate them to accept new teaching styles, learn to solve problems rather than repeat facts, and think for themselves rather than continue to follow the practice of rote memorization. Through persistence, American teachers have found that Chinese students are capable of vigorous classroom debates and learning through discussion.

Methods for evaluating student performance are usually left to the discretion of the American teacher. Whatever the number of papers assigned and examinations given in a course, it has been noted that students, including those who are already instructors, seem to be preoccupied with grades. This is an unfortunate but understandable concern because those selected to work with foreigners are very much aware that they have been given a special opportunity and that their performance is being carefully monitored by their units. Plagiarism is also a problem in China; the need to obtain good grades sometimes leads students to copy material written by others, misdemeanors that are not usually dealt with effectively by Chinese faculty.

WORKING CONDITIONS

Most school buildings are austere, unpainted, damp, and virtually unheated, but usually they are relatively clean and supplied with adequate lighting, blackboards, chalk, and standard classroom furniture. In some locations, electricity is erratic; in winter, when the electricity goes off, the heat goes off. Classes sometimes are rescheduled due to the lack of electricity. Upkeep on some buildings may not be adequate, and broken doors or windows may not be repaired promptly, allowing cold air to enter classrooms in the winter. Teachers survive the winters by dressing in layers of clothing. Classroom buildings are not air conditioned in the summer, but electric fans are used during the hottest months in some areas.

Some institutions assign private offices to their foreign teachers; in others, foreigners share a single work room. Offices are "not Madison Avenue plush, but they are embarrassingly spacious compared with those of our Chinese colleagues." Some teachers discover that many of their Chinese coworkers give up their own work space in order to make room for the foreign expert.

Physical surroundings are of little importance to most teachers, however, because their students are often extremely hardworking. One American wrote that he was "privileged to have students who are hungry to learn, who help themselves to knowledge the way harvest hands used to reach for mashed potatoes at my grandfather's table."

PROFESSIONAL RELATIONSHIPS

American teachers generally have found their Chinese students to be bright and able; they have also been surprised by how perceptive students have been in discussing a situation far removed from them in distance and experience and have been pleased that after overcoming an initial shyness, many students become active class participants, asking questions for clarification and presenting ideas for consideration. Many teachers described their Chinese students as extremely candid and friendly: "very fine—more studious than imaginative, but very friendly and a pleasure to work with"; the "brightest aspect of my experience in China"; "just about everything a teacher wants . . . [they] make this assignment one to be envied and coveted"; outstanding, extremely diligent, and highly motivated.

But there are other teachers who are not as enthusiastic. "About 60 percent of undergraduates had a good attitude, but they looked at their classes as a requirement to get a degree to graduate. They were not highly disciplined. They completed their assignments, but they didn't work up to their potential." "Chinese university students are not all hard working, disciplined, intelligent, and well prepared, which is the stereotype Americans bring to China. About 60 percent of the Chinese students reminded me of my American students, which was a surprise." "Extensive demands are made on students that cause them at times to shift attention from class work to other things such as preparation for TOEFL [Test of English as a Foreign Language]." "Students performed better than expected; it was difficult to get critical discussion in class as the students wanted to be told what they need to know; they like to be lectured." "Chinese students are mostly quite intelligent, but I was surprised by the lack of motivation of some; absenteeism is a big problem in China."

The relationships of American teachers with Chinese faculty members and administrators also varied. Some had excellent relationships with faculty in their departments and became good friends. There were visits by Chinese faculty to classes conducted by American teachers and vice versa. "Relationships with all administrators, faculty, and students were thoroughly professional and friendly; assistance was given and returned freely." "Contact with Chinese faculty was abundant, frequent, and very cordial. I only wished I had spoken more Chinese, as collegiality was limited only by the language barrier."

Other American teachers, however, had very little or no contact with Chinese faculty, nor were they invited to observe classes taught by the Chinese. And Chinese faculty in many cases did not visit classes taught by the Americans, even though they were invited. One American teacher explained that there was little opportunity to relate to Chinese faculty as many of them carried heavy teaching loads and taught extra classes at the host institution and other schools. Other teachers commented that they attempted to have seminars or discussions with Chinese faculty about the curriculum, teaching methods, and other areas of mutual interest. However, their efforts to discuss course changes, introduce greater flexibility, and employ different approaches to learning met with considerable resistance. Some teachers complained that efforts to change (improve) the teaching of a particular subject were ignored and that neither their colleagues nor the unit was willing to make changes that seemed both easy and desirable to foreign educators. Others were able to talk to their colleagues about such matters at least on an informal basis.

SOCIAL RELATIONSHIPS

Although many teachers have had to contend with frustrations in their work life, most have found more than compensating satisfaction in their less formal relationships with colleagues and students.

Students helped make the visitors' stay in China a pleasant and rewarding one by taking foreign teachers on shopping trips or visits to local points of interest, providing whatever translation assistance was needed, and informing them about activities that might be of interest—for example, band concerts, basketball games, and plays. Some teachers often ate with their students and were invited to participate in activities such as dances. (One teacher "highly recommends mastering a few 'traditional' dance steps before coming, as disco is still somewhat of an enigma to them; they feel more comfortable with the waltz or tango!") Others commented that their students constantly visited their homes for help and to practice their English. Still others had the opportunity to visit the homes and families of some of their students. A few teachers noted, however, that their students seemed hesitant to have informal contact with them. These teachers believe it is best to let Chinese students take the initiative in establishing relationships outside the classroom.

Many students and some faculty members are eager to attend schools in the United States and ask their American teachers for advice about the U.S. educational system and sometimes for letters of recommendation. Most teachers do not see such requests as an undue imposition but advise other Americans planning to teach in China to be prepared to play the role of adviser. They also caution Americans against making general comments about the possible assistance they or their home institution can render in helping Chinese students to study in the United States. Offhand comments can sometimes inspire unrealistic hopes for assured acceptance—and even a full scholarship to do graduate work in the United States. Teachers also caution newcomers on becoming involved with the selection of students being sent abroad by the work unit, as a word from a foreign expert or teacher is given a great deal of weight.

Relationships with Chinese colleagues generally are very cordial but a bit formal by American standards. Contact outside working hours is often limited to special ceremonial occasions, banquets, and outings planned by the host unit or department. Some foreign teachers have developed extremely close relationships with Chinese colleagues, frequently visiting their homes for meals and evenings of discussion or inviting their colleagues to their own homes. If the foreigner speaks Chinese, relationships tend to develop fairly easily—"knowing the language opens up an entirely different realm in relationships with Chinese people." Conversely, those who do not speak Chinese may interact most frequently with their English-speaking colleagues.

Relations with other foreign experts and teachers tend to be frequent and good as they often all share lodging and dining facilities. Some Americans, however, prefer to spend as much time as possible with their Chinese colleagues rather than with other foreign teachers.

CHINESE-LANGUAGE LESSONS

Many American teachers going to China would like to use the opportunity to learn Chinese or to improve their Chinese-language proficiency. Arrangements for a Chinese-language teacher usually can be made through the unit's foreign affairs office. From past experience,

Americans teaching in China note that a Chinese-language teacher is usually provided to them upon request; the American pays the teacher's fee and purchases any needed materials. Sometimes the department will pay for these expenses. Classes normally are held several times a week and might take place in the teacher's apartment or in the department in which he or she is teaching. One American who taught English in China had the following comments about learning Chinese: "If you want to learn Chinese in China, you must remember that there are a couple problems: (1) dialect—unless you are in the Beijing area or can find a 'pure' Mandarin teacher, it will be difficult; and (2) it's very hard to balance the role of English teacher and student of Chinese—some feel the responsibility to speak English only with their students, others with all personnel at the university, and others only in class."

GENERAL ADJUSTMENT ADVICE

Every teacher encounters problems in adjusting to life in China, but the individuals who provided information for this publication believe the satisfactions of working with intensely dedicated students, participating in Chinese life in a natural way, making a contribution to the quality of Chinese education, and feeling their way through the subtle nuances of friendships with Chinese people often outweigh the negative aspects. Some general pieces of advice offered to future Americans going to teach in China include the following:

> Get a good English-language map of the city you're in, and explore the city early and often. It quickly makes a very alien-seeming place begin to feel comfortable, and the feeling of ease helps immeasurably with the inevitable major cultural transition.

> Perhaps the greatest adjustment problem was having to learn Chinese-style decision making through consensus reached in informal discussions conducted before a formal meeting. Also, information and ideas came to me indirectly through the class monitor rather than directly from students. Everything happens slowly in China, so I had to learn to be more patient after making a request. And, although I had an apartment to myself, I had to learn to expect visits from students, colleagues, and the department chairman as early as 7 a.m. and as late as 10 or 11 p.m.; American-style privacy is nonexistent in China!

> Be as open and informal as your personality allows. Learn about and be sensitive to cultural differences. Spend as much time as possible with Chinese people, not other foreigners.

One American teacher's summary of the experience of living and working in China seems particularly appropriate: "Go planning to learn more than you teach, expecting a challenge, and above all, expect to enjoy China and its people—you won't be disappointed!"

6. Services Available

THE U.S. EMBASSY AND CONSULATES

The staffs of the U.S. Embassy in Beijing and the U.S. Consulates in Chengdu, Guangzhou, Shanghai, and Shenyang provide helpful services and in some cases assist in resolving specific problems. It is always best, however, to try to clear up any misunderstandings and resolve problems related to your activity in China with the appropriate officials at your host institution before seeking the help of U.S. diplomatic personnel. If other efforts fail, or if you need advice about how to deal with bureaucratic deadlocks, contact the Cultural Affairs Officer in the U.S. Embassy in Beijing (phone: 52-1161).

State Department regulations restrict the use of the diplomatic pouch and embassy medical facilities to diplomatic staff and their dependents. As noted earlier, however, the embassy does offer Japanese B encephalitis vaccine to any American in Beijing. (There is a series of three injections given one week apart; the cost is Y15 per injection.) Also, the embassy routinely issues letters of approval for Americans who leave China either for home or for short visits outside the country; but permission to travel within China must be secured from your host institution. With the new, more relaxed travel regulations, these letters generally are no longer needed.

When you arrive in China and each time you relocate, it is a good idea to register with the nearest U.S Embassy or Consulate. By doing so an emergency locator card will be kept on file in the event relatives need to reach you quickly. This card is also useful in case you lose your passport, develop a serious illness, or find yourself with other problems.

You must bring your passport with you when you register. Americans who register with the embassy or consulate nearest them may be included in functions open to all Americans: dances, movies, Friday afternoon cocktail hours, the annual Fourth of July gathering, and the like.

Although there is no reason to anticipate that you will need the assistance of U.S. consular officers, you should be aware of what to do and what to expect in an emergency—for example, a medical or financial emergency, difficulties with the police, or the death of a friend or relative in China. Within limits, consular officers can help in all such situations, and you should contact them for advice and assistance. For more information, consult the booklet *General Guidelines on Consular Services*, which is available free of charge from the:

U.S. Department of State
Bureau of Consular Affairs
Public Affairs Staff, Room 681
2201 C Street, NW
Washington, DC 20520

An officer in the U.S. Consulate General in Shanghai emphasized to a group of American teachers that the consulate personnel are there to help out in case of medical or personal emergency. They can get plane tickets out of the country fast, and, if necessary, can fly in a medical emergency plane or helicopter to take you to Hong Kong or Japan. One teacher reports that the consulate did this for an American who had a heart attack in Sichuan Province.

The U.S. Embassy in Beijing occupies three compounds near Ritan Park. The ambassador's residence and the offices of the press and cultural section (the U.S. Information Agency office in Beijing) are located at 17 Guanghua Lu (ask for *"yi ban"* when directing a taxi driver). The Bruce Building (*"er ban"*), located at 2 Xiushui Dong Jie, is a few blocks away and houses the consular section (where U.S. citizens register) and the administrative section. The new main building *"sanban,"* houses the embassy's executive offices and the offices of the political and economic sections as well as the Foreign Commercial Service and the Foreign Agricultural Service.

To inform Chinese students about study opportunities in the United States, the U.S. government donated reference collections to designated Chinese institutions containing information about U.S. colleges and universities, application procedures, and other pertinent details. See Appendix K for the locations and contents of these reference collections. The following list of U.S. Embassy and Consulate addresses and personnel is current for summer 1987.

U.S. Embassy/Beijing
Address: Xiushui Bei Jie #3
            Beijing, PRC
Telephone: 52-3831

Ambassador	Winston Lord
Deputy Chief of Mission	Peter Tomsen
Political Counselor	Raymond Burkhardt
Economic Counselor	Kent Weidemann
Commercial Counselor	Richard Johnston
Agricultural Attaché	David Schoonover
Science Attaché	Pierre Perrolle
U.S. Information Agency (USIA)	
Telephone: 52-1161	
Public Affairs Officer	McKinney Russell
Deputy Public Affairs Officer	George Beasley
Cultural Affairs Officer/Academic Advisor	Patrick J. Corcoran
Information Officer	Sylvia Rifkin

U.S. Consulate General/Chengdu
Address: Jinjiang Hotel
            180 Renmin Nan Lu
            Chengdu, PRC
Telephone: 28-24481

Consul General	William Thomas
Branch Public Affairs Officer	Vallerie Steenson

U.S. Consulate General/Guangzhou (Canton)
Address: Dongfang Hotel
            Renmin Bei Lu
            Guangzhou, PRC
Telephone: 66-9900; 67-7702 x1000

Consul General	Mark Pratt
Branch Public Affairs Officer (USIA)	Daryl Daniels

U.S. Consulate General/Shanghai
Address: 1469 Huaihai Zhong Lu
            Shanghai, PRC
Telephone: 37-9880

Consul General	Charles Sylvester
Branch Public Affairs Officer (USIA)	William Palmer

U.S. Consulate General/Shenyang
Address: 40 Lane 4, Section 5
Sanjing Lu
Heping District
Shenyang, Liaoning PRC
Telephone: 29-0045, 0034, 0054

Consul General   Eugene Dorris
Branch Public Affairs Officer (USIA)   William G. Crowell
Commercial Officer   Barbara Slawecki

POSTAL SERVICES

Every university campus and most hotels and neighborhood shopping areas have post offices or counters that provide standard postal services. Some of the smaller branch counters handle only cards, letters, and sales of stamps. International parcel post, registered mail, and other special services are usually offered in specified post offices—in Beijing, at the Friendship Hotel and at the International Post Office, which recently moved to Jianguomen, near the diplomatic quarter.

In summer 1986, airmail rates from China to the United States were Y1.10 for a letter and Y0.90 for a postcard. Internal airmail costs Y0.10. Internal surface rates are still inexpensive at Y0.08 outside the city and Y0.04 within any urban area. There is a special rate for seamail shipment of printed matter, which must be divided into 5-kilogram packages: Y31.00 each. Seamail rates for other materials average about Y7.50 per kilogram. Packages must be opened and inspected at the post office, which also provides customs forms and in some cases the paper and string for sealing the package. Most Chinese customers prefer to sew cloth bags or build wooden crates for their fragile parcels. (A supply of book mailers can be very useful for easy shipment of small parcels from China.) Film can be mailed out in special containers sold in the major post offices. Books can be mailed from any postal counter. Express mail is now available in major cities for about the same cost as similar services in the United States; it takes from four days to one week to reach most U.S. destinations. Air freight is handled through the Friendship Stores and the airlines.

Mail delivery in larger cities usually is quite reliable. Letters from the United States to Beijing take about 7 to 12 days and from Beijing to major U.S. cities, from 4 to 7 days. You should add a few days for mail that must reach smaller cities on either side. Mail in China sometimes shows evidence of tampering, but rarely goes astray permanently. A graduate student at Peking University comments on the handling of mail: "Many Chinese offices receive mail for students, faculty, and staff, which is either put into boxes for one or more persons or just laid out on a table or in a hallway. It is between this point and the intended recipient that much mail is opened and/or lost. The use of registered mail can help alleviate this problem. The post office will send a notice that the addressee must come to the post office with identification to pick up the package." If you move within China, you should not assume that mail will be forwarded to your new address; instead, resign yourself to returning to your original residence to search for undelivered mail.

You can expedite mail delivery from the United States by asking your relatives and friends to stamp letters and packages clearly as airmail and address them to you in the *People's Republic of China;* include the name of the city in *Pinyin** romanization and—even better—in Chinese characters. If you are literate in Chinese, you can write out the address in characters on a label that can be left at home and photocopied for multiple use. You should realize, however, that postal clerks are not always familiar with Pinyin, which may create delivery problems. Express mail between the United States and China cuts delivery time approximately in half and is reliable because it is held at the post office for pickup. As noted earlier, Chinese postal regulations prohibit mailing large amounts of used clothing into the country for other than personal use; and medicines of any kind may not be mailed to China except by special permission in emergency situations. See the postal regulations outlined in Appendix H for other such items. When a package arrives from abroad, the post office mails a notice to you; you can then pick it up at the designated local post office after producing proper identification—a passport or residence card—and pay duty on the contents. Foreigners may receive only four parcels per year, and no single parcel may be valued at more than US$30. Americans who are not members of the diplomatic community may not use the diplomatic pouch.

It is at the post office that periodicals also can be purchased and ordered for delivery. Postal workers usually have a list of periodicals that they are authorized to order for foreign customers; according to some reports the list varies among post offices. To subscribe to certain periodicals, permission is required from the foreign affairs office of your unit.

---

*Pinyin, the system of romanization now used in China, has replaced the Wade-Giles romanization system used prior to 1979. The Pinyin system more accurately reflects standard Mandarin names and pronunciations. Thus, Peking is now correctly rendered as Beijing, Canton is referred to by its Mandarin pronunciation—Guangzhou—and so forth. Maps and atlases published after 1979 should list the Pinyin romanizations of Chinese cities and provinces.

CURRENCY AND BANKING

The Chinese currency (*renminbi* or RMB) is based on a decimal system. The basic unit is the *yuan* (or Chinese dollar). The *yuan* is subdivided into 10 *jiao* (more commonly called *mao*, the Chinese dime) and 100 *fen* (penny). The largest paper RMB amount is the 10-*yuan* note (Y10); but there are also notes in amounts of Y5, Y2, Y1, and 1, 2, and 5 *jiao*. Coins, fashioned of light aluminum, come in denominations of 1, 2, and 5 *fen*. The official rate of exchange in January 1987 was Y3.71 to US$1.00. RMB is nonconvertible—it cannot be legally taken out of China and is not available for purchase outside the PRC.

The currency system became more complicated in April 1980 when the Bank of China began to issue a special convertible scrip, *waihuijuan* (the foreign exchange certificates or FEC discussed earlier), which was to be used by foreigners at designated places and for particular goods Initially, this scrip was the currency foreigners obtained in return for traveler's checks and foreign currency; they used it to pay for imported goods and for services in establishments that catered specifically to foreigners. *Renminbi* was the preferred currency for such transactions as taxi rides and meals in most restaurants.

In time, however, the demand for FEC, which the Chinese could use to purchase luxury goods, increased. Although the official rate of exchange between RMB and FEC remained equal, unofficially the demand for FEC grew to the point that in many cases in which domestic RMB should have been requested, FEC had to be used. Taxi drivers, for example, would refuse to accept RMB for payment or if paid in large denominations of FEC would give back change in RMB. Rail passengers who should have been able to use RMB for tickets would find no tickets available unless FEC were produced. Menus in some hotels carried two sets of prices: one for payment in RMB and one at nearly half the price in FEC. Long-term residents learned to carry only smaller denominations of FEC (which is issued in 50- and 100-*yuan* notes as well as in lower denominations corresponding with RMB) because it became so difficult to obtain change in FEC. In short, a black market developed and with it all of the ambiguity and tension that a dual currency system encourages.

The news in the Chinese press in the spring of 1986 that FEC was due to be abolished was greeted with joy by most foreigners—one student remarked that a return to a single currency system would make friendships between Chinese and foreigners easier. But at this writing it is not clear how and when the currency reform will be implemented, and the information that follows must be considered provisional.

Foreigners who receive currency from abroad in the form of bank checks or transfers will receive FEC, which can be taken out of the country at exit. Remember that when you leave China, you must show exchange memos equivalent to the dollar amount requested if you want to convert your remaining FEC into dollars.

The range of banking services in China varies; ask your host unit to direct you to the nearest Bank of China branch with full services for foreigners. In Beijing most Americans frequent the office on Dengshikou Xijie just north of Wangfujing Dajie. You can open a bank account (i.e., a savings that pays a low rate of interest) easily, in either U.S. dollars or FEC, and withdrawals can be made at any time. If your account is opened as a U.S. dollar account, you can withdraw funds in either U.S. dollars or FEC; but if it is opened using FEC, you can make withdrawals only in that form. All transactions are recorded in a passbook that must be surrendered when you leave the country. Bank drafts drawn on the Bank of China and issued in foreign currency can be sent out of the country, and there have been no reported problems cashing them in the United States. Wire transfers carry a minimal fee and have been smooth in most cases. As noted in the earlier chapter on preparing for your trip, it is important that your U.S. bank have correspondent relations with the Bank of China.

Banking transactions can be time-consuming, especially if you live far from the branch that handles foreign matters. It is wise to keep a supply of traveler's checks on hand since they can be converted quite easily at the Bank of China counter at any hotel or store that serves foreigners. Be aware, however, that in some hotels these counters are open only a few hours each day and that the larger branches stay open seven days a week in some cases but close for two hours at lunchtime. Finally, although it has been borne out that any Chinese city is safer than its Western counterpart, theft is not unusual, and many foreigners have been the victims of pickpockets, particularly on buses. For your own peace of mind and that of your hosts in China, it is wise to take reasonable precautions with valuables and currency. For information on credit cards in China, see the first chapter of this handbook.

CABLE AND TELEX FACILITIES

Cables can be used for internal communications and can be sent almost anywhere in the world from China. Post offices, postal counters at most hotels, and special communications offices handle cables. Many large cities have a main telegraph office that is open 24 hours a day. Cable rates for overseas range from Y1.20 to Y1.50 per word; rates are doubled for fast delivery (4 hours) and halved for overnight service in some hotels. Some hotels accept credit cards for payment.

Cables sent to foreigners in China are delivered to the foreign affairs office of their unit or to the reception desk at their hotel; notification usually is prompt. Sometimes names become garbled, however, and if you are expecting a cable, it is a good idea to check on it or—if you receive many cables and live in a hotel—to register a cable address. Cables are considered public and will sometimes be delivered opened.

Incoming telex facilities are becoming widely available at major hotels, although customers may have to punch their own tapes. The standard overseas rate is Y8.40 per minute with a three-minute limit. The rate to Hong Kong is about half the overseas rate.

THE TELEPHONE

Local calls within any city in China are free; long-distance calls are priced according to their destination and length with the minimum charge based on a three-minute call. Long-distance calls within China are expensive, and connections are usually poor. As strange as it seems, calls to anywhere outside China are almost always clearer than a connection anywhere within the country. In most hotels, if you speak Chinese, you can place calls directly by dialing the overseas operator. Many local operators still do not speak English. Be sure to check with hotel attendants for procedures. How long it takes to place a call depends on the time of day—at 9 or 10 p.m. Beijing time, for example, the wait can be up to two hours or more. It is advisable to book calls in advance and to try to call during nonbusiness hours in the United States. After your conversation is completed, the operator will call back to verify the time; in most hotels the bill is then paid at the service desk. Many Americans call the United States collect because calls are much less expensive when they are paid for there. If you are expecting a call from the United States, remember that at busy times overseas, the lines are sometimes congested and calls must be booked hours in advance. And be sure to let your friends and family know your room number as soon as possible because most foreigners are identified by room number rather than by name in most hotels. Except in the newest joint-venture hotels, there are no central registries listing names and room assignments.

In dormitories, incoming calls are received by workers in the office who notify the party being called by loudspeaker. Callers must know the student's Chinese name; dormitory personnel often speak no English. Placing a call from a dorm can take a great deal of time because many have only one telephone and many institutions have only one line to the outside. Some dormitories have a special long-distance telephone room; in others students must use the regular dormitory telephone. You can place an international call by dialing the overseas operator (in major cities, most of them speak English and are quite helpful) who will phone back after the call goes through. The bill can be paid to dormitory attendants.

All of China operates on one time zone: 13 hours ahead of U.S. eastern standard time and 16 hours ahead of Pacific standard time. In 1986 China began to use a new "summer time," which is equivalent to U.S. daylight savings time; the time difference now is the same year round. Because changes in the U.S. system are being discussed, confusion about time differences seems inevitable. China is in the same time zone as Tokyo and one hour ahead of Hong Kong during daylight savings time.

China	California	Washington, D.C.
8 a.m.	4 p.m. previous afternoon	7 p.m. previous evening
8 p.m.	4 a.m. same day	7 a.m. same day

Telephone books are hard to find in China, and they do not list residential or neighborhood phone numbers. Two directories that can be used as references for organizations are the *China Phone Book and Address Directory*, which can be ordered from:

The China Phone Book Company
Box 11581
Hong Kong

and the annual *China Telephone Directory* published by the Beijing Telecommunications Equipment Plant (their phone number is 47-16-55). Do not assume that your phone number is on record for public information, and be sure to collect the phone numbers of friends in China. Changes in important numbers for foreigners are sometimes noted in the *China Daily*.

MEDICAL CARE

The host unit in China is obligated to provide proper medical care for all its personnel, a responsibility that worries the Chinese host as much as the foreign guest. Colds and stomach disorders are common ailments. Seasoned residents advise that if remedies brought from home do not work, the first step is to go to your work unit's clinic. Medical personnel are almost always kind and concerned, but few speak English and at times, in their efforts to find a quick cure, they sometimes prescribe massive doses of antibiotics for any ailment that seems serious. As one teacher commented, "It helps if you can make a self-diagnosis, i.e., say whether you want penicillin or aspirin!" Wear a medical identification bracelet if you are allergic to any medications. As noted earlier, parents of school-age children warn newcomers with children to request that no medications be given in school without parental consent.

Chinese medicine is especially effective for the treatment of colds and diarrhea. Those who want to see a Western doctor, however, cannot rely on the U.S. Embassy, which treats only its own staff except in the case of encephalitis vaccine, which is offered to any American in China. The Japanese, Australian, French, and British Embassies usually have a physician on the staff who will see other foreign nationals, and they sometimes stock medications not available in Chinese facilities. You can call the general information number at these embassies to obtain phone numbers of their staff physicians. In case of serious illness the physician or the host unit will refer you to the foreigners' clinic at one of the large municipal hospitals: the Peking Union Medical College (formally the Capital Hospital), the Sino-Japanese Hospital, or the Friendship Hospital in Beijing; the Worker's Hospital in Nanjing; or the No. 1 People's Hospital in Shanghai. These hospitals have a special wing for foreigners and usually have at least one English-speaking physician on duty. Hospital pharmacies carry a limited supply of drugs and vaccines; however, immunoglobulin is *not* available. Note also that the Chinese do not have Rh-negative blood and thus do not stock it in their blood banks. For this reason it is extremely important that anyone with Rh-negative blood register at the U.S. Embassy so that blood can be located quickly from the foreign community in case of emergency.

Costs for medical care are nominal: an outpatient visit costs Y5 or less; an X-ray, Y10 to Y20. The cost of hospitalization varies according to the status of the patient and the quality and location of the hospital. For a researcher's spouse who contracted pneumonia in late 1985, a two-week hospital stay in Guangzhou totaled Y1,930 for medication and treatment and Y792 for lodging and food. The care was reportedly very effective. In another case a student who became ill with dysentery on a school trip with Chinese friends spent a week in the Worker's Hospital in Nanjing and paid a total of Y68. Although she describes the hospital facilities as barely adequate, she reports that the medical and nursing care were warm and attentive, and—in the case of a condition like dysentery, which is well understood in China—effective and inexpensive. She points out, however, that many provisions for daily life must be brought in by the patient—soap, toilet paper, washbasin, special foods, all of the necessities for dorm life that form every student's survival kit. Grain coupons also were required for the purchase of some foods. Most Chinese patients are fed and given extra care by family members—"Hospital food and services are very limited by Western standards. You will want someone to bring you soda, juice, fruit, extra toiletries, and reading material." In this student's case, these amenities and attentions were provided by the Chinese students traveling with her. She adds that it is of use to know the Latin names of drugs to which you are allergic because that is how they are identified by Chinese doctors. Services in hospitals that serve foreigners more frequently (such as the Peking Union Medical College) are more consistent with Western standards.

Useful tips for preventing and coping with illness abroad, including how to care for children who become ill, can be found in *Health Information for International Travel 1986*, which is available for $4.75 from:

The Superintendent of Documents
U.S. Government Printing Office
Washington, DC 20402
(202-783-3238)

URBAN TRANSPORTATION

Most people in China use one of three methods to get around in any city: taxi, bus, or bicycle. Walking is difficult for long distances because there are few sidewalks in the suburbs and traffic is intimidating. Taxis are expensive: from Y0.60 to Y0.90 per kilometer, depending on the model of the car. A variety of automobiles are now in use in China ranging from Volkswagen Rabbits to Toyotas and Mercedes. Be sure to ask the mileage costs *before* engaging a car. Some taxis are metered; all should have a sticker or information card that cites fares per kilometer.

Until recently taxi shortages in the major cities created headaches for foreigners who relied on this mode of transportation. In Beijing the creation of several new companies has alleviated the problem at major taxi stands, usually located at the larger tourist hotels, where you simply wait in line for a car. (Some taxi companies allow their drivers to pick up fares at places other than designated taxi stands.) For those who live on campuses or work units with no access to a taxi stand, the only recourse is to call the nearest taxi company and wait for a car to arrive, a nerve-wracking process that sometimes produces results only after a long wait or at times not at all.

In an entertaining article in the *China Business Review*, Carroll Bogart (now *Newsweek* correspondent in Beijing) offers tips on competing for taxis and explanations of the problems. For hailing a taxi, she writes that in Beijing you should be positioned on a major thoroughfare (not Tian'an Men, however): "A timid wave from the curbside will not do. It helps to plunge into traffic waving one's arms dramatically, or simply to open the door of an empty taxi waiting at a red light and hope that the driver agrees." The driver's agreement is not to be taken for granted, however, and securing a taxi requires negotiating skills. Bogart lists the 10 reasons taxi drivers refuse certain unlucky passengers: "a good

TV show, quitting time, mealtime, daily quota completed, short trip, wrong direction, bad weather, night trip, bad road, passenger without foreign exchange." Some of these excuses are inexcusable; others stem from very real constraints that the taxi drivers face. For example, because each driver must fulfill a daily kilometer quota, a short trip in heavy traffic is a waste of time. Some drivers also must earn a certain amount of FEC each day and will therefore refuse Chinese passengers—who now make up at least half of the customers—and foreigners without foreign exchange certificates. Finally, drivers are subject to dismissal for breaking traffic rules and lose their license for an accident involving a foreigner. As a result, inexperienced drivers are reluctant to drive in inclement weather because they fear the consequences of any mishap. Tips for hailing a taxi also include finding one that is returning to the station at your hotel or nearby and naming your ultimate destination to make the trip worthwhile, even if there will be stops along the way. Taxi waiting costs are calculated by five-minute intervals (five minutes equals one kilometer).

One solution to the taxi problem is to hire a car ahead of time—by bargaining with a driver for a half-day's worth of transportation, you can be assured that the car will wait for you as you conduct business or run errands. Some residents—for example, those with children who must be transported to school each day—engage a car by the week for as little as Y30 to Y100 daily, depending on the company and the size and make of the car. For large groups, mini-vans or *mianbaoche* ("bread trucks"), so named because of their supposed resemblance to a loaf of bread, can be engaged by the day or half-day. Some of these small vans serve certain bus stops and can be hailed from the road.

Buses go almost everywhere for a few *mao*, but they are slow and very crowded during the rush hours. It takes at least one hour to reach downtown Beijing from Beijing University, for example, and 30 minutes from Fudan to the center of Shanghai. In some cities the buses stop running rather early in the evening; a researcher in Wuhan notes that bus service there terminates at 9 p.m., and in Beijing many routes are not served after 10 p.m. A monthly bus pass can be convenient; ask your unit to help you apply for one. In Beijing a pass costs Y5 per month for unlimited rides.

Much of the time the most efficient way to get around is by bicycle. Although most foreigners relish the speed and freedom a bicycle affords, newcomers usually find traffic heavy and chaotic in many urban and suburban areas. In some cities, cars still flash their lights on and off to warn cyclists and pedestrians, but traffic accidents are on the rise. A recent article in the *China Daily* reports that traffic accidents killed 759 persons in Beijing in 1985, seven times the number of victims of criminal activities. The article attributes most of the traffic problem to the large number of bicycles on the road, although motorcycles, bad roads, increased truck traffic, and an inefficient traffic control system are also cited as causes of accidents. Safety also is a problem; women should be aware that females have been harassed while biking alone at night. Mechanical failure is less of a worry; bicycle repair shops and stands can be found in almost any neighborhood.

Some researchers and teachers find that their hosts strongly urge them to avoid cycling and public transportation. And in some work units, cars and mini-buses are used to transport foreign passengers.

RECREATION

Most university campuses have basketball and volleyball courts, track and soccer fields, and horizontal and parallel bars. Some have tennis courts and swimming pools. In Beijing, the International Club downtown and the Friendship Hotel each have a 50-meter pool and tennis courts; some of the joint-venture hotels have pools and exercise facilities. To use the International Club and Friendship Hotel pools, you must obtain a swimming card (which requires a minimal physical examination) to present for admission. Physical exams are given at the Friendship Hotel's clinic; the hotel also issues swimming cards. There is a charge for swimming at these facilities, but prices are nominal. On most campuses, foreigners are welcome to participate in team sports, and many consider this an excellent means to get to know Chinese colleagues.

Most dormitories have communal television lounges, and almost all hotels have color televisions in each room. Most colleges and universities also schedule movies. Some theater and opera tickets can be ordered by phone, but you must stand in line early in the day to buy tickets for popular performances. Recent reports indicate that tickets for performances at popular concert halls, such as the one just south of Zhongnanhai in Beijing, are notoriously difficult to obtain. Some units are willing to help their foreign guests obtain tickets for special shows, and students often are given tickets by their foreign affairs officials who also arrange for group transportation to the event itself.

Every city has at least one public park for outings and a few good restaurants (eating out is a favorite pastime in China). Ask your Chinese and foreign friends for restaurant recommendations. Some of the best finds these days are the small, family-owned eateries that serve genuine home cooking. In China "reserving a table" means you also order your meal ahead, and you pay a standard banquet price for the meal, which can be quite expensive. But if you go early (5 p.m.) and hope for a table, you can enjoy a meal in some of the finest restaurants for less than half the price quoted to foreigners.

Because so many foreigners visit Beijing at least once in their stay, a few favorite restaurants are listed here. Many foreigners like the deli-style atmosphere of the restaurant in Ritan Park, which is famous for its *jiaozi* (dumplings). The Shoudu Kaorouji Mongolian barbecue restaurant on the shore of Houhai behind the Imperial City features dining in an upstairs room with a balcony overlooking the lake in the summer. (This restaurant was closed for renovations in 1986.) The restaurant at the Bamboo Garden Hotel is located in a traditional courtyard, as is the famous Szechuan restaurant, which is situated in a house that once belonged to Yuan Shikai, the famous military man of late Qing and early Republican times. Alternatives to Chinese food can be found in the expensive but pleasant Japanese restaurant on the second floor of the Beijing Hotel; on the top floor of the Xinqiao Hotel you can order Western and Pakistani food. Finally, the offerings in the joint-venture hotels are fairly wide-ranging (from pizza and hamburgers to cheese fondue and curry buffets) but expensive.

INTERNAL TRAVEL

The possibilities for travel in China are so rich and varied that only general guidelines can be offered here—especially now that a wealth of travel lore exists in guidebooks and newspaper and magazine accounts, all of which can help you make the most of your travel opportunities. Travelers willing to "rough it" to economize and escape the confines of planned tours can consult two useful guides: *China—A Travel Survival Kit* by Alan Samagalski and Michael Buckley, and *China Off the Beaten Track* by Brian Schwartz (see Appendix L for publication information on all sources listed in this section). Academic travelers who do not speak Chinese report that these guides were invaluable for pointing out ways to save money and to see the "real China." For those interested in historical sites, *Nagel's Encyclopedic Guide to China* is scholarly and detailed. An up-to-date guide to historical and tourist sites that comes highly recommended is Evelyne Garside's *China Companion: A Guide to 100 Cities, Resorts, and Places of Interest in the People's Republic of China.*

In the spring of 1986, several regulations went into effect to ease the bureaucratic barriers involved in travel. The China National Tourist Office reported at that time that 244 cities and sites were opened to foreign travelers and that "foreigners with a valid visa or residence certificate can travel in areas open to foreign visitors without special travel permits." Areas that are not listed as open can be visited only with a travel permit issued by the Public Security Bureau or the *gonganju.* Foreign affairs officials usually will help secure these permits for the non-Chinese-speaking traveler. But as indicated by the recent detention of a journalist who traveled by motorcycle through parts of China not yet officially open to foreigners, there are limits to travel in China still—despite the new liberal policies.

The first step in arranging travel is to purchase train tickets at the local train station or airline tickets at the CAAC office in your city. For all practical purposes, only one-way tickets can be bought. Some travelers report being able to buy round-trip tickets but with reservations only for the leg of the trip from the city of origin to the city of destination. At each stop on your journey, you must buy tickets for the next leg; if you need help, consult the local *luxingshe* (China Travel Service) counter at your hotel. You can avoid the tourist surcharge if you buy tickets at the train station—but if you do not speak Chinese, the process can be confusing as few service clerks speak English. Timing must be carefully orchestrated. Train tickets usually cannot be purchased earlier than three days before departure, and you must literally have them in hand when you make hotel reservations. Train accommodations are of two types: soft and hard class; within each, you can choose seats or sleeping berths. For long or overnight journeys, soft-class (i.e., first-class) sleeping compartments have four berths with comfortable padded seats, a small table, doilies, pillows, a thermos of hot water, an overhead fan, and an overhead luggage compartment. These cars are no longer reserved for foreigners as they once were but also serve high-level Chinese officials. Hard class is just that—wooden benches for seats and thinly padded berths in sleepers that are not enclosed and are stacked three high. Prices for berths in this class depend on the level, with the highest price charged for the lowest berth. Hard-class tickets do not guarantee a seat, and many a traveler has sat out a long journey in the dining car—or stood, for lack of a seat. Some foreigners enjoy the lively atmosphere of the hard-class sections—where they are often the main amusement for their fellow travelers; others prefer a more sedate ride.

Train food varies in quality. Some trains are famous for excellent food, but usually foreigners do not make their travel plans on the basis of such amenities. About two hours before mealtimes, a service person will ask each foreign traveler about their dinner plans and will offer two or more grades (*biaozhun*) of food ranging in price from about Y6 to Y10 for four or five dishes. Most experienced travelers have noticed that there is no discernible difference in the amount or quality of the food in different grades, and they suggest you take the lowest *biaozhun*. You can skip the arranged fare altogether and opt for a noodle dish for half the price or the even cheaper boxes of hot rice with a few vegetables that Chinese passengers favor. Most passengers carry an assortment of food (from watermelons to peanuts) to be consumed along the way. Tea bags can be purchased on the train. Often there will be no English-speaking personnel on the train, which can be a problem for foreigners when ordering dinner. If you do not speak Chinese, you might want to take a supply of nonperishable goods.

Mix-ups are common about what kind of luggage is allowed on the train. It is a good idea to keep with you a small carry-on bag for essentials and to take seriously the regulation to lock checked bags. A number of travelers have reported items missing from outside pockets of luggage upon arrival at their final destination.

Internal air travel was once a bargain—most airline tickets used to cost about as much as a soft berth by train. However, a 30 percent increase applying only to foreigners (and excluding overseas Chinese visitors) went into effect in July 1986. But even with the increase, domestic service in China remains inexpensive by international standards. Reportedly, air cargo, air freight, and excess baggage costs also are going up.

Foreigners of different status are subject to different regulations, prices, and expectations about where, when, and how they should travel. Teachers and researchers are limited primarily by their work schedules and agreements with their unit about travel. Students are constrained by academic schedules and can travel only on weekends (which on some campuses begin at noon on Saturday); during the long national holiday at Spring Festival (*chunjie*) in late January or early February; or during summer vacation. These restrictions do not apply to students engaged in dissertation research under CSCPRC auspices or to those governed by university-exchange agreements.

Inexpensive casual travel is no longer limited to students. More and more, hardy travelers with no Chinese-language expertise are finding their way through China on their own. One colorful account accurately describes the flavor of the experience: "It was exhilarating to plan my own itinerary, to leave the beaten path and stir up a town with my presence, to eat and travel and suffer with the average Chinese. But it was also aggravating to cope with the lines and the language barrier while buying food or train tickets, and there were times when I was exhausted by 'hard-class' trains and spitting passengers and lying hotel staff who insisted that there was no room at the inn." The author Nicholas D. Kristof, in this special report to *The Washington Post* (February 26, 1984), goes on to describe the problems and possibilities of finding inexpensive accommodations despite the effort to keep foreigners in the fancier establishments: "But almost all hotels, even the finest, have 'dormitories' where a bed goes for a song—if the guest outlasts the cries of 'Mayo!' Dormitories are sometimes the barracks they sound like, but more often are comfortable rooms with perhaps four beds shared with other travelers. A bed typically costs the equivalent of US$2–$4." Kristof observes that you must insist on dormitory accommodations if you want them—they will not be offered immediately: "Usually the clerk gives in fairly quickly, but there is the famous story of the Frenchman who waited three days for a dormitory bed. And each night while waiting he slept in one of the many vacant beds—reasoning that he could not be charged for sleeping in beds that supposedly were already taken." Clearly, a sense of humor is essential for this kind of travel, but almost all who have struck out on their own conclude that the warmth and hospitality they received along the way far outweighed the frustrations.

Teachers and research scholars (or anyone of senior status) are expected to travel as tourists and pay tourist prices, although some American researchers who speak Chinese and can negotiate on their own have traveled hard class and dispensed with guides. Bicycles can be rented in most cities, but some travelers take their bikes along with them on trains for easy transportation. It is still a good idea, however, to book a room in advance from the local office of the China Travel Service especially in busy tourist times (May through October) in popular cities. Rooms, like train tickets, can be reserved only one leg at a time. Remember too that Chinese people are traveling more these days; as a result, national holiday times are not always ideal for travel.

Most teachers report that their hosts are willing to help plan and arrange for trips within China. But at times the host unit's eagerness to arrange for easy, comfortable, and accompanied travel conflicts with teachers' desires to plan their own trips and travel alone. If you want to dispense with guides and cars and soft accommodations on trains, you may prevail if you can speak Chinese fairly well and your hosts are confident that you can get along without help. It is important to note, however, that some foreigners have discovered that their Chinese colleagues expect to accompany them and in fact look forward to it because frequently it is their only chance to travel.

Often, students can take special tours sponsored by their unit. The tours usually cover five or more cities in three weeks at considerable savings over tourist rates—a typical three-week tour might cost as little as Y300 (frequently, students are put up in dormitories along the way). What these trips lack in spontaneity and comfort is compensated for in lower costs and sometimes opportunities to reach sites not always accessible to tourists. In some universities and colleges, researchers and teachers and their families also have been invited to go along on these trips.

Whatever the style or the itinerary, you are encouraged to travel at every opportunity. There is no better way to enlarge your perspective about China, to lift your spirits, and to meet Chinese people easily and naturally.

7. Leaving China

When you are ready to leave the PRC, one of the first things to do is decide how to ship back to the United States all the goods you have accumulated. Parcel post is one obvious way to ship your belongings home, but there are two other alternatives. One is air freight, which is convenient but expensive, especially in light of recent price hikes. Air freight is handled by the CAAC office. The other alternative is sea freight, which is inexpensive but slow—plan on about three months in transit. Sea freight is handled by the Friendship Store's transportation section; the store takes charge of building a crate for your shipment and moving it to a seaport city. Returning Americans who live in cities without this service and want to ship by sea freight have had to find someone to build the crate and accompany it to the coast personally, a rather cumbersome procedure. Ask your foreign affairs officials for help.

Changes in airline ticketing can be made in China, but during busy tourist seasons (from May through October) individual travelers have had difficulty booking flights. Flights must be confirmed through the airlines on which you hold the ticket or, if the airline has no direct representation in your city, through the CAAC office. Be sure to check with your travel agent about any restrictions that apply to your ticket, and be sure to reconfirm your flight. In most cases, reservations can be made 21 days before departure at the earliest, and reservations can be reconfirmed no more than 3 days before the flight. Remember to take your passport with you when you deal with the airlines on any matter. Some travelers actually find it easier to mail their ticket back to the United States for flight validations or itinerary changes; in that case, however, be sure to allow six weeks turnaround time. Be aware also that most tickets are valid only for one year from the issue date.

135

Exit visas are no longer required. The new travel regulations state that "foreigners leave by their valid passports or other valid travel documents." Regulations governing the kinds of materials that may be taken out of the country without permission are not clear, and if in doubt, you should check with your host unit. Student regulations (see Appendix B) state:

> Foreign students must observe the Chinese customs regulations concerning materials to be taken out of China or mailed abroad. The following items are allowable: textbooks, class handouts and related materials issued to them by the school, study notes, photographs, and audiovisual materials related to study. Any materials issued by the school which are not intended for outside circulation must be approved for exit by the school authorities, who will provide the student with an itemized certificate of authorization to present to the customs officer.

Although traditions vary from unit to unit and from place to place, generally it is difficult to leave expensive items with individual friends as gifts without inciting the envy of their colleagues. Radios, typewriters, tape recorders, and bicycles may be coveted by Chinese friends and coworkers, but you must be sensitive to the following regulations: (1) Technically, all hardware brought into the country must be taken out at departure. Customs officials pay particular attention to watches and cameras. (2) Some of the goods you might want to sell or give away could create problems because they are either rationed or, like bicycles, must be registered in the name of the owner who must present a sales slip as proof of purchase.

If possible, have someone from your unit accompany you to the airport—to help cut through the red tape and speed you on your way. To exit, you will need foreign currency exchange slips, your Bank of China passbook (if you have one), the customs declaration you filled out upon entry into China (any items listed but not taken out can be taxed), and Y15 for the departure tax.

As in other important activities, there is a ritual of leave-taking in China that begins a few weeks before departure: tea parties with colleagues and cadres from the unit, at least one farewell banquet, picture-taking sessions, exchanges of gifts, dinner invitations from Chinese friends, parties with foreign friends. The hectic schedule of arranging the myriad bureaucratic details and the rituals of departure also may be complicated by sudden professional opportunities as the host unit rushes to comply with longstanding requests. Nevertheless, the uncharacteristically fast pace that marks the end of a stay in China helps you overcome the sadness of leaving good friends and colleagues and appreciative students. Your adventure in China will soon be over—but not soon forgotten.

APPENDIXES

APPENDIX A

Interinstitutional Agreements Between U.S. and PRC Institutions

U.S. Institution	PRC Institution
University of Alabama, Huntsville	University of Science and Technology, Hefei
Appalachian State University	Northeast University of Technology
University of Arizona (under negotiation)	Beijing University
	Nanjing University
	Southwestern Jiaotong University
	Xinjiang University
Boston University	Huazhong Institute of Technology
Bowling Green State University	Xian Foreign Language Institute
Brigham Young University, Hawaii Campus	Jilin University
Brown University	Nanjing University
University of California, Berkeley	Beijing University
	Fudan University
	Nanjing University
University of California, Davis	Huazhong Agricultural College
	Beijing Medical College
	Henan Medical College
University of California, Los Angeles	Chinese University of Science and Technology, Graduate School, Beijing
	Zhongshan University
	English Language Center, Zhongshan University
	Beijing Institute of Foreign Trade, Institute of International Management

Adapted from *A Relationship Restored: Trends in U.S.-China Educational Exchanges, 1978–1984*, National Academy Press, Washington, D.C., 1986, Tables A-29 and A-30.

139

U.S. Institution	PRC Institution
University of California, San Diego	Chongqing University
	Huazhong University of Science and Technology
	Shanghai Jiaotong University
	Fudan University
University of California, San Francisco	Shanghai Second Medical College
University of California, Santa Barbara	Chinese Academy of Sciences
University of California, Santa Cruz	Beijing Language Institute
California Polytechnic University, Pomona	Yunnan University
California State University, Northridge	Heilongjiang University
	Beijing Institute of Technology
	Harbin Institute of Technology
	Jinan University
	Shaanxi Normal University
	South China Normal University
	Zhejiang University
Carnegie-Mellon University	Ministry of Education
	Academia Sinica
University of Chicago	Beijing University
City University of New York, City College	Nanjing Institute of Technology
	Shandong University
	Xibei University
	Zhongshan University
Colorado State University	East China Institute of Hydraulic Engineering
	Chinese Academy of Sciences, Gansu Province
	Gansu Grassland Ecological Institute & Gansu Agricultural University
University of Colorado Health Sciences Center	Hunan Medical College
Columbia University	Beijing University
	Shanghai Jiaotong University
Cornell University	Chinese Academy of Sciences
	Beijing University
	Fudan University
	Xian Jiaotong University
	Shanghai Jiaotong University
	Southwest Jiaotong University
	Nanjing Agricultural College
Eastern Illinois University	Northwest Polytechnic University
Eastern Michigan University	Chengdu Institute of Science and Technology
Emory University	Beijing University
Georgetown University	East China Normal University

U.S. Institution	PRC Institution
Hamline University	Beijing University
Harvard University	Beijing University
	Chinese Academy of Social Sciences
	Fudan University
	Nanjing University
	Shandong University
	Zhongshan University
University of Houston, University Park	Beijing Institute of Foreign Trade
University of Idaho	Ministry of Forestry
	University of Inner Mongolia
	Beijing Forestry College
	Northwest College of Agriculture
	Ministry of Agriculture
	Wuhan Geological College
	Changchun College of Geology
	Forestry College of Inner Mongolia
	Shanxi Agricultural College, Taiyuan
	Shaanxi Forest Research Institute
	Fujian College Forestry
University of Illinois, Chicago Circle	Jilin University of Technology
University of Illinois, Urbana	Fudan University
	Beijing University
	Chinese Academy of Sciences
Indiana University	Hangzhou University
	Shandong University
	Nankai University
Indiana University of Pennsylvania	Shanghai Foreign Languages Institute
University of Iowa	East China Technical University of Water Resources
	Wuhan Institute of Hydraulic & Electrical Engineering
Iowa State University	Shenyang Agricultural College
	Beijing Institute of Agricultural Mechanization
Johns Hopkins University	Beijing Medical Institute
	Chinese Academy of Medical Sciences
	Nanjing University
	Shanghai First Medical College
University of Massachusetts, Amherst	Beijing Normal University
	Shaanxi Teacher's College
	Fudan University
	Beijing Institute of Foreign Language
	Chinese Academy of Sciences, Institute of Systems Science

U.S. Institution	PRC Institution
University of Massachusetts, Amherst (*Continued*)	Beijing Teacher's College
	Foreign Language Press
	Central Translation Bureau
	Zhejiang University
	Tianjin University
Michigan State University	Beijing University
	Sichuan University
	Nankai University
	Guangxi University
	Xibei University
	Jiangsu Academy of Agricultural Sciences
	Heilongjiang Academy of Agricultural Sciences
	Northeast Agricultural College
	Chinese Academy of Sciences, Institute of Botany
	East China Normal University
University of Michigan	Beijing University
	Chinese Academy of Social Sciences
	Quinghua University
	Shanghai Jiaotong University
University of Minnesota	Chinese Academy of Sciences
	Jilin University of Technology
	Beijing Agricultural University
	Academy of Agricultural Science and Agricultural Engineering
	Nankai University
	Xian Jiaotong University
	Jilin University
	Fudan University
	Central South Institute of Mining and Metallurgy
	Changchun Institute of Geography
	Chongqing Architectural Engineering Institute
	Huazhong Institute of Technology
	Zhejiang University
	Beijing University
	Qinghua University
University of Missouri, Columbia	Anhui University
	Lanzhou University
	Zhengzhou University
	Xinhua News Agency
	Radio Beijing
	Foreign Language Publication and Distribution Bureau
	China Daily

U.S. Institution	PRC Institution
University of Missouri, Kansas City	Shanghai Second Medical College
	Wuhan University
	Harbin Medical University
University of Nebraska	South China Normal University
	Xibei University
	Sichuan University
	Beijing University
	East China Normal University
	Zhongshan University
University of New Mexico	Shanxi Teacher's College
Northeastern University	Beijing Polytechnic University
	Hunan University
	Shanghai University of Science and Technology
	Qinghua University
North Texas State University	Beijing Institute of Foreign Trade
Northwestern University	Fudan University
University of Notre Dame	Tongji University, Shanghai
Oberlin College	Taiyuan Institute of Technology
	Shanxi Agricultural University
	Beijing University of Iron and Steel Technology
Ohio State University	Hubei Bureau of Education
	Wuhan University
	Beijing Language Institute
Oregon State University	Shandong College of Oceanography
	Zhejiang Agricultural Institute
	Northeast Forestry Institute
Pace University	Beijing Institute of Foreign Trade
University of Pennsylvania	Beijing University of Iron and Steel Technology (with Penn's School of Engineering)
	Northwest Telecommunications Institute
	Shanghai Jiaotong University (with the Wharton and Engineering Schools)
Pennsylvania State University	South China Agriculture College
University of Pittsburgh	Tianjin University
	Northeast Institute of Technology
	Shandong University
	Xian Jiaotong University
	Zhongshan University
	Xinjiang University
	Shanghai Institute of Foreign Language
	East China Normal University
	South China Institute of Technology

U.S. Institution	PRC Institution
University of Pittsburgh (*Continued*)	Xian Foreign Language Institute Hubei Medical College
Pomona College	Nanjing University
Portland State University	Zhengzhou University Beijing Institute of Foreign Language
Princeton University	Fudan University
Rochester Institute of Technology	Shanghai University of Technology Zhejiang University of Hangzhou
Rutgers University	Jilin University
St. Mary's College of Maryland	Fudan University
San Francisco State University	Shandong Teacher's University
Seton Hall University	Beijing Institute of Foreign Trade Hangzhou School of Nursing Wuhan University
Siena Heights College	Jilin University
Simmons College	Wuhan University
South Dakota School of Mines and Technology	Kunming Institute of Technology
Southern Illinois University	Northeast Normal University Sichuan University Liaoning University
Stanford University	Beijing University Department of Chinese Language
State University of New York, Albany	Beijing Language Institute Beijing Normal University Fudan University Nanjing University Nankai University Beijing University
State University of New York, Cortland	Beijing Teacher's College Beijing Institute of Physical Education Chengdu Institute of Physical Culture
State University of New York, New Paltz	Beijing University
Temple University	Nankai University Tianjin Normal College
University of Tennessee	Lanzhou University Chongqing Institute of Architecture and English
University of Texas, Dallas	Qinghua University
University of Texas, Health Science Center, Houston	Beijing Second Medical College
Thunderbird Graduate School of International Business	Beijing Institute of Foreign Trade
University of Utah	Zhejiang University
Wake Forest-Bowman School of Medicine	Zhongshan Medical College

U.S. Institution	*PRC Institution*
University of Washington	Shandong University
	Nanjing Technical College Forest Production
	Chongqing Institute, Architecture and English
	Sichuan Medical College and Chongqing Medical College
Washington State University	Sichuan Foreign Language Institute
	Sichuan Agricultural College
	Chengdu University of Science and Technology
Washington University, St. Louis	Shanghai Jiaotong University
Wayne State University	Chinese Academy of Sciences
	Zhejiang University
	Chinese University of Science and Technology
	Shanghai Jiaotong University
Western Illinois University	Shandong College of Oceanography
	Yunnan Province
	Southwest Teacher's College
Western Michigan University	Guangxi University
	Xibei University
	Nankai University
University of Wisconsin, Madison	Harbin Medical College
	Harbin Teachers University
	Heilongjiang University
	Nankai University
	Harbin Institute of Technology (pending)
	Northeast Agricultural College (pending)
	Nanjing University (pending)
	Qinghua University (pending)
	Shanghai Jiaotong University (pending)
	Tianjin University (pending)
Yale University	Wuhan University
Yeshiva University	Beijing Medical College

APPENDIX B

Regulations Concerning the Admission of Foreign Students in Chinese Schools (1986)

Bureau of Foreign Affairs of the State Education Commission of the People's Republic of China

FOREWORD

The State Education Commission of the People's Republic of China is responsible for the admission and administration of foreign students. In order to promote exchanges in the fields of education, science and technology, and culture between China and other countries and to enhance international friendship, especially among young people, the Commission welcomes foreign students to study in China.

Apart from students sent by organizations in foreign countries, the Commission accepts foreign students mainly in accordance with agreements between the government of China and other governments. Colleges and universities in China are also encouraged to establish links with those of other countries and to exchange students.

At present about 70 colleges and universities in more than 20 cities accept foreign students. The specialities open to them are as follows: liberal arts, sciences, engineering, agriculture, medicine, fine arts and physical culture.

For the successful cooperation between the Commission and the organizations concerned of the students' home country and for the convenience of foreign students, the relevant regulations are set forth below.*

I. Categories of Foreign Students Eligible for Admission

A. Undergraduates: The applicant should be at least the equivalent of a graduate of senior middle school (high school) in China. He/she

---

*Information specific to the United States was provided by representatives of the Embassy of the People's Republic of China in Washington, D.C.

should be 25 years of age or younger. The program lasts from four to six years.

B. Candidates for a Master's degree: The applicant must come to China and pass the entrance examination for the Master's program at the institution to which he/she is assigned. If the applicant has been graduated with honors from a Chinese institution of higher education and wishes to work for an advanced degree at the same school, he/she may, upon recommendation by his/her department, be approved for the degree program without examinations. The applicant should be 35 years of age or younger. The program lasts from two to three years.

C. Candidates for a Doctorate degree: The applicant must be recommended by two of his/her professors and been approved for the doctoral program by the institution to which he/she has been assigned. The applicant should be 40 years of age or younger. The program lasts from two to three years.

D. General advanced students: The applicant should have completed at least two years of undergraduate studies in China or abroad, and should intend to continue studying in China a subject in which he/she already has some background (except for those wishing to study elementary Chinese). The applicant should be 35 years of age or younger. The program lasts from one to two years.

E. Senior advanced students: The applicant should have at least the equivalent of the Chinese Master's degree, or be a candidate for a Doctorate degree in another country. The student pursues advanced study independently under the direction of Chinese tutors. He/she should be 45 years of age or younger. The program generally lasts for one year.

II. Application Procedures

A. Applications from foreigners wishing to come to China to study under the auspices of their own government are dealt with by the Chinese Embassy or Consulate in the student's country, in consultation with the competent government authorities there; and/or by the Chinese State Education Commission, in consultation with the foreign diplomatic mission (embassy or consulate) or representative of the sponsoring organizations in China.

Foreigners who are already in China may apply for study through their countries' diplomatic missions or representatives of their sponsoring organizations in China.

Applications from Americans wishing to come to China to study as self-supporting students should be submitted to the Education Division of the Embassy of the People's Republic of China in Washington, D.C., or to one of the Chinese Consulates located in the United States. Addresses follow.

Education Division
Embassy of the People's
    Republic of China
2300 Connecticut Avenue, NW
Washington, DC 20008

Education Division
Consulate General of the
    People's Republic of China
3417 Montrose Boulevard
Houston, TX 77606

Education Division
Consulate General of the
    People's Republic of China
520 12th Avenue
New York, NY 10036

Education Division
Consulate General of the
    People's Republic of China
1450 Laguna Street
San Francisco, CA 94115

B. Applicants should submit the following materials:

(1) Application Form for Foreigners Wishing to Study in China, prepared by the Commission, to be completed by the applicant [see pages 162–165].

(2) Health Certificate, prepared by the Commission [see pages 166–167] to be completed by a medical doctor after a physical examination of the applicant, and should bear a seal of a clinic or a hospital. Those who fail to meet the health requirements will not be admitted to study in China. Should anyone who fails to meet the requirements come to China, he/she will be asked to leave the country within a month at his/her own expense.

(3) Duplicated copies of notarized diploma or certificate and school-certified transcript of complete academic records, in English or French or with a translation in English or French.

(4) Advanced students intending to pursue studies in the fine arts must also submit two letters of recommendation from teachers at or above the level of associate professor. Additional requirements are as follows:

> Art history: copy of an original term paper or other substantial piece of work on some aspect of art history;
> Graphic arts: three original pieces, or color photographs of six samples of the applicant's work;
> Music (performance): 30 minute tape recording of vocal or instrumental performance;
> Music (composition): copy of an original composition.

(5) Undergraduates in fine arts should submit the same material as above except that:

> —no letters of recommendation from teachers are required;
> —students of art history may submit a shorter criticism or commentary on some aspect of art history.

Time of Application:

(1) Undergraduates should apply during the period between April 1 and July 1 preceding the academic year for which application is made.

(2) All other applicants should apply during the period between March 1 and May 1 preceding the academic year for which application is made.

III. Entrance Examinations

A. After submitting their applications, undergraduates in the sciences, engineering, agriculture and medicine are required to take standard examinations in basic mathematics, physics and chemistry. Those intending to study management are required to take an examination in basic mathematics. In principle, these examinations are conducted by Chinese Embassies (or Consulates) in the students' home countries.

The provisions of this article may be replaced by those of an intergovernmental agreement, if there is one.

B. Candidates for graduate degrees must first come to China as advanced students. Candidates for Master's degrees must take written examinations in subjects required by the school in question (except for foreign languages and political studies). Candidates for Doctorate degrees will be examined orally by their faculty members. The school will notify students of the time of these examinations and of the subjects to be covered. Those who fail such examinations may nevertheless be permitted to stay on as advanced students at a level suited to their academic background. If they are recipients of Chinese government scholarships, the amount of their allowances will be reduced accordingly.

C. After they are enrolled, senior advanced students will undergo an evaluation by their tutors of their knowledge of their subjects. Those who do not meet the requirements must change their status to that of general advanced students. If they are recipients of Chinese government scholarships, the amount of their allowances will be reduced accordingly.

D. Undergraduates in liberal arts and general advanced students need take no entrance examinations. The admission decision will be based on the applicant's previous record.

IV. Admission and Registration Procedures

A. It is the State Education Commission that decides on admissions. The Commission will announce its decisions between the 1st of May and the 10th of August preceding the academic year for which application is made. The Commission will send to the sponsors (or applicant in the case of self-supporting students) via the Chinese Embassy or Consulate in each country the names of successful applicants from that country together with a notice of admission for each.

B. At the same time, the Commission will instruct the Chinese Embassy or Consulate in each country to issue the necessary visas. The successful applicant or his/her sponsor may obtain a visa from the Chinese Embassy or Consulate on presentation of the notice of admission. In general, students should not apply for visas at Chinese Embassies or Consulates in a third country.

C. The Commission will assign each foreign student to a school according to his/her particular field of study or subject of research. The Application Form for Foreigners Wishing to Study in China provides space for the applicant to indicate the subject he/she wishes to pursue in China and three choices of schools.* The Commission will try to take these preferences into account when making assignments. It cannot, however, arrange for foreign students to study in organizations not under its jurisdiction.

D. The Chinese academic year begins in September and foreign students who have been admitted are required to register, on the strength of the notice of admission, between September 1 and September 20. Those who fail to register within the time limit without valid reason will be disqualified.

V. Elementary Chinese and Preparatory Courses

A. Students who do not know Chinese, or whose knowledge of it is below the necessary level, are required to study the language and pass an examination in it before taking up their specialties. Undergraduates in Chinese language and literature, Chinese history, Chinese philosophy, history of Chinese art and Chinese medicine, are required to take a two year course in elementary Chinese. Undergraduates and advanced students in the sciences, engineering or other specialties are required to take a one year course in elementary Chinese.

General advanced students studying liberal arts who have attained an adequate level of competence in Chinese may enter their schools directly. Supplementary language courses will be organized for them by their schools, as necessary.

Senior advanced students studying liberal arts and candidates for advanced degrees should have attained a higher level of competence

---

*"The List of Specialities in Chinese Universities and Colleges Open to Foreign Students" is available for $2.50 postage and handling charges from the National Association for Foreign Student Affairs, 1860 19th Street NW, Washington, DC 20009.

in Chinese and be able to use it in pursuing study and research in their special fields.

B. Students who are required to take entrance examinations in mathematics, physics and chemistry under the provisions of Article III. A of these Regulations, and who reach a certain level in those examinations yet fail to meet the requirements for admission, may apply for a one year preparatory course in those subjects. Those who pass the final course examinations will be promoted to undergraduate classes; those who fail will be asked to withdraw.

The time spent in preparatory courses does not count toward the length of specialized studies.

VI. Academic Programs and Evaluations

A. All foreign students are expected to study hard, observe discipline and complete course work prescribed for them by their schools and teachers.

B. In principle, students are not permitted to transfer from one school to another, or to change either the subject or the duration of study that was agreed upon at the time of admission. In special cases, however, such changes may be approved by the Commission. For a change of subject, an application should be filed with the Commission before November 1 of the year in which the student is first enrolled, through the diplomatic mission or representative of the sponsoring organization in China of his/her country or through the sponsor in his/her home country. For extension of duration of study, an application should be filed with the Commission before March 1 of the year when the student is due to leave.

C. Undergraduates should, in principle, follow the regular academic program established by the school. If necessary, the school authorities will make adjustments in the student's program. Candidates for advanced degrees should, in principle, follow the same program as the Chinese students. General advanced students should follow the program originally agreed to; no tutors are allocated to them. Senior advanced students mainly study independently, with periodic guidance from the tutors assigned to them.

D. Schools are responsible for arranging field trips, field work and laboratory work in accordance with the needs of the academic programs. Students must observe the relevant regulations when they need to use reference books, archives and other materials.

E. With the exception of senior advanced students, who will receive written evaluations of their work from their tutors, all other students will be evaluated on the basis of their class work and of examinations taken at the end of each term. The schools will commend or reward those who excel in their studies and so notify their sponsors, if any. The sponsors may ask the school authorities for academic records of the students they are sponsoring.

F. Undergraduates who, in one academic year, fail a total of three subjects or two major subjects after taking make-up examinations are required to repeat the grade in question. They are allowed to repeat a grade no more than twice and to repeat the same grade only once.

Candidates for advanced degrees who fail in their examinations or thesis defense are allowed to extend the period of their studies in accordance with regulations formulated by the Chinese government.

General advanced students who fail in their final examinations for the academic year will be asked to withdraw from school. Schools using credit systems should follow relevant regulations.

VII. Class Attendance, Suspension of Studies, Withdrawal from Studies, Disciplinary Action

A. Foreign students are expected to attend classes regularly and are not allowed to be absent without valid reasons. If they are ill or have a special need to be absent, they should ask for leave in accordance with the school regulations.

B. Foreign students should abide by the academic calendar of the school in which they are enrolled. Chinese schools do not observe the national holidays or other festivals of foreign countries. However, on such occasions a foreign student concerned may, on request, be granted a leave of absence. Foreign students must not ask for leave to travel as tourists while school is in session.

C. A student who takes a leave of absence for more than two months at a time and cannot catch up with classes upon his/her return will be asked to suspend studies or to repeat the term. This must be done no later than the next academic year.

A student who is absent from class too often without valid reason will be subject to disciplinary action in accordance with the regulations of the school. In serious cases, he/she may be asked to withdraw from school.

A student who has an extended illness, or who is absent too often, or whose academic record is not satisfactory will be asked by the school authority to suspend study or to withdraw. The diplomatic mission and representative of the sponsoring organization in China of the student's country, or his/her sponsor at home, if any, will be notified of the action in writing.

If, for any reason, a foreign student wishes to suspend studies or to withdraw, or if the government or organizational sponsor decides to recall its students from China, the diplomatic mission in China of the student's country, or his/her organizational sponsor should submit a formal request to the Commission or to the school authorities.

D. A student who breaches the discipline of his/her school, damages public property, fights with others or behaves in other unacceptable ways, will be subject to disciplinary action by the school authorities. According to the circumstances and gravity of the offense, the student will be given a warning, a serious warning, or a demerit recording, be placed on probation, asked to withdraw or be expelled from school.

If a student on one year probation has clearly improved his/her conduct during the probation period, the disciplinary action against him/her may be rescinded. If a student fails to improve his/her conduct while on probation, he/she will be asked to withdraw from school.

When the school authorities take disciplinary action against a student, they will inform the student and also send written notification of the action to the diplomatic mission or representative of the sponsoring organization of the student's country in China, or to the student's sponsor at home.

VIII. Observance of Chinese Laws

A. Foreign students must obey the laws and decrees of the Chinese government, abide by the rules and regulations of their schools and respect Chinese ways and customs.

B. Foreign students coming to study in China should have ordinary passports. Before starting school, bearers of diplomatic, service or special passports should go through certain special procedures at Chinese public security departments and submit to them necessary documents issued by their countries' diplomatic missions or representatives of their sponsoring organizations in China. Such students will not enjoy diplomatic or other privileges during their studies in China.

C. Within a short period of time after their arrival in China, foreign students must obtain residence permits from the local public security departments.

When a foreign student wishes to travel to other countries, tour the Hong Kong and Macao regions, or return home for any reason, the diplomatic mission or representative of the sponsoring organization of his/her country in China should give written notification to the school ten days in advance, if possible. With the approval of the school, the student should go to the local public security department to apply for the necessary exit and reentry visas.

When a foreign student wishes to visit an area of China to which foreigners may gain access only with permission, he/she must apply to the local public security department for a travel permit.

D. Foreign students must observe the Chinese customs regulations concerning materials to be taken out of China or mailed abroad. The following items are allowable: textbooks, class handouts and related materials issued to them by the school, study notes, photographs and audiovisual materials related to study. Any materials issued by the school which are not intended for outside circulation must be approved for exit by the school authorities, who will provide the student with an itemized certificate of authorization to present to the customs officer.

E. Foreign students who have violated Chinese laws or regulations, endangered China's national security, disturbed public order or harmed the interests of others will be punished by the Chinese public security and judicial departments according to law.

IX. Board, Lodging and Medical Care

A. Chinese schools have separate dining halls for foreign students. However, foreign students may, if they wish, have meals in the canteens for Chinese students. They should observe the regulations of the dining halls and canteens and maintain order in them.

B. Chinese schools provide dormitories for their foreign students. In general, two students share one room. No special accommodations are available for married couples or for students' family members. Foreign students must abide by the school's regulations relating to housing.

C. Foreign students who fall ill during their studies in China may consult doctors in the school clinics, who will refer them to outside hospitals for treatment, if necessary.

Students on Chinese government scholarships enjoy free medical care. This, however, does not include the following: abortions, dentures, eyeglasses and diet supplements.

Self-supporting students are responsible for all their own medical expenses.

X. Extracurricular and Holiday Activities

A. Foreign students may take part in the activities organized by the student associations of their schools, as well as in the athletic and recreational activities of the Chinese students. They may join the various athletic and performing arts groups of their schools. They may also, if they wish, take part in activities organized by the Chinese to mark major holidays. Normal and friendly contacts between foreign students and Chinese teachers, students and people in general are encouraged.

B. If foreign students wish to organize activities in their school to celebrate their national days and major national festivals, they must obtain the approval of the school authorities. They must observe the rules and regulations of their schools in this connection.

C. Foreign students on Chinese government scholarships may join trips organized by schools during winter and summer vacations; every other year, the school will bear a portion of the expense for their travel and lodging. The schools will likewise pay parts of the expense for those scholarship students who are pursuing advanced studies for at least one academic year but less than two.

All self-supporting students and scholarship students who are pursuing advanced studies for less than one academic year may join these tours at their own expense.

XI. Academic Degrees and Certificates

A. Undergraduates and candidates for a Master's degree who pass the examinations at the end of their studies will receive certificates and, in accordance with the *Regulations of the People's Republic of China for Conferring Academic Degrees*, the Bachelor's and Master's degrees respectively. Candidates for a Doctorate degree who pass the final examinations and the thesis defense will be awarded Doctorate degrees. Those who fail such examinations will receive certificates of completion of studies.

General advanced students and senior advanced students who have completed the required work will receive certificates of advanced study. No degrees will be conferred upon them.

B. Students who withdraw from school before completing their programs will be issued certificates indicating the period of time during which they have studied.

C. Foreign students should leave China within 15 days after their graduation or conclusion of studies.

XII. Scholarships of the Government of the People's Republic of China

A. Scholarships of the Government of the People's Republic of China are awarded to certain foreign students by the Commission in accordance with bilateral exchange agreements between the governments concerned. The Commission provides a monthly allowance to the student in Chinese *renminbi* (*yuan*) and also allocates to the school a sum of money to cover his/her expenses for tuition, textbooks and class handouts, laboratory work, field trips, medical treatment, housing equipment, lodging and extracurricular activities. It provides an additional allocation to the school to cover the expenses of trips organized by the school on holidays.

B. The basic monthly allowance for living expenses of scholarship students is as follows:

—for undergraduate students: 180 *yuan*
—for Master's degree candidates and general
    advanced students: 200 *yuan*
—for Doctorate degree candidates and senior
    advanced students: 220 *yuan*

An additional monthly allowance of 30 *yuan* is provided to scholarship recipients in the following fields of study: physical culture, navigation, dance, theater and wind instruments. However, they will not receive this allowance until they start those studies.

An additional monthly allowance is provided to scholarship recipients studying in certain regions of China, as follows:

—in Guangdong and Fujian Provinces: 30 *yuan*
—in Gansu, Heilongjiang, Jilin and Liaoning Provinces: 10 *yuan*

C. Payment of allowances to scholarship students begins on the day of their arrival at school. Students who study for an entire academic year receive their allowances up to July 31 (including during the winter vacation). Those who study for more than one academic year will also receive their allowances during the intervening winter and summer vacations, even if they return home for a visit at that time. If a student remains absent from school without valid reason beyond the period of a prescribed vacation, no allowance will be issued to him/her for the period of unauthorized absence. Those who terminate their studies and return home before the end of the academic year will receive their allowances up to the month in which they return home.

Scholarships are discontinued during suspension of studies, and no retroactive payment is made after resumption of studies.

If a student withdraws from studies or is expelled from school, the scholarship is discontinued from the first day of the month following the withdrawal or expulsion.

XIII. Expenses Borne by Self-Supporting Students

A. Before coming to China, foreign students who are providing their own financial support must have a financial guarantor and must make sure that they have adequate resources to pay all expenses during the period of their studies here. All expenses must be paid in cash, according to the relevant provisions of the *Regulations Governing Grants to Foreign Scholarship Students and Fees for Self-Financing Foreign Students* (February 1985). [See Appendix C.]

B. For self-supporting students, school fees for tuition and housing are calculated in U.S. dollars and are to be paid after conversion into Foreign Exchange Certificates (FEC), according to the exchange rates of February 1 and September 1 of the year in which payments are made.

(1) Tuition fees for one academic year are as follows:
Students in the liberal arts
—Undergraduates and general advanced students: US$1,200
—Master's degree candidates: US$1,600
—Senior advanced students: US$2,000
—Doctorate degree candidates: US$2,500

Students in the sciences, engineering, agriculture, medicine, physical culture and fine arts
—Undergraduates: US$1,600
—General advanced students: US$2,000
—Master's degree candidates and senior advanced
    students: US$2,500
—Doctorate degree candidates: US$4,000

(2) Housing expenses are US$1.50 per bed per day for a double room in the school dormitory, two students sharing one room. The cost of a single room (available in some cases on request and with the approval of the school authorities) is US$4.00 per day.

(3) The student is responsible for his/her board, medical care, textbooks and class handouts. He/she is also responsible for expenses for additional laboratory work, field work and field trips which are not related to the teaching program, as well as the other expenses for transfer from one school to another.

C. Tuition is payable in two parts, half at the beginning of each term. Students who fail to pay tuition at the specified time will not be allowed to register. In special cases, students may apply to the school authorities for permission to delay payment. However, payment may not be delayed beyond one month after the beginning of the term, and a penalty will be charged for late payment in the amount of five percent of the total tuition for one term.

Students who stay at school for more than one term but less than a full academic year pay tuition for the entire academic year.

If, before the end of a term, a student transfers to another school for reasons not the responsibility of the Chinese, he/she will receive no refund of tuition, and no payments may be transferred to the new school. The student must pay tuition to the new school.

Housing expenses are also to be paid at the beginning of each term. However, if this creates a hardship for a student, with the approval of the school authorities, he/she may make monthly payments instead.

Students who terminate or suspend their studies, or who withdraw from school before the end of a term, must pay housing expenses only for the number of days they have actually lived in the dormitory.

Regulations Concerning Short-Term Study Courses for Foreigners (January 1983)

A. The State Education Commission of the People's Republic of China welcomes the voluntary participation of young people and others from countries outside China in short-term study courses in the Chinese language or any other specialty.

B. The Commission encourages the relevant Chinese institutions of higher education to sign bilateral agreements for the running of short-term courses directly with the relevant foreign institutions. The Commission also encourages relevant Chinese institutions to sign such agreements with friendly, non-profit, foreign organizations that are non-governmental. The kind of specialty, length of study and expenses of the short-term course may be negotiated through consultation by both parties. The agreement should be signed before December 1 of the year prior to the starting date of the course and it becomes effective only after approval by the competent authorities of the provinces, municipalities and autonomous regions where the relevant Chinese institutions are located.

C. The State Education Commission of China is also willing to hold discussions with governments of foreign countries on the matter of sending students to China to participate in short-term study courses. This item will be included in the bilateral exchange programs.

D. A short-term study course lasts at least four weeks and at most one normal school term, that is, around five months. Students of the course will receive a school badge and a temporary student's identity card from the relevant Chinese institution, so as to indicate their status during their stay in China. Upon completion of the course, students will receive a certificate stating their specialty and length of study and should return their school badges and/or identity cards to the relevant institutions in accordance with the rules.

E. The age limit for students in a short-term study course is 16 to 45.

F. Applicants should fill in the application form issued by the relevant Chinese institution of higher education which will decide on approval of the application. Those whose applications have been approved should hold ordinary passports. They must apply for an entry visa from the Chinese Embassy or Consulate in their own country, and not from a Chinese Embassy or Consulate in a third country.

G. The sponsoring party should appoint a leader among the students and send them to China together as a group.

H. Students in a short-term study course must observe the laws and decrees of the Chinese government, respect the Chinese people's customs and habits and abide by the rules and regulations of the relevant Chinese institutions of higher education.

I. Students in a short-term study course will bear their own tuition, lodging, textbook, travel and board expenses, which should be paid upon enrollment in accordance with the rules of the recipient institutions. In general, payment should be made directly by the students to the recipient institution. Should both sides agree, the expenses may be paid by the sponsoring party in one sum for all the students. The State Education Commission of China does not provide scholarships for students of short-term courses.

J. Students in a short-term study course can participate collectively in the trip organized by the recipient institutions in accordance with the relevant agreement. On such a trip, they enjoy the same preferential terms as long-term students. The recipient institutions are not responsible for arranging individual trips and a student making such a trip does not enjoy any preferential terms. No arrangements will be made by the State Education Commission of China or the relevant institutions for relatives and friends of students who wish to come to China to make a visit.

K. The students should return to their own countries as soon as possible after the conclusion of their study and organized trip. As a general rule, the State Education Commission of China and the relevant institutions will not transfer a student from a short-term course to a long-term one, nor extend his or her entry visa.

SHORT-TERM STUDY COURSES IN CHINA

The following is a 1986 list (incomplete) of institutions of higher education in China which offer short-term courses to foreigners:

Architecture
1. Nanjing Institute of Technology
2. Qinghua University (Beijing)
3. Tianjin University

Arts
1. Central Academy of Fine Arts (Beijing)
2. Central Institute of Arts and Crafts (Beijing)
3. Sichuan Academy of Fine Arts (Chongqing)
4. Zhejiang Academy of Fine Arts (Hangzhou)

Chinese Language and Culture

1. Anhui University (Hefei)
2. Beijing College of Iron and Steel Technology
3. Beijing Foreign Languages Institute
4. Beijing Institute of Post and Telecommunications
5. Beijing Language Institute
6. Beijing Normal University
7. Beijing Second Foreign Languages Institute
8. Beijing Teachers College
9. Beijing United University
10. Beijing University
11. Central China Teachers College (Wuhan)
12. Central Institute for Nationalities (Beijing)
13. Dalian Foreign Languages Institute
14. East China Normal University (Shanghai)
15. Fudan University (Shanghai)
16. Fujian Normal University (Fuzhou)
17. Guangxi Teachers College (Guilin)
18. Hangzhou University
19. Harbin Institute of Technology
20. Heilongjiang University (Harbin)
21. Inner Mongolia University (Hohhot)
22. Jilin University (Changchun)
23. Jinan University (Guangzhou)
24. Liaoning Teachers University (formerly College) (Dalian)
25. Liaoning University (Shenyang)
26. Nanjing Teachers University (formerly College)
27. Nanjing University
28. Nankai University (Tianjin)
29. North China Jiaotong University (Beijing)
30. Northeast Normal University (Changchun)
31. Northwest China University (Xi'an)
32. People's University of China (Beijing)
33. Shaanxi Normal University (Xi'an)
34. Shandong University (Jinan)
35. Shanghai International Studies University (formerly Shanghai Institute of Foreign Languages)
36. Shanghai Jiaotong University
37. Shanghai Teachers University (formerly College)
38. Shanxi University (Taiyuan)
39. Sichuan Teachers College (Chengdu)
40. Sichuan University (Chengdu)
41. Southwest China Jiaotong University (Emei County)
42. Southwest Teachers College (Chongqing)
43. Suzhou University (formerly Jiangsu Teachers College)
44. Tianjin Foreign Languages Institute
45. Tianjin Teachers University (formerly College)
46. Tianjin University
47. Wuhan University (Wuchang)
48. Xiamen University
49. Xi'an Foreign Languages Institute
50. Xi'an Jiaotong University
51. Yunnan Institute for Nationalities (Kunming)
52. Yunnan University (Kunming)
53. Zhongshan University (Guangzhou)

Law
1. East China Institute of Politics and Law (Shanghai)
2. Jilin University (Changchun)
3. Wuhan University (Wuchang)
4. Zhongshan University (Guangzhou)

Medicine
1. Beijing College of Chinese Medicine
2. Chengdu College of Chinese Medicine
3. Chongqing Medical University (formerly College)
4. Jinan University Medical College (Guangzhou)
5. Kunming Medical College
6. Nanjing College of Chinese Medicine

Music
1. Shanghai Music Conservatory

Veterinary Acupuncture
1. South China Agricultural College (Guangzhou)

Additional information about short-term study courses in China from the January 1983 publication of the then Ministry of Education, now State Education Commission, includes:

(1) Chinese is the language of instruction in Chinese language courses. The majority of teachers in these courses can use a foreign language to give explanations when necessary.

(2) Chinese institutions of higher learning conduct short-term courses of various kinds according to inter-institutional exchange programs. Subjects, durations, number of students, fees and other terms can be negotiated. No individual applications will be accepted.

(3) No scholarships from the Chinese government are granted to students of short-term study courses. All expenses will be borne by students themselves.

BUREAU OF FOREIGN AFFAIRS, STATE EDUCATION COMMISSION OF THE PEOPLE'S REPUBLIC OF CHINA

Application Form for Foreigners Wishing to Study in China

1. NAME (As for passport All block capitals)			ATTACH A RECENT PHOTOGRAPH HERE
2. NATIONALITY		3. SEX	
4. RELIGION		5. SINGLE MARRIED	
6. DATE AND PLACE OF BIRTH			
7. CURRENT ADDRESS			

8. EDUCATION HISTORY (In chronological order)	Institution	Dates attended	Degree or diploma received
	Category of secondary school attended	(1) General secondary school (2) Secondary school emphasizing liberal arts (3) Secondary school emphasizing sciences	
	University training	(1) Major subject (2) Minor courses	

9. STUDENT STATUS SOUGHT IN CHINA	(1) Undergraduate (2) General advanced student (3) Senior advanced student	
10. FINANCIAL RESOURCES	Scholarship granted by Chinese government	
	Scholarship granted by home-country government	
	Financial support from other organs	Guarantor's name Guarantor's address
	Self-paying	Guarantor's name Guarantor's address
11. PROPOSED DURATION OF STAY IN CHINA	Period of further elementary Chinese language study	
	Period of specialized study	
12. ACADEMIC REQUIRE-MENTS IN CHINA	(1) Undergraduate speciality	Names of proposed institutions I. II. III.
	(2) Speciality of General Advanced Student	Names of proposed institutions I. II. III.
	(3) Research topic of Senior Advanced Student	Names of proposed institutions I. II. III.
13. PERSON OR ORGAN IN CHINA RESPONSIBLE FOR YOUR AFFAIRS	(1) Home-country's Embassy in Beijing	
	(2) Other person or organ: Name of person or organ: Address and tel. no. in China:	

14. PRESENT CHINESE LANGUAGE LEVEL	(1) Duration of previous Chinese language study: (2) Place of study: (3) Present level 　　Reading　　　Listening　　　Speaking
15. OTHER LANGUAGES	
16. RELEVANCE OF PRO-POSED STUDY IN CHINA TO FUTURE WORK	
17. PREVIOUS WORK EXPERIENCE	

TO BE FILLED IN BY SENIOR ADVANCED STUDENTS ONLY	
18. DETAILED DESCRIP- TION OF RESEARCH TOPIC	
19. TITLE OF DOCTORAL THESIS YOU EXPECT TO COMPLETE	
20. TITLES OF ARTICLES, THESES AND OTHER PUB- LICATIONS	

NOTICE:

1. The State Education Commission of China, taking note of your preference, will determine the university or college where you are to study. Inconvenience is caused if you refuse its arrangements.
2. Please choose your speciality from the List of Specialities in Chinese Universities and Colleges Open to Foreign Students provided by the Ministry of Education of China.
3. Relevant academic certificates are required of students of all categories.

DATE: SIGNATURE:

HEALTH CERTIFICATE

Name		Sex	
		Age	
Personal medical history			
Family medical history			

E.N.T.	Eyesight	left	Ability to distinguish colours	
		right		
	Auditory ability	left	Disease of the ears	
		right		
	Tonsils			

Surgery	Lymph glands	
	Thyroid gland	
	Vertebral column	
	Limbs	
	Joints	
	Skin	
	External genital organ	
	Hernia	

Medicine	Heart and blood vessels		Blood pressure	
	Lungs			
	Abdomen		Liver	
			Spleen	

Nerves and mentality

Fluoroscopy of the chest

Blood	Hemoglobin		Leucocyte	Blood type
	GPT		T.T.T.	HAA
	Wassermann and Kahn			

Urine	Albumin		Microscopic examination	

Stool	Worm eggs

Others

Remarks of the doctor:

Seal of the hospital
Signature of the doctor
Date

APPENDIX C

Regulations Governing Grants to Foreign Scholarship Students and Fees for Self-Financing Foreign Students (February 1, 1985)

State Education Commission
People's Republic of China

1. Starting February 1, 1985, the State Education Commission of the People's Republic of China will apply the following standards in extending financial aid, denominated in *renminbi*, to foreign scholarship students:

a. Monthly living stipend: 150 *yuan* for undergraduates; 170 *yuan* for general advanced students and master's degree students; 190 *yuan* for senior advanced students and doctorate degree students.

b. Monthly supplements for students majoring in physical education, navigation, dance, theater and wind instruments is 30 *yuan*.

c. Monthly regional differential: 30 *yuan* for students in Guangdong and Fujian provinces; 10 *yuan* for students in Gansu, Heilongjiang, Jilin and Liaoning provinces.

The following expenses are covered directly by universities and colleges for foreign scholarship students (and are not included in grants given to the students):

a. 90 *yuan* for lodging for each student, 20 *yuan* for medical care, 12 to 14 *yuan* for activities per month, 40 *yuan* per semester for books.

b. Other expenses, such as for furniture, bedding, water and electricity, central heating, cooling devices, laboratory equipment, field trips and subsidies for winter clothing are covered by universities and colleges, subject to certain regulations.

The total cost of such a scholarship is 6,000 *yuan renminbi* per academic year.

2. The fee scale for self-financing foreign students set by the then

Ministry of Education (now the State Education Commission) in 1980 is obviously too low. The fees being paid by self-financing foreign students are not covering the cost of their studies to their universities and colleges. Therefore, starting September 1, 1985, Chinese universities and colleges will charge self-financing foreign students the following fees: (Calculated in U.S. dollars. Foreign currencies must be paid in Foreign Exchange Certificates.)

a. Tuition (per person per academic year) Liberal arts: $1,200 for undergraduates; $1,600 for master's degree students; $2,500 for doctorate degree students; $1,200 for general advanced students; $2,000 for senior advanced students.

Science, engineering, agriculture and medicine as well as physical education and arts: $1,600 for undergraduates; $2,500 for master's degree students; $4,000 for doctorate degree students; $2,000 for general advanced students and $2,500 for senior advanced students.

Elementary Chinese language courses, and pre-university courses in mathematics, physics and chemistry: $1,200.

b. Lodging fees: $1.50 a day per student in a double room (two beds) in a campus dormitory. $4 per day for a single room, assuming the college can provide this. If a student leaves the university or college, either because he or she has completed his or her studies or has suspended or discontinued them for any reason, his or her rent will be assessed according to the days he or she has used the room.

c. Apart from the above-mentioned fees paid to the college by the self-financing foreign students themselves, the Commission will continue to provide subsidies to universities and colleges that enroll self-financing foreign students.

d. All expenses for board, medical care and field trips as well as for field work, laboratory experiments and professional trips outside the scope of the study program are to be paid by the self-financing foreign students themselves.

e. Tuition and lodging fees may be paid in installments during the academic year. However, half of the total must be paid before the start of each semester. Students enrolled for more than half a year but less than one year must pay a full-year's fees. Those enrolled for one semester or less must pay a half-year's fees. Those who have not paid by the required time will not be permitted to register. Payment may be delayed in special cases only after the student's request in this regard has been approved by university or college authorities. But five percent of the total fee will be added on for late payment, a fee which must be paid no later than one month into the semester.

f. The foreign currency paid by self-financing foreign students for college expenses will be converted into Foreign Exchange Certificates according to the exchange rates in effect on February 1 and September 1, respectively.

g. Those who transfer to another university or college on their own initiative may not receive a refund for fees paid. Fees for their studies at the new university or college will be assessed according to regulations.

h. These regulations do not apply to research scholars in China. Those who enjoy mutual exemption from tuition or other expenses under bilateral agreements are subject to the terms of their special arrangements.

i. The fee scale for self-financing foreign students already studying in China remains unchanged. Undergraduates enrolled in programs leading to degrees may continue their studies under the old regulations through graduation and advanced students may finish their predetermined course. Anyone who wants to continue his or her studies beyond the current program will do so according to the new regulations.

When these new regulations take effect, the old regulations governing fees for self-financing foreign students will be terminated.

APPENDIX D

Regulations Concerning Applications by Foreign Research Scholars to Engage in Scientific Research in Institutions of Higher Education in China (September 1985)

State Education Commission People's Republic of China

1) In order to promote academic exchanges and enhance friendship between the peoples of China and other countries, the State Education Commission of the People's Republic of China welcomes foreign research scholars to come to China to conduct scientific research in a special field.

2) The term "foreign research scholars," here, applies to those who come to conduct scientific research in a Chinese institution of higher education open to foreigners. They should hold the professional title of professor or associate professor, or possess the equivalent status, or be in China for post-doctoral research.

3) In general, foreign research scholars coming to China should do so through government exchange programs (except for those who come on inter-university exchange programs). The State Education Commission will make arrangements for foreign research scholars who come to China under government exchange programs or any other special agreements to conduct scientific research in higher education. No arrangements will be made by the Commission for those who intend to conduct research in organizations other than institutions of higher education.

4) *Application procedures:* The State Education Commission will send a copy of the "Application Form for Foreign Research Scholars to Conduct Scientific Research in Chinese Institutions of Higher Education" to foreign embassies in China, foreign sponsoring departments or individuals in accordance with relevant agreements. At least four months

171

prior to their arrival in China, the applicants should fill out the application form in duplicate in Chinese and send one copy to the State Education Commission of China and the other to the host Chinese institution of higher education. The details will be worked out by foreign sponsoring departments or the individual research scholars themselves through direct consultations with the relevant institutions of higher education in China.

The host Chinese institution will send a formal invitation to the applicant after it approves the application. Meanwhile, the Commission will authorize the relevant Chinese diplomatic mission abroad to issue a visa to the applicant. After being registered, applicants will be granted a "Foreign Research Scholar Card" by the host institution.

5) *Expenses:* A monthly research fee of $300 in the form of foreign exchange certificates is to be paid by self-supporting foreign research scholars (based on the exchange rate of foreign currency to Chinese *renminbi* on the day applicants are registered). For those staying less than half a month, the fee will be calculated for half a month; for those staying more than a half a month but less than a month, the fee will be calculated for a whole month. Should the $300 be insufficient to cover the research expenses, an extra fee will be charged according to the regulations of the host institution. In addition, board, lodging, travel, medical, photocopying, and field trip expenses will be borne by the individual research scholars themselves.

Self-supporting foreign scholars who are exempt from the research fee according to relevant agreements will pay their own board, lodging, transportation, medical, photocopying, and field trip expenses. If their monthly laboratory fee exceeds $300, they should pay the difference.

Foreign research scholars sponsored by the Chinese side in accordance with the relevant agreements are exempt from the research fee, the expenses covering a single room on campus, medical [care], and transportation in the city related to academic activities. Each month, the relevant Chinese institutions will provide them 250 *yuan* in *renminbi* for board and pocket money. During their stay in China, they will be offered 500 *yuan* in *renminbi* for academic field trips. The costs of photocopying and any field trip expenses over 500 *yuan* in *renminbi* must be borne by themselves. All expenses for foreign research scholars' family members should be paid by themselves.

6) Foreign research scholars must observe laws and decrees of the Chinese government, abide by the rules of the recipient institutions and respect the Chinese people's customs and habits.

7) The Chinese institution of higher education chosen by a research scholar for his or her research must be in a place open to foreigners. As a rule, no change in place should be made during the stay in China. If the necessity arises to conduct research in another institution or take

field trips in other places, a separate plan should be worked out through consultation by the recipient institution and the research scholar.

8) Foreign research scholars should submit their research plans to relevant host institutions and carry out independent scientific research with the consent of the host institutions. Generally, the plan will not be changed after it is made. After the conclusion of their research work, they should submit to the host institutions a brief report of their research and a list of the material they intend to take home. Only material which falls within the limits set by the host institutions and Chinese customs can be taken out of China.

Foreign research scholars wishing to have Chinese assistants help in their independent scientific research should state their specific requests on the application form, and the salaries of the Chinese assistants should be determined through consultation with the host institutions. The Chinese assistants are selected by the Chinese side. The publication of the results of their research should include an acknowledgment of the role of the Chinese assistants.

9) Research studies and field trips by foreign research scholars can be conducted only in places open to foreigners. As a general rule, the Commission and relevant institutions do not arrange such activities in areas not open to foreigners. In general, the field trip will last two weeks in every half year.

10) If foreign research scholars require data or other written material, they should apply to the recipient institutions and their requests will be dealt with in accordance with the decrees of the Chinese government and regulations of the departments concerned.

11) Foreign research scholars are expected to be able to use Chinese as a working language. The Chinese side will not be responsible for providing translators or interpreters.

12) Foreign research scholars will generally be provided with accommodations in hotels while in China. Where conditions permit, they can also board and lodge at the relevant institutions with the latters' consent. From the port of entry to the final destination, the sponsor or the foreign research scholars themselves will be responsible for their own board, accommodations, and transportation.

13) Foreign research scholars are advised not to bring their families during their stay in China. Should their families come to China, the Chinese side will not be responsible for arrangements regarding their work, schooling or enrollment in nurseries.

14) The above regulations do not apply to those foreign scholars who come to China to give lectures, make short-term visits, or conduct special joint research projects according to other relevant agreements. All arrangements for them in China, including their expenses, will be dealt with in accordance with the relevant agreements.

APPENDIX E

Information on the Recruitment of Foreign Experts (1985)

Foreign Experts Bureau of the State Council
People's Republic of China

Chinese institutions of higher learning, the press, radio and publishing houses wish to recruit foreign scholars and specialists for work in China to help train the qualified personnel needed for building socialism. The information in this regard is as follows:

I. Recruitment Range and Work Assignment

Lecturers and professors who wish to teach foreign languages, science and technology, finance, trade, banking, business management and law in Chinese institutions of higher learning and those who wish to do editing, translating, and polishing in press, radio, and publishing departments may apply to either the Foreign Experts Bureau of the State Council or the nearest Chinese Embassy or Consulate.

A. Lecturers or professors of foreign languages recruited for institutions of higher learning are expected to perform the following assignments:

To upgrade the professional skill of Chinese foreign language teachers;

To teach undergraduates and postgraduates;

To counsel and guide Chinese teachers;

To offer advice on extracurricular language training activities and to supervise graduates in writing academic papers;

To compile and edit teaching and reference material when required;

To give general knowledge lectures about their own countries and on topics in the fields of culture, history or other subjects as required.

174

B. Senior lecturers or professors of science, engineering, finance, trade, banking, business management, law and the like are expected to perform the following duties:

To upgrade the professional level of Chinese instructors;

To train Chinese teachers and teach senior students in specialized subjects;

To give guidance to postgraduates on scientific research projects;

To advise on carrying out experiments in their specialties and in laboratory work;

To compile and edit teaching and reference materials when required.

Language personnel recruited for press, radio and publishing institutions are expected to take on the following responsibilities:

To translate Chinese articles or scripts or revise or polish translations of such material;

To re-edit or re-write articles;

To improve the efficiency and language skills of Chinese translators.

II. Qualifications for Foreign Experts

A. Language lecturers and professors:

(1) Should have a relatively high attainment in their own language and literature.

(2) Should have been engaged in regular language teaching or the teaching of literature at university or college levels or should have been regular language or literature teachers for five years or more in senior high schools, and possess a senior high school teacher's certificate.

(3) Should have obtained an MA or higher degree.

B. Translators, polishers and editors:

(1) Should have had at least several years experience in journalism or editing.

(2) Should have a relatively high attainment in their own language and literature; or have had experience in creative writing or in translating literary works.

(3) Are expected to understand English or Chinese in addition to their own languages if their mother tongue is not English.

C. Lecturers or professors of science, engineering, trade, finance, banking, business management and law:

(1) Should be qualified with an MA degree or higher with the rank of lecturer, engineer, research fellow or higher.

(2) Should have relatively high attainments in the basic theory of their specialty (or specialities).

(3) Should be familiar with the latest development of their specialty; should be qualified to compile and edit teaching materials, or to assume the responsibility in guiding laboratory work and give direction on scientific research in their special fields.

D. All experts working in China are expected to observe the laws and decrees of the Chinese government, and the relevant rules and regulations of the locality and their host organization.

They are expected to fulfill the obligations drawn up and signed in the contract. All experts are expected to respect Chinese social and moral norms.

E. Foreign experts in press, radio and publication institutions are expected to work six days a week, eight hours a day. Those who assume responsibilities at institutions of higher learning for compiling, editing or revising reference materials are likewise expected to work six days a week, eight hours a day.

Teaching loads at colleges or universities should be no less than 12 classroom hours in addition to compiling, editing or revising teaching materials; recording; counselling and other teaching activities. The total work load for a teacher should be no less than 20 hours besides the time needed for preparing classes.

F. Experts recruited as above must provide personal health certificates. The same applies to family members who accompany them to China.

G. Experts so recruited should have no unfinished business or legal entanglements in their own countries.

III. Procedures to Be Followed by Applicants

A. Persons having the above-mentioned qualifications may submit an application in writing to the Foreign Experts Bureau of the State Council, the People's Republic of China or to any Chinese Embassy or Consulate. [See page 148.] Applicants are to furnish their curriculum vitae (see Appendix I to these regulations) and to supply their credentials and other references (see Appendix II to these regulations).

All such information must be authentic. If false information is given by the applicant, the host organizations have the right to cancel the agreement or to terminate the contract, and to demand financial compensation for costs sustained by the host.

B. When a candidate's application has been preliminarily approved, the Foreign Experts Bureau will recommend the applicant to the prospective host organization for further consideration. The host organization will communicate with the applicant by correspondence. An interview or a written examination may be conducted for applicants when necessary.

Given the willingness of both the inviting and invited parties, a contract will be sent abroad to the approved applicant for signature. This will serve as an initial agreement before the expert comes to China to report for duty.

The contract is legally valid. Both parties should observe them [it].

Applicants who do not receive a reply within three months can assume that the application has not been accepted.

C. The invitee, after signing the draft agreement, is expected to go through the necessary formalities for leaving for China at the nearest Chinese Embassy or Consulate. The host organization will inform the embassy or consulate concerned in advance.

IV. Remuneration and Accommodation

Remuneration for the invited party consists of two parts, namely net income which is the expert's monthly salary, and benefits which include lodging, transportation to and from work to the place of residence and medical service provided by the host organization. Following are the concrete terms:

A. The salary of the invited expert is determined by work accomplished and professional ability, with due consideration for the expert's record, experience and education.

Any foreign expert who has completed one calendar (or academic) year's service shall be given half a month's extra salary.

B. Monthly salary ranges from Y500 to Y1,500.

For well-known scholars, professors and persons with special skill the salary is negotiable.

C. An expert whose spouse or family has been brought to China may have 30 percent of the agreed salary converted into foreign currency. For those who do not bring any family member, 50 percent of the salary may be converted into foreign currency.

D. During the term of service the invited experts and their family members shall enjoy free medical service in accordance with China's medical system.

E. Those whose term of service is at least one calendar (or academic) year are provided direct route tourist class air tickets to and from China. If the invited expert wishes to purchase his/her international air ticket to China, reimbursement will be made in Chinese *renminbi* (equal to the cost of economy-class flight, as aforesaid).

An expert who has worked less than half a year and then discontinues the contract must pay his/her own return international travel expenses, and also repay the travel expenses the host organization has already provided for his/her coming to China.

F. An expert who has worked a calendar (or academic) year shall be entitled to one month's vacation, the vacation time of those working in colleges and universities shall correspond with the Chinese academic vacation in those institutions. The expert will then receive his/her regular salary, plus an additional annual Y800 vacation allowance.

Those who have worked half a year (or a semester in succession but less than one year) shall be entitled to a two-week vacation and Y400.

An expert who works less than half a year is not entitled to any vacation allowance.

G. Foreign experts whose term of service is a calendar (or academic) year or longer may bring their spouse and children under 12, whose round-trip and housing in China will also be paid for by the host organization.

H. All expenses for a short visit to the invited expert by his/her family members or close relatives shall be borne by themselves.

I. If an expert and his/her family come to China by air, the host organization will pay for overweight air luggage, not exceeding twenty-four (24) kilogrammes per person or seventy-two (72) kilogrammes for a family of more than three. This extra luggage must be shipped as unaccompanied luggage if the cost is to be paid by the host organization.

All correspondence should be addressed to:

The Foreign Experts Bureau of the State Council
P.O. Box 300
Beijing, People's Republic of China

APPENDIX I

Contents of Curriculum Vitae

1. Personal Information: Name, sex, nationality, place and date of birth, present address and present place of employment.

2. Academic Qualifications: Pre-college, college or university, graduate school, major subject(s), assessment of academic paper, degree(s).

3. Professional Experience: Name of institution(s) and professional title(s), academic rank(s).

4. Publications: List of materials published, dates and names of publication, brief description of content of major works.

5. Health: Any illnesses or any physical handicaps. Present state of health.

6. Proposed time for coming to China; probable term of stay in China.

7. Type of work unit, or region preferred.

8. Name of spouse, date of birth, nationality, education and state of health.

9. Accompanying Children: Name, sex, date of birth, education and state of health.

10. Travel experience.

11. Have you other special skills or qualifications?

12. Knowledge of foreign languages and degree of proficiency.

APPENDIX II

Credentials Requested

1. Academic Credentials: Copies of scholastic records such as diploma(s) or certificate(s), university or college transcripts.

2. Professional Credentials: Descriptions of previous professional activities.

3. Three Letters of Recommendation: One is from a university chancellor or president of educational institution, and two are from the deans (chairpersons) of your department, or the heads of your place of work.

4. Publications: Sample sections from your published articles or books.

5. Health Report: A health certificate including that of spouse issued within the last two months by an accredited doctor or a hospital.

WORK APPLICATION

Full Name	Photograph
Nationality	
Date of Birth	
Place of Birth	

Marital Status	Wife's (Husband's) Name

Present Address

Present Occupation
  and Place of Work

Academic Background

Work Experience

Publications

Knowledge of Languages

Possible Time for Coming to China

Term of Stay in China
State of Health
Accompanying Children (If Any)
Remarks
Remarks

Date

Signature

APPENDIX F

Japanese Encephalitis Vaccine Investigators in the United States

ALABAMA
Richard J. Whitley, M.D.
University of Alabama in
Birmingham
Department of Pediatrics
Children's Hospital Tower,
Suite 653
Birmingham, AL 35294
205-934-5316

ALASKA
Rodman Wilson, M.D.
Room 319
825 L Street
Anchorage, AK 90502
907-264-6724

ARIZONA
Joseph Rea, M.D.
1145 N. Warren Ave.
Tucson, AZ 85719
602-626-7900

CALIFORNIA
Smith Adron Ketchum
Overseas Medical Center
No. 10 California Street
San Francisco, CA 94111
415-982-8380

Victor L. Kovner, M.D.
12311 Ventura Blvd.
Studio City, CA 91604
818-762-1167

David A. Mathison, M.D.
Scripps Clinic & Research
Foundation
10666 N. Torrey Pines Road
La Jolla, CA 92037
619-457-8616

Charles McKinney, M.D.
Assistant Director
Occupational & Preventive
Medicine
Cowell Hospital
University of California at Davis
Davis, CA 95616
916-752-2300

Ronald M. Schwartz, M.D.*
Occidental Petroleum Corporation
10889 Wilshire Boulevard
Los Angeles, CA 90024
213-208-8800;
213-879-1700

Bob Young, M.D.
29 West Anatamu
Santa Barbara, CA 93101
805-965-0052

183

COLORADO
Steven K. Mostow, M.D.
Assistant Chairman
Department of Medicine
Rose Medical Center
4567 East 9th
Denver, CO 80220
303-320-7277;
303-320-2974

Jack D. Poland, M.D.
Centers for Disease Control
P.O. Box 2087
Ft. Collins, CO 80522-2087
303-221-6429

CONNECTICUT
Michele Barry, M.D.
Director (Medicine)
Tropical Medicine and
    International Travellers Clinic
Yale-New Haven Hospital
New Haven, CT 06504
203-785-2476

Kenneth R. Dardick, M.D., FACP
Mansfield Professional Park
Storrs, CT 06268
203-487-0002

DISTRICT OF COLUMBIA
Donald Burke, M.D.*
Division of Communicable Diseases
Walter Reed Army Medical Center
Washington, DC 20307-5100
202-576-3757

Lawrence J. D'Angelo, M.D., MPH
International Health Service
Georgetown University Hospital
3800 Reservoir Road, NW
Washington, DC 20007
202-625-7379-Georgetown
202-745-2178-CHWMC

Andre LeBrun, M.D.*
Medical Department of the World
    Bank
1818 H Street, NW
Washington, DC 20433
202-477-4733

Dr. David M. Parenti
Assistant Professor of Medicine
The George Washington University
2150 Pennsylvania Avenue, NW
Washington, DC 20037
202-676-5558

Martin S. Wolfe, M.D.
2141 K Street, NW, Suite 408
Washington, DC 20037
FTS 632-3401

FLORIDA
David Dodson, M.D.
Travelers Medical Service
Palm Beach Medical Group
705 North Olive Avenue
West Palm Beach, FL 33401
305-832-8531

Caroline MacLeod, M.D.
Institute of Tropical Medicine
1780 NE 168th Street
Miami, FL 33162
305-947-1722

GEORGIA
A. Walter Hoover, M.D.*
Employee Health Service Clinic
Building 4, Room 121
Centers for Disease Control
1600 Clifton Road, NE
Atlanta, GA 30333
404-329-3385

HAWAII
Steven Berman, M.D.
Suite Number 810
1380 Lusitana Street
Honolulu, HI 96813
808-524-0066

ILLINOIS
Pierce Gardner, M.D.
University of Chicago Hospitals
5841 S. Maryland
Chicago, IL 60637
312-962-1448

Dr. Ronald Massarik
M.C. 3805
AMACO Corporation
200 E. Randolph Drive
Chicago, IL 60601
312-856-2814

John Phair, M.D.
Department of Medicine
NW University Medical School
303 E. Chicago Avenue
Chicago, IL 60611
312-649-8196

Barbara Z. Surmaczynska, M.D.
200 E. Randolph
Chicago, IL 60601
312-856-5406

INDIANA
Joseph Jackson, M.D.
Family Practice Center
Indiana University Medical Center
1100 West Michigan
Indianapolis, IN 46223
317-264-2169

IOWA
Laverne A. Wintermeyer
Iowa Department of Health
Robert Lucas State Office Building
Des Moines, IA 50319
515-281-5605

KANSAS
Larry Rumans, M.D.
Medical Consultant, P.A.
Institute of Medical Infectious
    Diseases
631 Horne, Suite 420
Topeka, KS 66606
913-234-8405

LOUISIANA
Joseph A. Bocchini, Jr., M.D.
Chief, Pediatrics Infectious Diseases
Department of Pediatrics
School of Medicine in Shreveport
LSU Medical Center
1501 Kings Highway,
P.O. Box 33932
Shreveport, LA 71130-3932
318-674-6072

George A. Pankey, M.D.
1514 Jefferson Highway
New Orleans, LA 70121
504-838-4005

MARYLAND
Major Gilcin Meadors, III, M.D.*
Department of the Army
U.S. Army Medical Research
    Institute of Infectious Diseases
Fort Detrick, MD 21701-5011
301-663-7655

C. J. Peters, M.D.*
Disease Assessment Division
USAMRIID
Fort Detrick
Frederick, MD 21701
301-663-7193

Gerald V. Quinnan, M.D.
8800 Rockville Pike, Room 2D-24
Bethesda, MD 20205
301-496-3144

Captain Brian Rothstein, M.D.*
Department of the Army
U.S. Army Medical Research
    Institute of Infectious Diseases
Fort Detrick, MD 21701-5011
301-663-7631

Dr. R. Bradley Sack, Director
Division of Geographic Medicine
Department of International Health
School of Hygiene and Public
    Health
The Johns Hopkins University
615 North Wolfe Street
Baltimore, MD 21205
301-955-6931

MASSACHUSETTS
Dona Felfenstein, M.D.
Infectious Disease Unit
Gray-4
Massachusetts General Hospital
Boston, MA 02114
617-726-3813

Dr. Leonard Marcus
148 Highland Avenue
Newton, MA 02160
617-527-4003
    and
154 East Main Street
Westboro, MA 01581
617-366-0060

Dr. Michael Sands
Baystate Medical Center
Infectious Diseases Service
759 Chestnut Street
Springfield, MA 01199
413-787-5376

Joan Savitsky, M.D.
Outpatient Department
Mount Auburn Hospital
330 Mount Auburn Street
Cambridge, MA 02238
617-492-3500, X1266

MICHIGAN
Louis Saravolatz, M.D.
Division of Infectious Diseases
Henry Ford Hospital
2799 West Grand Blvd.
Detroit, MI 48202
313-876-2573

B. Sugarman, M.D.
ATTN: Maureen Chajnack
Internal Medicine
MSU Clinical Center
138 Service Road
East Lansing, MI 48824
517-353-3049

MINNESOTA
Wallace R. Anderson, M.D.
Boynton Health Service
University of Minnesota
410 Church Street
Minneapolis, MN 55455
612-373-3742

MISSOURI
Helen Aff, M.D.
Pharmacy
601 S. Brentwood
Clayton, MO 63105
314-854-6630

NEW HAMPSHIRE
Anthony Lopez, M.D.
Hitchcock Clinic
25 South River Road
Bedford, NH 03102
603-624-1313

Robert Smith, M.D.
Assoc. Professor of Clinical
    Medicine
Dartmouth-Hitchcock Medical
    Center
Hanover, NH 03756
603-646-5279

NEW JERSEY
Dr. Jerome F. Levine
Infectious Disease Section
New Jersey Medical School
Hackensack Medical Center
30 Prospect Avenue
Hackensack, NJ 07601
201-441-2000

NEW MEXICO
Dr. Donald A. Romig
1482 C St. Francis Drive
Santa Fe, NM 87501
505-984-1981

Michael Wilder, M.D.
1456 St. Francis Drive
Santa Fe, NM 87501
505-988-9849

James Windeck, M.D.
Lovelace Medical Center
5400 Gibson Blvd. SE
Albuquerque, NM 87108
505-262-7008

NEW YORK
Louis C. Abelson, M.D.
Kennedy Medical Office
Bldg. 198
Kennedy Airport
Jamaica, NY 11430
718-656-5344

Mary Fleissner, M.D.
(See Sillman)

John Frame, M.D.
120 East 62nd Street
New York, NY 10021
212-838-8498

Eugene Sillman, M.D.
Rath Office Building
95 Franklin Street
Buffalo, NY 14202
716-846-7656

Eileen Hilton, M.D.
Long Island Jewish Hospital
Department of Infectious Diseases
Room B202
New Hyde Park, NY 11042
718-470-7290

Warren Johnson, M.D.
International Health Care Service
440 East 69th Street
New York, NY 10021
212-472-6803
212-472-5100 Evenings

NORTH CAROLINA
Jerry Withrow, M.D.
c/o The Family Doctor
151 Rams Plaza
Chapel Hill, NC 27514
919-968-1985

OHIO
Richard Olds, M.D.
Division of Geographic Medicine
University Hospital
University Circle
Cleveland, OH 44106
216-844-3205

Tennyson Williams, M.D.
Chairman, Department of Family
    Medicine
456 Clinic Drive
Columbus, OH 43210
614-421-8007

OREGON
David N. Gilbert, M.D.
4805 N.E. Glisan
Portland, OR 97213
503-230-6086

Mark O. Loveless, M.D.
10535 N.E. Glisan
Portland, OR 97220
503-254-8812

David White, M.D.
2460 Willamette Street
Eugene, OR 97405
503-687-1163

PENNSYLVANIA
Dr. Caryn Bern
Student Health Service
Hospital of the University of
    Pennsylvania
University of Pennsylvania
Philadelphia, PA 19104
215-662-2850

Dr. Mathew Levison
(Envel. add. to Dr. David Kaufman)
Division of Infectious Diseases
Medical College of Pennsylvania
3300 Henry Avenue
Philadelphia, PA 19129
215-842-6975

Nalini Rao, M.D.
Park Plaza Building
Suite 217
128 North Craig Street
Pittsburgh, PA 15213
412-681-1633

Frans J. Vossenberg, M.D.
Medical Associates of King of
    Prussia
491 Allendale Road, Suite 307
King of Prussia, PA 19406
215-265-2240

TENNESSEE
David Bell, M.D.*
5120 Yale Road
Memphis, TN 38134
901-373-2100

Dr. Joseph M. Bistowish
Metropolitan Health
311 23rd Ave., N.
Nashville, TN 37203
615-327-9313

TEXAS
Charles Haley, M.D.
1936 Amelia Court
Dallas, TX 75235
214-920-7899

David E. Miller, M.D.
Senior Medical Director, Functions
Shell Oil Company
P.O. Box 2463
Houston, TX 77001
713-241-4639

Thomas Sloan, M.D.
2201 Cedar Crest
Abilene, TX 79601
915-676-9260

VERMONT
Paul Young, M.D.
1 South Prospect
Burlington, VT 15401
802-656-4696

VIRGINIA
Garth B. Dettinger, M.D.
Assistant Health Director
Fairfax County
4080 Chainbridge Road
Fairfax, VA 22030
703-691-2433

WASHINGTON
Robby Eaves, D.O.*
P. O. Box 862
Steilacoom, WA 98388
206-967-8489

Michael A. Heath, M.D.*
P. O. Box 862
Steilacoom, WA 98388
206-967-8489

Elaine Jong, M.D.
Tropical Med. Travel Clinic
Room 16, University of Washington
Seattle, WA 98195
206-543-7902

R. M. Nicola, M.D.
Tacoma-Pierce County Health Dept.
3629 South "D" Street
Tacoma, WA 98408
206-593-4104

WISCONSIN
Donald J. DeBruyn, M.D.
The Manitowoc Clinic
601 Reed Avenue
P. O. Box 3008
Manitowoc, WI 54220
414-682-8841

Robert E. Dedmon, M.D.
Staff Vice President
Medical Affairs
Kimberly Clark Corp.
2100 Winchester Road
Neenah, WI 54956
414-721-5994

Dr. Paul McKinney
Medical College of Wisconsin
8700 West Wisconsin Ave.
Milwaukee, WI 53226
414-259-2712

---

*Private agency—cannot give vaccine to general public.
ID2725D: 08/06/86.

APPENDIX G

Approximate Costs of Hotel Rooms and Food, Internal Travel, Services, and Clothing

The figures below are based on reports current in March 1986. Prices are subject to change and continue to rise. The quotations are merely estimates to help you plan your trip. All prices are in *yuan* (Y), at a rate of Y3.00 to the dollar.

HOTEL RATES AND FOOD COSTS

Beijing
Beijing Hotel   Y265/day
Friendship Hotel (2-room suite)   Y144/day
Jianguo Hotel (joint venture)   Y285/day
Xiyuan Hotel   Y210/day
    Food in hotel dining rooms runs from Y8.00 for breakfast to Y15.00 for lunch and dinner and is much higher in the joint-venture hotels, where a dinner for two might cost Y150.00 and a hamburger in the coffee shop, Y15.00.

Changchun
South Lake Hotel   Y90/day

Guangzhou
Beiyuan Hotel   Y55/day
Food   Y60/day

Hangzhou
Hangzhou Hotel   Y120/day
Food   Y60/day

Lanzhou
Lanzhou Guesthouse   Y60/day
Food   Y10/day

Shanghai

Shanghai Hotel   Y100/day
Jingan Guesthouse   Y100/day

Turpan

Turpan Hotel   Y38/day
Food   Y3–Y5/day

Urumqi

Urumqi Guesthouse   Y45/day

NOTE: Students who have traveled recently advise that it is *not* possible in most cases to get discounts at hotels with student cards—so count on paying Y50 each night in the cities.

DORMITORIES AND FOREIGN EXPERT BUILDINGS

Beijing

Beijing University, Shaoyuan Lou
 Building no. 4, single room, communal bath, at
  student rates   Y360/month paid in advance each semester
 Building no. 5, two rooms, bathroom, TV, air-conditioner, at
  researcher's rates   Y2,100/month
 Food   Y10–Y20/day
Central Arts Academy Dormitory
 Student rates   Y20/day
 Food   Y3/day

Chongqing

Sichuan Fine Arts Academy
 Student rate   Y30/day
  (room rate was reduced by half when researcher traveled)
 Food   Y30/day

Hainan

Xinglong State Farm Guesthouse   Y50/day

Hangzhou

Hangzhou University, Foreign Experts Dormitory   Y360/month

Guangzhou

South China Institute of Technology Guesthouse   Y30/day
 Food   Y15/day

Nanjing

Nanjing Foreign Languages School Dormitory
 (room with bath)   Y25/day

Shanghai
Shanghai College of Traditional Medicine
Researcher rate   Y30/day
Student rate   Y24/day
East China Normal University, Foreign Experts
Dormitory   Y30/day

Tianjin
Tianjin University Guesthouse   Y75/day
Food   Y15/day

TRANSPORTATION COSTS

Airfares (one-way)
Beijing–Shanghai   Y150
Beijing–Urumqi   Y429
Beijing–Kunming   Y360
Chongqing–Xi'an   Y90

Train
Beijing–Xi'an (soft sleeper)   Y124
Turpan–Beijing (soft sleeper, student rate)   Y189
Beijing–Guangzhou (hard sleeper)   Y21.90
Guangzhou–Beijing (soft sleeper)   Y120

NOTE: In general airfares and soft sleeper accommodations on trains are about the same price. Students with a student card can obtain discounts on trains but not on planes. See the section in Chapter 6, "Available Services," on internal travel for a discussion of the different modes of train travel in China.

Reserved Car
Beijing, Institute car for daily use   Y25–Y80/day

Taxis
Calculated by distance and quality of car   Y0.6–Y0.8/km
Beijing examples:
Peking University to Friendship Store (one-way)   Y20
Downtown to Friendship Hotel   Y15

Bus Pass
Beijing (all buses and trolleys)   Y5/month

Bicycle
New   Y80–Y200
Used   Y80

RESEARCH TRAVEL

A scientist who traveled with his spouse for two months to cities that included Xining, Xi'an, Shanghai, Hangzhou, Nanchang, Jinggangshan, and several small cities in Guangzhou spent Y22,533 for local hotels, guesthouses, plane fare, trains, and cars.

An art historian who itemized her research travel expenses to Buddhist sites in out-of-the-way places in Northwest China, including Datong and Wutaishan, Taiyuan, Loyang, Xi'an, and environs, spent a total of Y4,000 for two people. Her costs for 3½ weeks break down as follows:

Train fare   Y227
Airfare   Y162
Hired cars (calculated by kilometer and not number of passengers) Y1,230
Food (for two)   Y876
Hotels and guesthouses (calculated by room and not number of guests)   Y1,077
Miscellaneous items (including educational materials and small charges for driver's room and food at Wutaishan)   Y370

SERVICES

Postage
Airmail letter overseas   Y1.10
5-kg Package of printed matter seamail   Y31.00

Film Processing
36 Color prints   Y21.00
36 Color slides   Y7.50

Photocopies (per page)
Hotels
    Letter size   Y0.50
    Legal size   Y0.70
Neighborhood copy shops   Y0.15–Y0.20
Shaoyuanlou   Y0.15
Peking University Library   Y0.10
CSCPRC office   Y0.10
Microfilm reproduction, No. 1 Archive
    One sheet   Y0.90
    One roll of microfilm copied   Y28.00

Laundry
Average per person per week   Y25.00

Kindergarten (Chinese school)
Per child per month   Y75.00

Medical Care
Clinic visits   Y0.50–Y2.00
Hospitalization (two weeks) in Guangzhou for pneumonia, December
    1985 (researcher's spouse)
    Medicine and treatment   Y1,983
    Lodging and food   Y792
Hospitalization (three days) in Nanjing for dysentery,
    1986 (student)   Y68

NOTE: Although these prices are calculated at an exchange rate of
Y3.00 = US$1.00, the exchange rate as of January 1987 was Y3.71 =
US$1.00.

CLOTHING, LUGGAGE, AND SPORTS EQUIPMENT

Easy to Find

Woolen long underwear   Y35
Silk undershirt   Y15–Y20
Men's cotton underwear   Y5–
    Y7
Terry-cloth bathrobe   Y40
Plastic shower shoes (essential
    for dormitory dwellers)   Y5
Woolen sweater   Y40–Y60
Cashmere sweater   Y100–Y120
Down jacket   Y70–Y100
Down vest   Y50
Chinese overcoat   Y45–Y150
Padded silk jacket   Y55
Fur hat   Y40
Woolen and cashmere
    scarf   Y30
Leather shoes   Y40
Cloth shoes   Y5
Sneakers   Y15–Y30

Cotton shirt and blouse   Y10–
    Y15
Sweatshirt and running
    suit   Y30–Y50 for both
Canvas and leather bags of all
    sizes   Y15–Y50
Luggage (fabric and
    leather)   Y45–Y100
Sheet, cotton   Y15–Y20
Quilt, cotton   Y40
Quilt, down   Y100–Y150
Woolen blanket   Y40–Y60
Volleyball and
    basketball   Y25–Y30
Baseball, tennis equipment,
    and other sports items are
    available for reasonable
    prices
Umbrella, collapsible and
    regular   Y8–Y12

Difficult to Find

Men's walking shorts
Large-sized men's clothing and
  shoes
Bathing suits
Good running shoes
Sturdy leather shoes and boots
Woolen socks
Warm slippers

Lined leather boots for winter
Western-style dresses and
  women's slacks
Flannel nightgowns
Shower caps
Inexpensive watches
Diapers and plastic pants

APPENDIX H

Selected Information on Postal and Customs Regulations of the People's Republic of China

Since postal and customs regulations are subject to change at any time, it is prudent to check with the U.S. Postal Service and/or the Chinese Embassy as you prepare to mail or carry specific items to China. To help you plan, *selected* regulations in effect as of 1981 are summarized below.

POSTAL REGULATIONS

The following items may *not* be mailed to China:

- currency, checks, securities, and other financial instruments
- perishable biological materials (except for serums, vaccines, and required medications that cannot be obtained easily in China)
- arms, ammunition, and explosives of all kinds
- radio telegraph receivers and transmitters
- narcotics and poisonous drugs
- large amounts of used clothing for other than personal use
- used bedding
- material that is "harmful politically, economically, culturally, or morally to China"

Gift parcels are admitted without an import permit if the value of the parcel does not exceed 50 *yuan*. Each family can receive no more than four gift parcels per year, with no single parcel valued at more than 50 *yuan*.

All parcels must be sealed. Combined length and girth of parcels is not to exceed six feet.

CUSTOMS REGULATIONS

The tariff on selected items is as follows:

- medical and scientific instruments, electronic calculators ... 20%
- medicines and patent medicines 50%
- household and office equipment, tape recorders, cutlery,
hand tools, spare parts, and accessories 50%
- sporting goods and musical instruments 50%
- radios, record players, spare parts, and accessories 100%
- bicycles, other types of vehicles, spare parts, and
accessories 100%

APPENDIX I

Sample Contract for Teachers
(July 1985)

A sample contract for Foreign Experts is reprinted below. An American teaching in China, who sent this contract to the National Association for Foreign Student Affairs, indicated that particular items to be noted in the Annex, "Regulations Concerning the Living Conditions of Foreign Experts Working in Cultural and Educational Institutions" (pp. 200–203), include—

Section II.A: "Only tickets from the Civil Aviation Administration of China (CAAC) shall be provided if its international flights are available. . . ."

Section II.C: The items to be provided in the housing facilities are specified, but individuals should be aware that these sometimes do not function properly and that electricity and water supplies are very erratic.

Section II.D: Americans teaching in China should not expect to teach and be able to do a great deal of traveling. The only long vacation is Spring Festival, which is about four weeks in late January, February, or early March, depending on the date of the Chinese New Year, which is determined by the lunar calendar. At that time, the trains are terribly crowded, and it is very cold. Since indoor heating is rare, travel can be quite uncomfortable at that time. In the summer, at the end of the academic year, it is quite hot. So individuals whose objective is to travel should consider teaching only in the fall semester and traveling in the months of March, April, and May.

CONTRACT (FORM)

PREFACE   The form of the Contract and the Annex, "Regulations Concerning the Living Conditions of Foreign Experts Working in Cul-

198

tural and Educational Institutions," are sample copies. Subsequently, Party A and Party B can, before signing the contract, submit amendments and supplements to the sample copies according to their specific conditions. The contract will come into force only after both sides have, through consultation, established in written form and confirmed through signature the content and the living conditions therein.

Party A ———— wishes to engage the service of Party B ———— as (teacher, compiler, translator, etc.). The two parties, in a spirit of friendly cooperation, agree to observe this contract.

I. The period of service will be from ———— to ————.

II. The duties of Party B are as follows:

III. Requirements for Party B to fulfill.
   A. Party B shall observe the laws, decrees, and relevant regulations enacted by the Chinese government and Party A's work system.
   B. Party B shall cooperate with Party A and make every effort to complete the tasks agreed on.
   C. Party B shall accept Party A's arrangement and direction in regard to his/her work. Without Party A's consent, Party B shall not render service elsewhere or hold concurrently any post unrelated to the work agreed on with Party A.
   D. Party A shall pay Party B a salary of ——— yuan (renminbi) each month and provide him/her the benefits stipulated in the "Regulations Concerning the Living Conditions of Foreign Experts Working in Cultural and Educational Institutions."
   E. Neither of the two parties shall terminate the contract ahead of time or altar it without mutual consent.
   If Party A wants to terminate the contract before it expires, Party B must be given thirty (30) days' notice and reasons for breaking the contract. During Party B's term of service, his/her salary shall be paid as agreed on for the term of the contract. Party A shall also pay for the return air tickets of Party B and his/her family [i.e., Party B's spouse and child(ren) under twelve (12) who have been permitted to come and remain with Party B in China for the whole duration of the contract; they will hereafter be referred to as Party B's family] and for the transportation of their luggage.
   If Party B wants to terminate the contract before it expires, he/she should hand in a written request with his/her reasons for breaking the contract thirty (30) days in advance. Party A shall stop paying Party B's salary and providing any benefits for Party B starting from the day

when Party A consents to the request. Party B shall bear all the expenses involved in traveling back home together with that of his/her family. Party A is entitled to claim compensation for any loss brought about by Party B's termination of the contract.

Both parties shall continue to execute this contract until the request for termination has been agreed upon.

F. Party A has the right to cancel the contract in any of the following cases:

1. If Party B violates either Regulation II or Regulation III of the contract and fails to correct the error after Party A's mentioning it to him/her, Party A has the right to terminate the contract and arrange for him/her to return home within thirty (30) days. Party B shall pay for his/her and his/her family's air ticket(s) and the cost of the transporation of their luggage.

2. If Party B cannot resume work after a doctor's certified sick leave of two months (60 days), Party A may arrange, in consideration of Party B's health, for Party B and his/her family to return home within a month (30 days). Party A shall pay for the air ticket(s) of Party B and his/her family and the transportation of their luggage.

G. The contract takes effect when Party B reports for work and becomes void automatically upon the expiration of the contract. Either party that makes a proposal for the extension of the contract should put forward his/her request three months (90 days) prior to the expiration of the contract. A new contract on an extension of the period of service shall be signed by both parties if they agree to it after consultation.

All stay expenses incurred after the contract expires shall be borne by Party B.

H. The contract is written in both Chinese and English, both texts being equally valid.

Signed on the _____ day of _____, 19_____.

Party A   Party B
(Signature)   (Signature)

ANNEX: Regulations Concerning the Living Conditions of Foreign Experts in Cultural and Educational Institutions

I. Salary

A. Party A shall fix Party B's salary according to his/her professional abilities, the work assigned, his/her educational and professional background. Party A shall inform Party B of the amount of salary before he/she consents to accept the position.

B. Party B's salary shall be paid regularly by the month. It shall begin from the day of Party B's commencement of his/her work in China until the expiration of the contract. If the work to be done will take less than a month, the payment shall be made by the day, each being one-thirtieth of the monthly salary.

C. Party B's salary shall be paid in *renminbi*, which can be changed into foreign currency under the following conditions:

If Party B comes to China alone, he/she may change fifty percent (50%) of his/her monthly salary into foreign currency.

If Party B comes with his/her family [spouse and child(ren) under twelve (12) who come and remain in China with Party B at Party A's consent; hereafter referred to as Party B's family], he/she may change thirty percent (30%) of his/her monthly salary.

If Party B's spouse is invited as a foreign expert at the same time and they have no children living in China, each may have fifty percent (50%) of his/her salary changed into foreign currency.

Party B may change his/her foreign currency allowance either every month or all at once at the expiration of the contract.

II. Traveling Expenses

A. If Party B's period of service is over one year, he/she may bring with him/her, at Party A's consent in advance, his/her spouse and child(ren) under twelve (12) to come and remain in China. Party A shall provide Party B and his/her family with economy-class air return tickets from the airport nearest to the city where Party B is when he/she accepts the invitation from Party A (or Party B's permanent residence) when coming to the place of work in China and when returning home upon the expiration of the term of Party B's service. Only tickets from the Civil Aviation Administration of China (CAAC) shall be provided if its international flights are available in Party B's country.

Party B shall bear all the expenses of his/her family on temporary visits to China.

B. Party A shall pay for the cost of transportation of twenty-four (24) kilograms (kg) per person [no more than a total of seventy-two (72) kg for a family of more than three] of luggage by nonaccompanied air freight incurred by Party B and his/her family for the same distance as mentioned above, both when coming and on their return after the expiration of the period of service. Expenses for packing and delivering the luggage between Party B's temporary residence at the time of his/her application for the post (or his/her permanent residence) and the airport when coming to China or on his/her return home shall be borne by Party B.

At the request of Party B, for sending his/her luggage by sea instead of by air, Party A shall pay for the cost of one cubic meter of unaccompanied luggage per person (but no more than two cubic meters for a family of over two people) by sea, including the expenses charged for delivering the luggage to and from Party B's place of work and the seaport in China. Expenses incurred for packing and delivering luggage outside of China between the temporary residence at the time of Party B's application for the post (or his/her permanent residence) and the seaport on coming to China and on returning home shall be borne by Party B.

The cost of transportation of incoming luggage within the stipulated limits can be reimbursed only on presentation of receipts.

C. During Party B's period of work in China, Party A shall bear the following expenses on behalf of Party B.

1. Housing (with furniture, bedding, a bathroom, a television set, a refrigerator, and the facilities for heating and air conditioning).

2. Transportation to and from work.

3. Medical care to be subsidized in accordance with China's medical system except for expenses incurred in registration, doctors' home visits, fitting false teeth, cleaning teeth, undergoing cosmetic surgery, buying spectacles, boarding in hospital, and nonmedical tonics.

D. Vacations

1. In addition to China's national holidays, such as New Year's Day, the Spring Festival (three days), May 1, and National Day (two days), Party B is entitled to 30 days' vacation in China every year. The vacation time of those working in colleges and universities shall correspond to the summer and winter vacations. Those working in institutions of information and publication shall not be entitled to a vacation until after they have worked for half a year. After Party B has worked for a year, he/she shall be given an additional eight hundred (800) *yuan renminbi* vacation allowance. If the term of service is over half a year but less than a year, Party B shall enjoy a vacation of two weeks and be given an additional four hundred (400) *yuan* vacation allowance.

The vacation allowance cannot be changed into foreign currency.

Party B shall receive his/her salary as usual for the vacation period.

2. If Party B comes to China alone and is on a contract for two years, he/she may spend the vacation visiting his/her home country once at the end of one year's work. Party A shall pay for an economy-class return air ticket. Only tickets of CAAC shall be provided if its international flights are available. In such cases, Party B shall no longer be given a vacation allowance that year, but his/her salary for the month when he/she is on vacation at home can all be changed into foreign currency.

If Party B gives up such opportunity to go for a vacation in his/her home country, he/she shall be given a sum in *renminbi** equivalent to a one-way economy-class air ticket instead of the vacation allowance for that year. If the price of the ticket is less than eight hundred (800) *yuan*, Party B shall be given the difference.*

E. Sick Leave or Absence from Work

1. If he/she is ill, Party B shall ask for sick leave and produce a doctor's certificate. His/her salary shall be paid as usual if the sick leave is up to sixty (60) days in succession. If Party A does not exercise the right stipulated in Item F. 2. in the Annex (i.e., if Party A does not propose termination of the contract), Party B shall receive seventy percent (70%) of his/her salary from the sixty-first day until the day he/she resumes regular work or to the expiration of the contract.

2. If Party B asks for leave of absence and obtains Party A's consent, a deduction in salary shall be made according to the number of days Party B is absent.

F. Severance Pay

Severence pay shall be granted to Party B when Party B leaves China at the end of his/her service, namely an additional half a month's salary for each full year's service. No severance pay shall be granted if Party B has worked less than one year.

Severance pay may be changed into foreign currency.

---

*Nonconvertible.

APPENDIX J

Protocol Between the Government of the United States of America and the Government of the People's Republic of China for Cooperation in Educational Exchanges

The Government of the United States of America and the Government of the People's Republic of China [represented by the United States Information Agency and the State Education Commission of The People's Republic of China], hereinafter referred to as "the Parties," recognizing the role of education in furthering progress in both nations and in building understanding between the people of the two countries, subject to the "Agreement on Cooperation in Science and Technology between the Government of the United States of America and the Government of the People's Republic of China" and in accordance with the principles of the "Cultural Agreement between the Government of the United States of America and the Government of the People's Republic of China," have, with a view to promoting educational exchanges, agreed on activities of educational exchanges described in this accord.

ARTICLE I—GUIDING PRINCIPLES

The Parties agree and affirm that the principal objective of this accord is to provide opportunities for cooperation and exchange in educational fields based on equality, reciprocity and mutual benefit. Recognizing differences in the societies and systems of the two countries, both Parties will initiate educational exchange activities based on their own as well as mutual interests. The receiving side will facilitate and assist in implementing those educational exchange projects to every extent possible to assure that the requests of the sending side for study and research opportunities are met to the extent required in each case in accordance with each country's laws and regulations.

Both Parties will undertake measures to enhance educational exchange objectives. Scholarly data and information derived from activities under this accord may be made available to the world scholarly community through customary channels in accordance with the normal procedures the participating institutions and individuals would follow in their own countries.

Receiving institutions of each country will have final approval of students and scholars applying from the other country. Both Parties will, however, use their best efforts to assure the fulfillment of the principles of this accord.

The Parties further agree that the principles of this accord will be the basis of all official educational exchanges. While recognizing the independence of non-official arrangements, the Parties agree these principles should also be extended, to the degree applicable, to the full range of educational exchanges between the two countries.

The Parties will reach detailed agreement on specific programs through regular exchanges of letters or other instruments on at least an annual basis.

ARTICLE II—OFFICIAL EXCHANGES OF INDIVIDUALS

The Parties agree on the following categories of official exchanges of individuals:

(A) RESEARCH SCHOLARS   Each Party may select and sponsor scholars from its own country to engage in research in the other country. Each Party may select and sponsor scholars from the other country to engage in research in its own country. Scholars may be placed in association with educational research or other institutions relevant to the accomplishment of research objectives or may, with the approval of the host government, engage in independent research. Research fields will include the humanities, the social sciences, the natural sciences and the technological sciences.

(B) GRADUATE STUDENTS   Each Party may select and sponsor qualified graduates of institutions of higher learning or equivalent of its own country to pursue degree or non-degree graduate programs of study and research in the other country. Each Party may select and sponsor qualified graduates of institutions of higher learning or equivalent from the other country to pursue degree or non-degree graduate programs of study and research in its own country. Fields of study will include the humanities, the social sciences, the natural sciences and the technological sciences.

(C) TEACHERS AND LECTURERS   The Parties agree to encourage and sponsor teachers, lecturers, professors and other qualified people of the institutions of higher learning of their respective countries to teach or to give a series of lectures in the other country. Fields of teaching and lecturing will include the humanities, the social sciences, the natural sciences and the technological sciences.

ARTICLE III—OFFICIAL DELEGATIONS AND GROUP PROJECTS

The Parties agree to exchange delegations and groups in various educational fields which may include participation in joint meetings such as conferences and symposia in the areas of mutual interest as agreed.

ARTICLE IV—EXCHANGE OF MATERIALS

The Parties agree to encourage and facilitate the exchange of scholarly and other educational materials between educational and research institutions of both countries and individuals. Materials may include books, periodicals, monographs and audio-visual materials.

ARTICLE V—NON-OFFICIAL EXCHANGES

The Parties agree to continue to encourage and promote direct educational exchanges and cooperation between educational organizations, universities, colleges, schools, research institutions and individuals of their respective countries. The assistance to these exchanges should be facilitated in accordance with each country's laws and regulations.

ARTICLE VI—FINANCIAL PROVISIONS

(A) The Parties agree that the expenses for official delegations and groups under the auspices of Article III of this accord will be as follows: The sending side shall bear the two-way international travel expenses of the delegation or group. The receiving side shall bear the expenses of board and lodging, transportation, and medical care or health and accident insurance when the delegation or group is in its territory; any exception to these provisions shall be determined by written agreement of the Parties.

(B) The Parties agree that the necessary expenses for the official exchange of individuals under the auspices of Article II of this accord shall be based on the principle that the sending side pays the costs associated with its participants. Exceptions to this principle will be by agreement of the Parties.

(C) The Fulbright and university-to-university affiliation programs, and other designated programs shall share certain costs mutually agreed by the Parties and the participating institutions.

(D) The financial provisions for non-official exchanges shall be determined by the participating institutions, the Parties recognizing that public and private institutions of both countries have limited capacity to support educational exchange activities.

(E) The Parties agree that activities under this accord shall be carried out subject to the availability of funds.

ARTICLE VII—EXECUTIVE AGENTS

(A) The Executive Agent of this accord on the United States side shall be the United States Information Agency. The Executive Agent of this accord on the People's Republic of China side shall be the State Education Commission of the People's Republic of China.

(B) Upon signature, this accord will become a part of the official agreements concluded under Article 5 of the Agreement between the Government of the United States of America and the Government of the People's Republic of China on Cooperation in Science and Technology signed January 31, 1979, extended January 12, 1984.

(C) As agreed by the Executive Agents of the Parties, the representatives of agencies or organizations concerned in both countries will exchange visits for the working out of plans and programs of educational exchange and for discussing progress, problems and matters related to educational exchange projects. These meetings may be held in the United States of America or in the People's Republic of China as agreed.

(D) This accord will supersede "The Understanding on the Exchange of Students between the United States of America and the People's Republic of China" reached in October 1978, and be the guiding document for educational exchange of the two countries.

This accord shall enter into force upon signature and remain in force for a five-year period. It may be amended or extended by the written agreement of the two Parties; it may be terminated by either Party by giving six months' written notice to the other Party of its intention to terminate.

Done at Washington, this 23rd day of July 1985, in duplicate in the English and Chinese languages, both equally authentic.

RONALD REAGAN	LI XIANNIAN
For the Government of the United States of America	For the Government of the People's Republic of China

APPENDIX K

Locations of U.S. Educational Reference Collections in China and Their General Reference Contents

COLLECTION LOCATIONS

Active Centers (Offer personal guidance services in addition to reference materials)

Advisory Center of Foreign
  Educational Information
Beijing Languages Institute
Beijing

IIE-Guangdong American Study
  Information Center
Ground Floor
46-1 Dezheng South Road
Guangzhou

Study Abroad Training
  Department
Shanghai International Studies
  University
Shanghai

Study Abroad Training
  Department
Guangzhou Foreign Languages
  Department
Guangzhou

Study Abroad Training
  Department
Sichuan Foreign Languages
  Institute
Chongqing

Study Abroad Training
  Department
Dalian Foreign Languages
  Institute
Dalian

Study Abroad Training
  Department
Xi'an Foreign Languages
  Institute
Xi'an

Study Abroad Training
  Department
Chengdu University of Science
  and Technology
Chengdu

Study Abroad Information
  Service
Bureau of Higher Education of
  Guangdong Province
Guangzhou

Passive Centers (Stock reference works and possibly have personnel familiar with the materials but do not offer personal guidance services)

Beijing National Library
Beijing

Beijing Youth Overseas
    Educational Information
    Center
Quianmenjie Middle School
A5 Hepingmen East Street
Beijing

Shanghai Municipal Library
Shanghai

Guangzhou Municipal Library
Guangzhou

Liaoning Provincial Library
Shenyang

Hubei Provincial Library
Wuhan

Sichuan Provincial Library
Chengdu

Heilongjiang Provincial Library
Harbin

Jilin Provincial Library
Changchun

GENERAL REFERENCE WORKS CONTAINED IN THE COLLECTIONS

Accredited Institutions of Postsecondary Education, 1984–85
Accredited Programs Leading to Degrees in Engineering, 1984 (with 1985 addendum)
Accredited Programs Leading to Degrees in Engineering Technology, 1984 (with 1985 addendum)
Adviser's Manual of Federal Regulations Affecting Foreign Students and Scholars (with 1983 emendations)
Allied Health Education Directory, 1985
American Universities and Colleges, 12th edition
The American University—A World Guide
Arrival Information Requests
The College Handbook and Index of Majors (two volumes)
Costs at U.S. Educational Institutions, 1985–86
Directory of Graduate Programs: 1986 and 1987 (four volumes)
    Volume A: Agriculture, Biological Sciences, Psychology, Health Sciences, and Home Economics
    Volume B: Arts and Humanities
    Volume C: Physical Sciences, Mathematics, and Engineering
    Volume D: Social Sciences and Education
Directory of Overseas Educational Advising Centers
Directory of Residency Training Programs, 1985–86

The Doctor of Philosophy Degree

Engineering Education (March 1985 issue: Engineering College Research and Graduate Study)

English Language and Orientation Programs in the United States

Entering Higher Education in the United States—A Guide for Students from Other Countries

Financial Aid Available to Students and Scholars from the People's Republic of China for Study and Research in the United States, 1987

Financial Planning for Study in the United States—A Guide for Students from Other Countries

Foreign Teaching Assistants in U.S. Universities

A Guide to COPA Recognized Accrediting Associations, 1984–86

A Handbook for Foreign Students

Higher Education Directory, 1985

Lovejoy's College Guide, 17th edition

The Master's Degree

Map of Colleges and Universities in the United States

NAFSA (National Association for Foreign Student Affairs) Directory, 1985

NHSC (National Home Study Council) 1985–86 Directory of Home Study Schools

Occupational Outlook Handbook, 1984–85

The Official Guide to MBA Programs, Admissions, and Careers

Open Doors: 1984/85—Report on International Educational Exchange

Peterson's Annual Guides to Graduate Study, 1986 (five volumes)

   Graduate and Professional Programs: An Overview (Book 1)

   Graduate Programs in the Humanities and Social Sciences (Book 2)

   Graduate Programs in the Biological, Agricultural, and Health Sciences (Book 3)

   Graduate Programs in the Physical Sciences and Mathematics (Book 4)

   Graduate Programs in Engineering and Applied Sciences (Book 5)

Pre-Departure Orientation Handbook for Students from the People's Republic of China Planning to Study in the United States

Profiles: Detailed Analyses of the Foreign Student Population, 1983/84

Specialized Study Options USA

Trade and Technical Careers and Training—Handbook of Accredited Private Trade and Technical Schools

Additional centers may be open in the future, and new reference works will be added to the collections as they become available. Check with the nearest U.S. Embassy or Consulate in China for an up-to-date list of locations and contents.

APPENDIX L

Selected Reading List

General

Bonavia, D. *The Chinese.* New York: Lippincott, 1980.

Congressional Quarterly. *China: U.S. Policy Since 1945.* Washington, D.C.: Congressional Quarterly, 1980.

Fairbank, J. K. *The United States and China.* 4th ed. Cambridge, Mass.: Harvard University Press, 1979.

Fraser, J. *The Chinese: Portrait of a People.* New York: Summit Books, 1980.

Frolic, M. B. *Mao's People.* Cambridge, Mass.: Harvard University Press, 1980.

Hinton, H. C., ed. *The People's Republic of China: A Handbook.* Boulder, Colo.: Westview, 1980.

Hooper, B. *Inside Peking: A Personal Report.* London: MacDonald and Jane's, 1979.

Kaplan, F. M., J. M. Sobin, and S. Andors. *Encyclopedia of China Today.* New York: Harper and Row, 1979.

Kapp, R. A. *Communicating with China: Five Perspectives.* Washington, D.C.: The China Council of the Asia Society, 1981.

Lo, R. E., and K. S. Kinderman. *In the Eye of the Typhoon.* New York: Harcourt Brace Jovanich, Inc., 1980.

Matthews, Jay, and Linda Matthews. *One Billion: A China Chronicle.* New York: Random House, 1983.

Meisner, M. *Mao's China: A History of the People's Republic.* New York: Free Press, 1977.

Oxnam, Robert B., and Richard C. Bush, eds. *China Briefing 1981.* Boulder, Colo.: Westview, 1981.

Salzman, Mark. *Iron and Silk.* New York: Random House, 1987.

Schwartz, Vera. *Long Road Home: A China Journal.* New Haven, Conn.: Yale University Press, 1984.

Shell, O. *Watch Out for the Foreign Guests.* New York: Pantheon, 1980.

Terrill, R., ed. *The China Difference.* New York: Harper and Row, 1979.

Townsend, J. R., and R. C. Bush, eds. *The People's Republic of China: A Basic Handbook.* New York: The China Council of the Asia Society and the Council on International and Public Affairs, 1981.

211

Yue, Daiyun, and Carolyn Wakeman. *To the Storm: The Odyssey of a Revolutionary Chinese Woman.* Berkeley: University of California Press, 1985.

Zongren, Liu. *Two Years in the Melting Pot.* San Francisco: China Books, 1984.

Politics and Economics

Barnett, A. D. *China and the Major Powers in East Asia.* Washington, D.C.: Brookings Institution, 1977.

Baum, R., ed. *China's Four Modernizations: The New Technological Revolution.* Boulder, Colo.: Westview, 1980.

Eckstein, A. *China's Economic Revolution.* New York: Cambridge University Press, 1977.

Fingar, T., ed. *China's Quest for Independence: Policy Evolution in the 1970s.* Boulder, Colo.: Westview, 1980.

Kallgren, J., ed. *The People's Republic of China After Thirty Years: An Overview.* Berkeley, Calif.: University of California Press, 1979.

Prybyla, J. S. *The Chinese Economy: Problems and Policies.* Columbia, S.C.: University of South Carolina Press, 1980.

Snow, E. *Red Star Over China.* New York: Vintage Books, 1971.

Townsend, J. R. *Politics in China.* 2d ed. Boston: Little, Brown and Company, 1980.

U.S. Congress, Joint Economic Committee. *Chinese Economy Post-Mao.* Washington, D.C.: U.S. Government Printing Office, 1978.

Education

Barlow, Tani E., and Donald M. Lowe. *Chinese Reflections: American Teaching in the People's Republic.* New York: Praeger, 1985.

Chen, T. H. *Chinese Education Since 1949.* New York: Pergamon, 1981.

Fingar, T., ed. *Higher Education in the People's Republic of China.* Stanford, Calif.: Northeast Asia-United States Forum on International Policy, 1980.

Lampton, David M., with Joyce A. Madancy and Kristen M. Williams for the Committee on Scholarly Communication with the People's Republic of China. *A Relationship Restored: Trends in U.S.-China Educational Exchanges, 1978–1984.* Washington, D.C.: National Academy Press, 1986.

National Association for Foreign Student Affairs. Rev. ed. *An Introduction to Education in the People's Republic of China and U.S.-China Educational Exchanges.* Washington, D.C.: National Association for Foreign Student Affairs, forthcoming.

Pepper, S. "Chinese Education After Mao: Two Steps Forward, Two Steps Back and Begin Again." *China Quarterly,* no. 81 (March 1980):1–65.

Pepper, S. *China's Universities: Post-Mao Enrollment Policies and Their Impact on the Structure of Secondary Education.* Ann Arbor, Mich.: Center for Chinese Studies, University of Michigan, 1984.

Shirk, S. "Education Reform and Political Backlash: Recent Changes in Chinese Educational Policy." *Comparative Education Review.* 23, no. 2 (June 1979):183–217.

Taylor, R. *China's Intellectual Dilemma: Politics and University Enrollment, 1949–1978.* Vancouver: University of British Columbia Press, 1981.

"Teaching in China: What We Give, What We Get." *Asian Survey* 23, no. 11 (November 1983):1182–1208.

Thurston, Anne F., and Burton Pasternak, eds. *The Social Sciences and Fieldwork in China: Views from the Field.* Boulder, Colo.: Westview, 1983.

White, D. G. *Party and Professionals: The Political Role of Teachers in Contemporary China.* Armonk, N.Y.: M. E. Sharpe, 1981.

Science

Orleans, L. A., ed. *Science in Contemporary China.* Stanford, Calif.: Stanford University Press, 1980.

Sigurdson, J. *Technology and Science in the People's Republic of China: An Introduction.* New York: Pergamon, 1980.

Suttmeier, R. P. *Science, Technology, and China's Desire for Modernization.* Stanford, Calif.: Hoover Institution Press, 1980.

Travel Resources

Customs Hints for Returning U.S. Citizens: Know Before You Go. Washington, D.C.: U.S. Government Printing Office, 1986.

Garside, Evelyne. *China Companion: A Guide to 100 Cities, Resorts, and Places of Interest in the People's Republic of China.* New York: Farrar, Straus & Giroux, 1981.

General Guidelines on Consular Services. Washington, D.C.: U.S. Department of State.

A Guide to Living, Studying, and Working in the People's Republic of China and Hong Kong. New Haven, Conn.: Yale China Association, 1986.

Health Information for International Travel. Washington, D.C.: U.S. Government Printing Office, 1986.

Henderson, Gail, and Myron Cohen. *The Chinese Hospital: A Socialist Work Unit.* New Haven, Conn.: Yale University Press, 1984.

Kaplan, Frederick M., and J. Sobin. *Encyclopedia of China Today.* New York: Eurasia Press, 1982.

Kaplan, Frederick M., J. Sobin, and Arne J. de Keijzer. *The China Guidebook.* New York: Eurasia Press, 1986.

Nagel's Encyclopedic Guide to China. Geneva: Nagel Publishers, 1986.

Samagalski, Alan, and Michael Buckley. *China—A Travel Survival Kit.* Berkeley, Calif.: Lonely Planet, 1985.

Schwartz, Brian. *China Off the Beaten Track.* Hong Kong: St. Martins Press, 1983.

Index